THE REAL WORLD OF COLLEGE

THE REAL WORLD OF COLLEGE

What Higher Education Is and What It Can Be

WENDY FISCHMAN AND HOWARD GARDNER

The MIT Press
Cambridge, Massachusetts
London, England

The MIT Press would like to thank the anonymous peer reviewers who provided comments on drafts of this book. The generous work of academic experts is essential for establishing the authority and quality of our publications. We acknowledge with gratitude the contributions of these otherwise uncredited readers.

This book was set in Scala and ScalaSans by New Best-set Typesetters Ltd. Printed and bound in the United States of America.

Library of Congress Cataloging-in-Publication Data

Names: Fischman, Wendy, 1971– author. | Gardner, Howard, 1943– author.
Title: The real world of college : what higher education is and what it can be / Wendy Fischman and Howard Gardner.
Description: Cambridge, Massachusetts ; London, England : The MIT Press, [2022] | Includes bibliographical references.
Identifiers: LCCN 2021014609 | ISBN 9780262046534 (Hardcover)
Subjects: LCSH: Education, Humanistic—United States—Case studies. | Educational change. | Alienation (Social psychology) | College students— Mental health—United States. | College students—Psychology.
Classification: LCC LC1011 .F475 2022 | DDC 378.1/980973—dc23
LC record available at https://lccn.loc.gov/2021014609

10   9   8   7   6   5   4   3   2   1

May young people everywhere have the kind of education that we were fortunate to have received.

CONTENTS

CONTENTS

INTRODUCTION

Books about higher education in the United States appear almost daily. Typically, they focus only on a single sector or specific issue; and all too often, their claims—whether celebratory or damning—are not supported sufficiently by relevant data.

In this book, we report on a study of nonvocational higher education in the United States that may be unparalleled in its ambition and scope. Along with our research team, we spent five years visiting ten disparate campuses, carrying out over two thousand intensive, semi-structured interviews. On each campus we interviewed approximately fifty incoming students and fifty graduating students, and smaller numbers of faculty, senior administrators, trustees, young alums, parents, and job recruiters. These interviews—which typically lasted an hour or more—covered a wide swathe of the undergraduate college experience. The campuses we visited range from highly selective private schools to less selective public institutions; they differ in terms of region, demography, and declared missions. We spent the subsequent two years carrying out quantitative and qualitative data analyses on these interviews; identifying the principal findings and themes; and then (and only then) arriving at recommendations for the entire sector. We've written over fifty blogs, given dozens of public presentations, and published several articles in scholarly and wide-circulation publications. Now, in this book, we have the opportunity to detail our findings, conclusions, and recommendations.

We ourselves benefited from a broad higher education and we have been associated with individuals and with institutions that share a belief in the value (and the values) of this form of education. This approach has been described by various phrases: "liberal arts,"* "liberal arts and sciences," "general education," and "core curriculum." It typically requires students to select courses from the arts and humanities, social sciences, and the natural or physical sciences; and it may well mandate a course in writing, mathematics, or coding. Training for specific jobs is not featured and may even be discouraged. Or to put it positively, in the spirit of this book, such a broad education constitutes the best possible

---

*For many readers, this form of education will immediately evoke the descriptors "liberal arts" or "liberal arts or sciences." However, as we explain in box 3.2 (in chapter 3), this phrase is widely misunderstood; so we do not use it in reporting on our study.

preparation for a wide range of positions and opportunities in the society of the future.

We had hoped (and indeed had assumed) that—while under some threat and some criticism—an appreciation of this capacious conception of higher education would nonetheless be widely shared. But in fact, while there remains much to admire in US higher education, we have concluded—on the basis of our comprehensive study—that the sector has lost its way and stands in considerable peril. And this conclusion was reached well before the COVID-19 pandemic, which has proved disruptive for all institutions of higher learning, in this country and abroad, most especially for the less affluent ones.

We did not anticipate many of our findings and conclusions; we suspect that many of them will likewise come as a surprise to our readers. To begin with, more than a thousand students across disparate campuses turn out to be more similar than different; indeed, they generally use the same vocabulary and discuss the same themes, often in similar ways. Contrary to what one gathers from the press and from certain alarmist books, students are *not* preoccupied with political correctness, free speech issues, or the cost of college. (To be sure, we know of other studies in the last few years that suggest greater sensitivity with respect to such issues; we don't know whether this is a temporary or long-lasting phenomenon.)* Instead, we find that students are worried about their GPAs and resumes. Indeed, well before the onset of

---

*For examples, see Jonathan Rauch, *The Constitution of Knowledge: A Defense of Truth* (Washington, DC: Brookings Institution Press, 2021).

the pandemic, the biggest issues with which students struggle have been mental health challenges. Notable as well is the widespread feeling on the part of many students that they (and others) don't belong—far too many students feel alienated from peers, the academic agenda, and/or the ethos of the institution as a whole. While those adults who are "off campus"—parents, trustees, alums—acknowledge these problems, they, like a great many students, are preoccupied with issues of jobs and/or institutional reputation. In contrast, faculty and administrators—those presumably in contact with students on a daily basis—have significantly different and more aspirational ideas about the purpose(s) of college.

As we sought to understand the perspective of students and the other constituencies whom we interviewed, we developed a number of concepts that we believe are useful.

First, we introduce four ways of thinking about the experience of attending college: *inertial, transactional, exploratory,* and *transformational.* Fortunately, few of the individuals with whom we spoke saw college inertially—only as the "next step" after high school. But less happily, far too many students have a transactional view of college, and in that stance, they are customarily joined by parents, alums, and trustees. Interest in breadth of learning, having new educational experiences, and thinking of oneself and the world in new ways is limited, and is not the purpose for which most people go to college.

We also introduce a measure of the kind of analytic, synthesizing, and communication skills that we believe college should inculcate in all students. Terming it *Higher Education Capital*

(HEDCAP, for short), we conceive of it as the abi
analyze, reflect, connect, and communicate on issues ~. ...
and importance. We analyze the factors that contribute to development of high HEDCAP, or, less happily, maintain low HEDCAP.
While on the whole, more graduating students have higher HED-
CAP than first-year students, in many cases the academic benefits
of a college education prove difficult to demonstrate. This state of
affairs should concern all who care about the strength of a sector
that—so crucial to the thriving of any contemporary society—is
under considerable strain.

While we focused on this view of higher education and its pre-
sumed benefits (beyond the degree itself), we also determined
that students face major barriers to an effective education. Issues
of mental health loom large on every campus and with every
constituency—and, as noted, this was true well before the stressful period ushered in by COVID-19. Even over the course of our
study, large swathes of students reported that they (and often their
classmates) felt that they did not belong: many students feel alienated from their studies, from their peers, and from the institutions in which they are matriculating. Clearly, the challenges of
mental health and alienation require attention and redressing.

Throughout our discussion, we illustrate and summarize what
we have learned and what we think it means. As noted, certain
findings stand out. And yet, it's important to indicate that findings never speak directly to what they mean. As one example, we
find that about one-third of students report one or another form
of alienation from their collegiate experience. One could either
celebrate this finding (two-thirds don't signal alienation, therefore

we should celebrate); or one could point out that this means at least one million current college students are alienated—and perhaps those who are most alienated chose not to participate or did not even know about our study. As another example, we find that nearly half of US college students have an essentially transactional view of college. But that finding in itself does not reveal whether such a view is appropriate, troubling, or neutral; how it differs across different kinds of campuses; and, importantly, whether and in what ways it shifts from the first year of college to the later years. As yet one more example, we often find that students' views are better aligned with the views of off-campus than those of on-campus adults (faculty or staff); but whether this is expected or surprising, and what one should do about this misalignment, does not emerge directly from our data.

Given such puzzling and intriguing findings, we offer two major recommendations. To put it sharply, except for faculty and administrators, the academic goals and means of college are not salient for most students, nor for the other stakeholders we interviewed. To put it extra sharply, we suggest that most participants have "missed the point" of nonvocational higher education. Of course, this finding raises the vital question of *why* we need higher education at all—and given our own interest in a broad, general education—why offer *any* higher education that is not strictly vocational?

Our regretful conclusion: Many, perhaps most, US colleges have lost—or lost sight of—their principal reason for being. By virtue of the many activities available on campus, multiple motivations for attending college, often unhelpful expectations generated in secondary school, and the myriad of mixed messages on traditional media and social media, colleges are overwhelmed by mission sprawl. The understandable proclivity to create additional programs and additional administrative roles leaves students confused and unable to take advantage of what should be the chief focus—indeed, the *raison d'être*—of college. And, alas, as our investigation of various constituencies confirms, this confusion is not restricted to students.

On the basis of our study, we recommend a reframing, a reconfirmation of college today. From the day of admission, if not before, unless they are attending an explicitly vocational institution, students need to be introduced and guided toward the primary academic goals of their campus; and, equally, they need to be encouraged to draw on the academic resources—faculty, library, museums, research labs, writing centers—on their campus. All too often, such key introductory experiences (e.g., college tours, sketched in our opening chapter) serve mainly to foreground—if they are not limited to—dormitories, food, clubs, sports, and other pointedly nonacademic features. From the start, the campus needs to *onboard* the students—helping students to understand and belong to an entire community of learners, dealing with their health issues as much and as soon as possible, and supporting them throughout. Otherwise, the academic agenda cannot even be reasonably pursued.

We recommend a swift end to *projectitis*, the seemingly endless proliferation of offices, positions, and centers that bewilder students, when they are even noticed.* Instead, guided by determined leadership, undergraduate campuses need a laser-like focus on the academic mission of higher education. At most, a school should have *one* other focus that is not exclusively academic. And if the school determines that it wishes to feature such an emphasis—say, a civic, ethical, religious, or vocational orientation—that emphasis needs to be carefully *intertwined* with the central academic mission. For example, if a school wants its students to carry out public service, those enrolled should be given the necessary scholarly background and orientation—historical, political, economic, social, and quantitative concepts and skills; only then is it likely that they will be able to carry out such service in a knowledgeable and effective way. Absent such grounding, such public service may well be a diversionary experience, one that may even prove counterproductive for both the student and the public that is allegedly being served. Similarly, if part of a school's mission is to foster substantive contact and conversations with individuals from diverse backgrounds and interests, these opportunities should be featured in classroom work and assignments—not sidelined to incidental encounters elsewhere.

To anticipate the question that is doubtless on the mind of many readers: How is the picture we obtained and the recommendations we suggest affected by the recent pandemic? Of course, we cannot know for sure how the picture presented here might

---

*We are referring primarily to the various offices that attempt to address student issues—not to research centers, an important part of undergraduate as well as graduate and professional education.

have differed had we carried out the study half a decade later. But we can assert our strong conviction: a major world trauma should motivate every institution, every profession, every sector, indeed every entity, to reexamine its fundamental reason for being and to consider how best to sustain that central mission, those core values, in light of inevitable (and sometimes needed or even desirable) changes. Further, we believe that recent events—political as well as pandemic related—strengthen our case: it is imperative to place academic values and approaches at the center of the college experience.

We conclude that if higher education in the United States is to be successful in the twenty-first century, it needs to be sharply reframed. Pervasive issues of mental health and belonging must be addressed; extensive onboarding is needed with respect to the centrality of the academic educational agenda; any goal that is not strictly tied to learning needs either to be excised or to be clearly *intertwined* with the academic agenda.

In what follows, we invite you to join our research team.

In Part I, we detail what we did in our study. In chapter 1, we ask you to accompany us on a typical visit to a college—the college is hypothetical, but the experiences are all too real. In chapter 2, we present the background of our research: the earlier work that led to the rationale for the current study as well as the methods and concepts that guided our work. Then, in chapter 3, we describe our research methods in some detail and indicate where the reader can find additional technical information.

This background information should help the reader make sense of our findings and help our recommendations come alive.

But those eager to learn about our findings can proceed directly to Parts II and III; and those hungry for our recommendations can skip to Part IV, the concluding portion of the book.

In Parts II and III, we adopt the roles of cultural anthropologists, presenting our observations and findings in detail. Chapters 4 and 5 detail our major findings about how students think about college (introducing the four mental models); and whether, as a result of their college experiences, students develop the habits of thought and mind that we would hope to cultivate in young adults (our measure of Higher Education Capital).

In Part III, we present two formidable barriers to an effective education: chapter 6 details the pervasive mental health issues that arise on every campus; chapter 7 documents the failure of many students to secure and exhibit a sense of belonging. The academic goals of college would be far easier and more straightforward to achieve if students felt healthy in mind as well as part of a community; but in the absence of these desirable starting points, we need to do all we can to ensure a healthy mind and spirit.

At the start of Part IV in chapter 8, we offer a synthesis of those concepts that have proved most important for our understanding of the sector. Thereafter, we shift roles. In place of observing and analyzing (in the manner of social scientists), we offer our recommendations and prescriptions (in the manner of clinicians).

We do so in two ways: in chapter 9, we give presentations of four "ideal type" colleges, each illustrating different challenges and thus benefiting from different interventions; in chapter 10, we craft specific messages to the various stakeholders, who have kindly shared with us their thoughts, anxieties, and aspirations. In both cases, we keep in mind the often different goals and orientations of the various stakeholders and suggest ways of bridging those misalignments.

In the epilogue, we present our own personal reflections, as well as our aspirations for the sector that has provided so much value to us and our families, and to so many persons for so long a period of time.

I WHAT WE DID, WHY WE DID IT, AND HOW WE DID IT

Preparing for our first visit to yet another college, we meet at Boston's Logan Airport for an early morning flight. Howard, already at the gate, is reading a pile of student papers. As Wendy walks over, she runs through a mental checklist of interview essentials that should be in her carry-on bag: two recording devices, biographies for each interview participant, laptop for interview notes, several copies of interview questionnaires, consent forms, campus map, and a package of extra batteries for the recorders. It looks to be a busy week ahead at Greenly College (our literary invention, but the scenario draws on experiences that we had repeatedly in the course of our study). We are navigating our first visit, during which we expect to carry out approximately thirty interviews.

Having received approval from the school's president several months ago to carry out our study, we have already taken care of various logistics of travel and scheduled numerous interview appointments. During this initial trip, we will focus on interviews with faculty and administrators, along with some students sprinkled throughout our crowded schedule. Months ago, we scoured the school's website pages for information about each department, reading descriptions of faculty and administrators in order to identify individuals whom we hoped to interview.

In letters to these select individuals, we requested an hour of their time to solicit their views on the "college experience," including queries about curriculum, pedagogy, and campus life. As we put it, "We hope that your views will help us to provide valuable suggestions for how best to provide a quality education in the twenty-first century." In the case of Greenly, we sent over fifty email queries in the hopes of securing four full days of interviews. We sent gentle reminders if we did not hear back regarding the first invitation, but we did not continue correspondence after this second attempt. We are persistent, but also respectful of people's time.

As we received positive responses, we carefully curated the agenda. It was important to secure a representative sample from the school—faculty representing as many different departments as possible; and administrators focused on academic matters, as well as those focused on other facets of campus life. Having reached out to more than fifty individuals, we were able to schedule thirty of them, a manageable number of interviews for our first trip.

For their part, the students we plan to interview responded to an advertisement placed in the campus newspaper—promising a $50 gift card to either Amazon or DonorsChoose for those willing to share their perspectives. (As a token of appreciation, faculty and administrators received books.) Hoping to recruit additional students for a later time, Wendy also brought along some fliers that we were permitted to post around campus.

Other than the information on the web, we know little about the texture of the school. After consulting informants, we selected Greenly because of its size, location, and mission, as well as some intriguing academic and student life features. We carefully examined the mission statement of the school to understand important features of the school—or at least the features that the institution has chosen to emphasize. We were especially struck by two components. First, the school highlights its lengthy history as a leading institution of higher learning. Second, the school underscores its openness to students of "diverse" backgrounds and its goal of developing an "inclusive" and "healthy" community.

Before beginning our week on campus, we could easily generate some hypotheses about what we would find—rates of participation, language used, issues raised, and the like. But as social scientists, we know how important it is to approach our research in as *disinterested* a manner as possible—avoiding preconceived notions of what we might find. We strive to visit the campus with open minds—eager to listen as carefully as we can to the beliefs, desires, and needs of all whom we encounter.

DAY 1: GETTING TO KNOW THE CAMPUS

Having avoided the traveling researchers' peril—flight cancellations or delays—we arrive midday at Greenly College. Because our interviews don't begin until tomorrow, Wendy decides to attend an information session and take a college tour. Howard plans to go to the bookstore, the library, and the campus center, on the lookout for sites, events, postings, and human interactions that might inform our research.

Two remaining members of our team arrive mid-afternoon. As has become our custom, we gather before dinner to share initial impressions and prepare for the next day's interviews. Wendy reports that the tour was given by a graduating student, majoring in economics, which he claimed is the most popular major, alongside biology, political science, and psychology. The student guide first walked the group by the "most famous" dining hall on campus (where students can purchase an unlimited meal plan), the comfortable theater, and the new, state-of-the-art athletic center, complete with an Olympic-size swimming pool, basketball and squash courts, and an indoor track. Rugby and frisbee are the most popular clubs on campus. After traipsing through a residence hall and describing Greek life on campus, the guide pointed out the recently renovated science quad. He explained that as part of the "general education program" at Greenly, every student must fulfill certain requirements, like natural science courses and quantitative courses, most of which are "easy to complete." More than half of the students study abroad. The tour guide mentioned a wellness center but did not show it to the group.

A separate information session was facilitated by an admissions staff member and another graduating student, majoring in biology. The audience consisted mostly of parents and prospective students, with a few siblings. Most of the session focused on campus life—especially, the variety of clubs available for students (nearly three-quarters of the students participate in at least one club); access to current and classic movies shown in the new campus auditorium; and the campus center café open around the clock. The facilitators also mentioned several off-campus opportunities available to students—volunteer activities, internship programs, travel abroad, and laboratory initiatives on the school's private island, as well as day-long or weekend-long hiking and canoeing trips for members of the outing club.

As for services *on* campus, facilitators highlighted the fully staffed advising and tutoring centers, career center workshops, and dining hall options. Toward the end of the session, the speakers underscored the importance of "student well-being"—and described a recently expanded mental health center, a nutrition office, the wide range of clubs ("more than one can count"), and the centrally located Office of Diversity, Equity, and Inclusion, which had just appointed a new dean as well as a new associate dean.

Throughout the session, admissions facilitators repeated the words "inclusive" and "community service," which, they reminded us, "reflect the institutional priorities" of the school.

Asked about his stroll across campus, Howard offers a few comments. Whereas other campuses had not had newspapers available, Greenly College gives away free copies of the *New York Times* and the *Wall Street Journal*. But even on a Monday, as students bustled around campus, the piles of papers outside of the library and the bookstore remained high. In the library, groups of students were seated together, working on problem sets and—as he overheard—helping each other prepare for an upcoming exam. The bookstore housed and displayed more literary fiction than bookstores on most other campuses. Outside the store, students gathered to pick up a shuttle—in splendid isolation, each glued to their phones.

Howard also shares another observation: the plethora of new buildings on campus, bearing the names of the school's wealthiest alums. Wendy notes that she heard detailed information about several new initiatives (and recently hired administrative staff) focused on student well-being—recalling the school's mission statement, which focuses on inclusivity and well-being. A member of our team asks, "What's the evidence that Greenly equally values scholarship, also claimed in the mission of the school?" And the other member follows up: "How much of the information session and the tour was focused on academics? Did any parents focus specific questions on the curriculum, or only on student services?"

With this background, researchers are ready for the first set of interviews.

DAY 2: FIRST SET OF INTERVIEWS

At an early breakfast, the team gathers again to discuss the schedule for the day. There are ten scheduled interviews: five with faculty members (two in the sciences, three in social sciences and humanities); three with senior administrators (the assistant head of athletics, director of admissions, and a student life administrator in charge of Greek life); and two students—one involved in student government and the other on the soccer team. Two members of our team participate in each interview—one researcher primarily to pose questions from the interview protocol, the other to take notes, keep track of important questions to ask, note the time remaining, and monitor the digital recorders (two—one as backup). Pairs of interviewers change throughout the day so that we all have an opportunity to experience each other as interviewers, and to share the roles of interviewer and note taker.

In the early evening, after several unplanned encounters throughout the day, we congregate in a conference room at the hotel—thereby ensuring that no one can eavesdrop (happily, all ten of our scheduled interviews worked out—otherwise we would have had to do some quick reshuffling of our plans). We begin at once to talk about the apparent prevalence of mental health topics in our disparate interviews. One by one, each of us reports that across interviews, most participants rank "mental health issues" as the most important problem on campus (relative to other problems such as alcohol and substance abuse, academic dishonesty, safety issues, and relationships with peers). One member of the team recounts seeing several students chatting casually outside the wellness center yesterday. We are curious whether on this campus, as compared to some others, mental health issues might be destigmatized.

As our conversation continues, Wendy remarks that the word "stress" came up a lot with the two students she interviewed (see box 4.1).* In response to the question: "What, if anything, keeps

---

* All box numbers are yoked to the chapter in which they appear.

you up at night?" one student said: "I definitely have trouble sleeping when I have an exam the next day or something like that . . . I get super stressed out about . . . stuff that has a heavy weight on my grade . . . I have not been sleeping well this week . . . It's just a lot of stress about getting it all done."

Howard chimes in: the first faculty member he interviewed—a political scientist who has been teaching at this school for nearly thirty years—brought up the lack of sleep among students as a major concern. This professor claims that students here "vastly underrate" the importance of sleep in terms of being able to "think about material, and to be able to read carefully, to make it to class, and get the most out of class." In fact, when asked for three pieces of advice that he'd offer to a hypothetical incoming student, "adequate sleep" headed the list.

The team arrives at an insight: whether talking about sleepless nights, or overall stress and anxiety—*not a single participant* mentioned finances or the cost of higher education. This surprises us. We speculate that we might hear more on these topics from parents or trustees when we ask them the same questions, in the coming months. Or perhaps we would have heard more in the period immediately following the financial crash of 2007–2008.

THE REST OF THE WEEK: SMOOTH SAILING

Each day follows the same general structure. Supplementing the digital recordings, researchers prepare detailed notes about each interview; write personalized thank you notes to each participant;

scan online biographies of the next day's participants (when available); and confirm locations of faculty offices on the campus map for the next day's interviews (no time to get lost!). Team members also explore different spaces on campus—sitting in the library, working out in the gym, and trying out almost every coffee shop on campus. These experiences help us to understand the campus culture and give us the opportunity to listen inconspicuously to conversations among those on campus—about which courses to choose next semester, the perils of parking, and how to juggle hefty reading assignments with heavy work or athletic responsibilities.

By the end of the week, we have accumulated eight digital recorders full of thirty interviews, approximately sixty pages of notes, and folders of forms to file when we get back to the office, including consent forms and book selections. Importantly, we also have secured far more knowledge about this campus—everything from where to get the tastiest sandwich, to policies governing promotion and tenure, to the biggest struggles reported by students. Of course, these are just our initial impressions. They will be nuanced and perhaps revised in light of our three or four subsequent visits to campus, our interviews of other constituencies, and in-depth coding at a future point in our study.

We are left with many more questions than we had on our official interview questionnaire. We wonder which of our impressions are transitory or idiosyncratic, and which will be reinforced by other visits to this or other campuses. In our minds, we have begun to compare Greenly College to its peer schools in our study, as well as contextualize what we have heard and observed here with respect to what we have learned from publications and postings on higher education.

Over the course of five years of data collection, we and the hard-working members of our team will have spent forty weeks working across campuses just like this. It's a good thing we've taken lots of notes!

2 THE "WHY" QUESTION: BACKGROUND AND CONTEXT FOR OUR STUDY

At the time of writing this book (2021), we have spent many years working on this study: five years visiting ten different campuses and interviewing more than two thousand individuals, and more than two years analyzing the interviews and our observations. To our knowledge, in recent years, no other study of American higher education with this size and scope has been conducted. And, while both of us have conducted research in education for many years, this is our first time focusing on higher education. You might well wonder: *why*, nearly a decade ago (during the first term of Barack Obama's presidency), did we undertake this ambitious, wide-ranging study, and *why* did we proceed the way we did?

There was a method to our madness.

Even though we strove to be objective and to avoid any pre-conceived notion, of course, no research project springs up in an instant—like Athena from the head of Zeus. We (Wendy and Howard) are psychologically trained social scientists who, since 1995, have worked together at Project Zero, a research consortium at the Harvard Graduate School of Education. For the first full decade, we worked side-by-side on an ambitious research project called the "Good Project" (for details, see box 2.1). The current study emerged in large measure from the findings and surprises of that project.

As part of the Good Project, Wendy led a study of how adolescents and young adults thought about work generally, as well as the particular professional niches to which they aspired. Wendy and colleagues confirmed that those young participants—aspiring or budding professionals—knew and admired "good work"—a sense of responsibility with respect to the kind of work carried out, and to the individuals being served by that work. Yet at the same time—indeed repeatedly—young people admitted to ethical misconduct: not checking sources before turning in a story, lying about research methods in scientific reports, or engaging in work that violated personal standards; for example, taking a lead role in a theater production that promoted racial stereotypes that they otherwise deplored.[1]

Surprisingly, students displayed little to no embarrassment or shame in sharing these values and beliefs; they felt justified, validated. They never asked us to turn off the recording devices, nor did they request that their testimony remain confidential. Repeatedly, young people told us that they had worked too hard to be on the cusp of success, and accordingly it would not be "fair" if others got ahead of them. For these young professionals, "good work"

Box 2.1

The Good Project and the Concept of Alignment

In 1967, Nelson Goodman, an eminent analytic philosopher, launched a research group at the Harvard Graduate School of Education. The avowed purpose of this scholarly inquiry was to study learning in the arts. As Goodman quipped, "there's lots of lore about artistic learning, but little systematic knowledge. And so, we'll call our enterprise Project Zero."

Goodman retired in 1971, and Howard joined David Perkins as codirector of the Project. Over that time span, Project Zero expanded in scope from the arts to the range of scholarly disciplines, from early childhood education through secondary education, and grew increasingly international. Now, over fifty years old, Project Zero remains an influential educational research center, known for its innovative ideas and practices, as well as its conferences and online learning opportunities.

Wendy joined the staff of Project Zero in 1996. For a decade, in collaboration with psychologists Mihaly (Mike) Csikszentmihalyi and William (Bill) Damon and other colleagues, Howard, Wendy, and a sizable multisite staff carried out a large-scale research project to understand the values of work across nine professions, including education, genetics, journalism, and law. While such professions had once occupied a hallowed niche in the US workplace, we discerned a definite decline in a professional sense of responsibility for "good work"—reflecting the increasing centrality of technology, powerful market forces, the absence of countervailing forces, and, all too often, the lack of firm ethical standards (including sanctions) that would allow the professions to continue to thrive. The "Good Work Project," since renamed the Good Project, launched several additional lines of inquiry (Good Play, Good Collaboration, Good Digital Citizenship).

The investigative methods we used in the present study were drawn in significant measure from our earlier Good Project. In that endeavor, Wendy and Howard, along with a team of researchers, interviewed over 1,500 individuals—investigating individual beliefs, values, and responsibilities for work. We carried out intensive interviews with a wide-ranging, open-ended interview questionnaire; recorded and transcribed the interviews (which was more difficult to do in the 1990s than in 2020); coded the responses using an in-depth qualitative approach; secured reliability; and then looked for patterns within and across the several professions.

The earlier project yielded our key concepts of *alignment* and *misalignment*. Briefly, "good work" is much more likely to emerge when the various interest parties in any profession are *well aligned*—when the different stakeholders have similar values and work toward the same goals. Alignment contrasts with a less fortunate situation, when the various constituencies surrounding a profession have different, even clashing, sets of values—in short, when they are *misaligned*. In the present study, we chose to compare the testimony and the stances of eight separate constituencies, and to ascertain to what extent they were aligned or misaligned with one another. Our concept of alignment (and misalignment) helped us to make recommendations to individuals, institutions, and, indeed, to the entire sector.

We should note one major difference between the Good Project and our study of higher education. In the earlier study, we focused on individual practitioners and professionals, not on institutions. In the current study of higher education, we interviewed over 2,000 individuals in order to investigate campuses as a whole, and to secure the views of the various stakeholder groups on each campus (students, faculty, administrators, etc.).

was an aspiration for *later* in life—for what commentator David Brooks has dubbed "the second mountain."[2]

Our collaboration on the Good Project stimulated considerable curiosity about the "mental set" of students on the cusp of adulthood. We wondered: Why were young people so "transactional"? Why were they willing to kick the "good work" can down the road? And, importantly, can anything, or *should* anything, be done about it?

As researchers, we might simply have pondered these puzzles or moved on to other ones. But instead, we decided to proceed from careful research to modest interventions. And so, in the next few years, we created a "Good Work Toolkit," which teachers and researchers could draw upon, and we carried out courses and interventions at schools nearby—Colby College in Maine, Amherst College in Western Massachusetts, and Harvard College, for first-year students at our own campus.

As we and our colleagues developed and facilitated many reflection sessions across these campuses, we became keenly aware of the struggles and tensions students face in college in the early twenty-first century. And as we—longtime researchers at Project Zero—switched the focus of our research from K–12 to higher education, we surveyed the plethora of writings about US colleges and universities—some of them by close colleagues, others by experts in fields ranging from economics and business to historical and literary studies. At the same time, news outlets in the United States began to headline often searing critiques of higher education—raising questions about its "value," as costs were rising and students were seen as unmotivated or immature, as faculty were seen as careerist rather than classroom oriented, and as leftist rather than centrist or conservative. It's easy to add to this list of complaints. We read and learned from these books, articles, and podcasts. Yet we were also impressed by the ratio of strong opinions in comparison with carefully collected and analyzed data. To borrow an old phrase, we wished that we were as sure of *one* thing as some of these authors were of the *entire* landscape.

And so, we gradually constructed an ambitious project, the results of which we present in these pages. The *scope* of the project: to carry out an empirical study of undergraduate higher education in the United States, covering a range of campuses; to collect and distill what the diverse stakeholders on each of these campuses think about the value of nonvocational education—traditionally, what we and others have called "liberal arts and sciences" (see box 3.2). We wanted to collect considerable—perhaps, indeed, unprecedented—data about the college experience: what it is and what it could be.

It is our good fortune that our colleague Richard Light agreed to be the senior adviser to the program and to provide invaluable guidance and recommendations throughout the entire period. Over the course of our project, many other outstanding educational thinkers have guided us—their names, along with our gratitude, appear in the acknowledgments.

TWO HELPFUL ANALOGIES

In carrying out this research, we assumed the stances of *anthropologists* (more accurately, budding or aspiring anthropologists or ethnographers)—as can be gleaned from the description of our week at Greenly College. We traversed campuses, made all sorts of observations, spoke to a wide range of individuals associated with the campuses, took careful notes (as well as occasional photographs and videos), and described what we saw and heard as carefully and faithfully as possible. We saw ourselves as attempting to "capture the culture" on various campuses, and, as far as possible, on US college campuses in the aggregate.

But given our concerns about what is happening—or not happening—on college campuses, we went beyond the purely descriptive mission of the traditional anthropologist. In describing the arc of our work, we have also found it useful to think of ourselves as *physicians* (less presumptuously, budding or aspiring *clinicians*)—the characterization that we will use going forward—investigating a patient. In our case, the "patient" is that segment of the higher educational system in the United States that is not avowedly vocational; that is troubled, but whose symptoms are vague; and whose future course of treatment is accordingly uncertain. In making the shift from anthropologists to clinicians (in the spirit of the subtitle of this book), we shift from describing *what is* to prescribing *what can be*.

Armed with an "analytic stethoscope," so to speak, we wanted to probe the various organs of college, in the hopes of determining the nature of the "ailment(s)" and identifying interventions that are most likely to restore overall health. Of course, the sector of higher education in the United States is quite complex; it might be more useful to think of us as a group of clinicians armed with a variety of stethoscopes and other instruments, investigating many campuses and constituencies. Or, in the aggregate, as medical anthropologists.

As with clinicians, our mission transcends diagnosis. Even as we were recording what we noticed across campuses, we were on the alert as well for programs, projects, and perspectives that could address the various ailments that we diagnosed—the promising interventions that would enhance the health of different constituencies on campus, and the health of the sector as a whole to bring about better alignments. Indeed, in the concluding parts of this book, we detail some of the most effective treatments about which we have learned.

A nuance to our approach: while we are interested in the entire higher education system, we believe that it's important to focus on specific units. And of course, in the United States, the units are specific colleges—either stand-alone colleges or ones embedded in larger universities. And so, while we are actually interested in the "symptomology of" and the "treatment for" the entire sector, our descriptions and, in particular, our recommendations and "prescriptions" are often directed at specific colleges, and occasionally at specific departments or a particular constituency within a college.

Accordingly, in the manner of responsible clinicians, we planned to present our findings on each campus at "rounds"—discussions with the various constituencies on campus. We would showcase the data, answer questions, engage in discussion, and make specific suggestions about how best to improve the health of that college. And, indeed, in chapter 9, we give brief examples of such rounds. There, drawing on our observations, we present four "ideal type" campuses—each "presenting" with a particular set of strengths and challenges. And in each case, we include specific recommendations designed to strengthen the profession of higher education going forward—"the health of the sector," so to speak.

For now, we'll put the analogy of budding anthropologist and clinician on hold until the later part of the book; but if it proves helpful, please keep it in mind as we describe more specific approaches, analyses, and findings.

THE BROAD CONTEXT DEFINED

We've indicated the factors that have led us—as longtime researchers—to undertake our large, national study of higher education. But, of course, a study like ours should be seen—albeit briefly—in context.

For at least a century, higher education in the United States has been a source of national pride—and indeed, an institution admired in much of the world.[3] But recently and, seemingly, for the first time, large segments of the American public indicate that they are dissatisfied with higher education and, indeed, many go so far as to assert that higher education is not in the national interest.[4] We are unsure of the reasons for this (to us) alarming finding—directed particularly at colleges—and we hope that it proves to be transient. This disaffection could come from the costs of higher education, the belief that higher education is tilted politically to the left, skepticism that education that is not avowedly vocational is a waste of time and/or of money—or perhaps a thoughtful, or casual, or even thoughtless blend of these reasons (see box 10.1), which addresses concerns raised by skeptics of higher education.* If there were ever a time for a careful study of higher education in the United States, it has arrived.

How did higher education get to this point?

Historical Context

In North America, institutions of higher education date back to the colonial era—schools like Harvard, William and Mary, and Yale were launched well before the American Revolution. These institutions were patterned after the colleges in England (and Scotland); their curricula consisted largely of classical languages, mathematics, and the sciences of the day. Indeed, they bore a family resemblance to the trivium and quadrivium of the Middle Ages foregrounded at the earliest universities in western Europe—the *original* liberal arts, as it were. A primary ambition of these American colleges was to develop religious leaders, though preparation for other professions and for leadership roles in the society also took place.

Once the colonies had broken away from England, colleges took on a civic as well as a religious emphasis. Toward the end of the

---

*This critique applies particularly and often specifically to colleges; the role of universities, with their professional and scientific training, is less frequently the subject of critique. See Steven Brint, *Two Cheers for Higher Education: Why American Universities Are Stronger Than Ever—and How to Meet the Challenges They Face* (Princeton, NJ: Princeton University Press, 2019).

eighteenth century and in the first half of the nineteenth century, a plethora of schools—many religious in origin—were launched across the expanding nation. Small and without much funding, their existence was perilous, but familiar names like Amherst, Mount Holyoke, and Williams in New England, and Kenyon College and Ohio Wesleyan in the Midwest, date from that era. Students were expected to master the knowledge and skills needed to participate in the activities and the decisions of their communities and perhaps assume the mantle of leadership—locally, regionally, even nationally.

The latter half of the nineteenth century—the period during and after the Civil War—ushered in major changes in the landscape of higher education. Under President Lincoln, land grant public colleges were launched—the beginnings of agricultural, technological, vocational, and more general institutions of higher education date to this time. Then, following the impressive model in Germanic (Humboldtian) institutions of higher education, several leading colleges evolved into universities that granted doctoral degrees in specific subjects; postgraduate-oriented schools, notably Clark University, Johns Hopkins, and the University of Chicago, were also established. This development marked the start of the research university—classical studies and languages were on the wane, surveys of science (as distinct from technology) on the rise. Also, along with these factors of public funding and a greater emphasis on emerging lines of scholarly inquiry, the religious mission declined, and, indeed, had become nearly invisible in many schools by the twentieth century—including the ones we've just named.[5]

Before the twentieth century, education beyond primary and secondary schools was restricted largely to individuals from comfortable financial and social backgrounds, with only a few highly deserving students receiving the small number of scholarships. (Significant financial endowments were virtually unknown.) Moreover, with few exceptions, the school population was white and male. But as the United States became a world power, especially after the World Wars, colleges and universities expanded greatly. With the activation of the GI Bill at the end of the Second World War, an ever-increasing proportion of the population continued its education beyond high school. More places were open to women and minorities; more colleges—including the oldest and most storied ones—became coeducational. In many cases, there were explicit efforts to recruit, enroll, and support Black, Hispanic, Native American, and other historically marginalized groups. A religious focus remained at only a small minority of schools. (Indeed, as we detail in chapter 8, missions either proliferated or waned; schools sought to address an ever-expanding variety of constituencies with a concomitant variety of foci.) And perhaps most notably, this was the era par excellence of major public universities, led by the flagship California system. Community (junior) colleges, state schools, and major research universities were publicly—and, for a time, generously—funded by several jurisdictions.[6]*

---

*Clark Kerr was a key figure in developing public universities. After serving as the Chancellor of the University of California System of Higher Education, he chaired the Carnegie Council of Policy Studies in Higher Education, an institution that issued a series of landmark reports.

Contemporary Context

Scholars generally agree that the period of the 1950s to the 1970s marked a high point for higher education—both within the United States and with respect to its status relative to the rest of the world. (The once-admired German universities were still recovering from the disastrous political events in the first half of the twentieth century.)[7] Colleges expanded, students of diverse backgrounds and demographies flocked to them, the job market was growing—both for students who were headed directly for the marketplace and for students who wanted additional study for the professions, including the profession of college or university teacher.

But in recent decades, the sector has been ever more troubled. Because education has traditionally not benefited from an economy of scale, costs of almost every facet have risen steadily.[8] And even as costs have risen, the percentage of the budget provided by the state to public institutions has declined, often precipitously. At the University of Massachusetts, for example, state support dropped from roughly 60% to 35% during this time, while at the University of Illinois at Chicago, state support declined from 53% to less than 17%.[9] Indeed, were there not legal obstacles, proud flagship public universities like the University of Virginia, the University of Washington, the University of Michigan, and the Berkeley and Los Angeles campuses of the University of California would clearly benefit from becoming private institutions. They would be freer to raise money and no longer subject to the whims of trustees, many of whom have been selected for political reasons and are often uninformed or misinformed about substantive issues of higher education.

Especially notable are the costs for individuals who want to attend college but are not eligible for scholarships or federally funded Pell Grants. The average tuition for public institutions (in state), not including room and board, in 1970 was $394; in 2000 it was $3,501; and in 2017, according to a recent report, tuition was $9,037. At the same time, the average tuition for private institutions, not including room and board, in 1970 was $1,706; in 2000 it was $15,470; and in 2017, according to the most recent report, tuition was $30,731.[10] Meanwhile, while continuing to rise, average family incomes have grown much more slowly. These are the figures that haunt families and inevitably raise the economically (and politically) charged question of higher education's "return on investment."*

Once one moves away from purely financial considerations, other trends can readily be documented. Yet their causes are more difficult to ascertain—especially for those who are immersed in, if not overwhelmed by data, as well as for those who are inclined toward skepticism. There is little question that grade inflation is rampant—in many places a B is considered a mediocre grade, and a C as *de facto* failure. One could argue that perhaps students

---

*The price of college is a complex issue. See Michael McPherson and Morton Owen Schapiro, eds., *College Access: Opportunity or Privilege?* (New York: College Board, 2003); Caroline M. Hoxby and Kevin Stange, eds., *Productivity in Higher Education* (Chicago: University of Chicago Press, 2016); Robert B. Archibald and David H. Feldman, *Why Does College Cost So Much?* (Oxford: Oxford University Press, 2010); and Ron Lieber, *The Price You Pay for College: An Entirely New Road Map for the Biggest Financial Decision Your Family Will Ever Make* (New York: HarperCollins, 2021).

are getting smarter or working harder. But considerable evidence indicates that students are devoting far less time to their studies than they did in earlier eras.[11]

Another trend concerns the areas of study. Fifty years ago, college students took general education courses, accepted (and, indeed, often welcomed) distribution requirements, and enrolled in significant numbers in courses and majors in the humanities (English, foreign languages, history, philosophy, the arts) and the "softer" social sciences (sociology, anthropology, certain areas of psychology and government). But over recent decades, the appeal of the humanities has steadily declined, while majors in business (an avowedly direct route to a vocation) or economics (often the privileged student's entry to business or finance) have risen. STEM (science, technology, engineering, and mathematics) courses and majors are also more popular, with courses in computer science, data science, artificial intelligence topping the list.[12] Undoubtedly these trends are driven by uncertainty about the job market; it is also possible that the more traditional disciplines have failed to make an adequate case for their significance, or that they are indeed less central in the landscape of knowledge than they were in earlier eras.[13]

Yet another trend concerns the ways in which academic material is presented. There are modest trends toward less lecturing and more "hands on" and "project-based" learning, particularly at schools with more resources.[14] A far larger factor is the advent of online learning. No doubt this form of learning will both increase globally and, if more gradually, will improve in quality (which appears to have happened far more quickly in the wake of the

COVID-19 epidemic). But at the time of our study, online learning was still not a major factor for most students enrolled in two-year or four-year US colleges—those of a more skeptical frame of mind challenge its effectiveness and its depth, except for students who are quite motivated. And even those students value—perhaps overvalue—the importance of living on campuses or at least rubbing elbows with their peers.

Other trends concern how students use their time and how they feel about their lives. As already indicated, many students today spend less time reading, studying, and preparing for examinations than they used to. In contrast, students are spending (perhaps too) much time online, particularly on social media; and our own data also suggest much time spent watching television and movies—and not primarily with academic learning in mind.[15]

Most dramatically for our own study is students' desire for help in coping with stress, anxiety, and other symptoms of mental illness. On every campus (and well before the recent pandemic), many students report these symptoms, and many students want help in dealing with them. On a related point, many students express a lack of sense of belonging in their respective campus communities. The extreme skeptic might counter that these conditions always existed, but that students either denied them, coped with them when they arose, or outgrew them over time. But here we are *not* extremely skeptical. We believe that these trends and statistics are irrefutable, and they constitute an enormous challenge for higher education today. Hence, in the pages that follow, they occupy much of our attention.

Box 2.2

A "Free Week" on Campus: The Greatest Gift of All

Katie Abramowitz

Imagine you are a college student who has been mysteriously given a "free" week on a college campus. Unburdened by your 8 a.m. chemistry class, afternoon study group, and other obligations and time commitments, you are free to explore the new gallery in the campus's prestigious art museum, stop by a professor's office hours, or maybe attend that interesting live lecture series that you never had time for before. Curious about how students think about and use unstructured time on campus, we asked students the following question: "If you were given a free week on campus, without obligations, but with all of the resources, how would you spend your time?" None of our expectations—catching up on work, making some extra money, or seeking advice about future life choices—were borne out.

What *did* we find?

Almost half of all students (46%) state that they would use campus facilities, but students describe time on a quad, lawn, or the gym.

For example, a first-year student pursuing a double major in nursing and psychology comments: "I would definitely go to the gym . . . and maybe go to the health center or get a massage therapy . . . but I definitely think the gym is one of the biggest things and is in your tuition so you don't have to pay for it . . . so I'd definitely make really good use of the gym."

Indeed, artistic performances, research centers, or residence hall convening spaces are hardly mentioned in students' descriptions of how they would use free time on campus. Only a quarter of these students who describe campus facilities talk about the library.

At the same time, while approximately a third of students (34%) talk about using the time to socialize with others, nearly a quarter of students (21%) talk about relaxing on their own—watching movies or even "doing nothing."

A first-year student on the school's rugby team says: "Well, I'd fear that I would probably spend the majority of it sleeping in my bed watching Netflix."

A graduating senior admits: "I think I would sit in my living room and play The Sims all day long. And then maybe go out to the dining hall for meals. Or maybe I would take food out of the dining halls, and eat it in my apartment, and never leave. That's probably what I would end up doing, with naps mixed in. Because my life is so stressful, any chance that I would have to have no obligations, I would just really enjoy it and do nothing."

As reflected by these responses, unstructured time is viewed by many students as a necessary, even cherished opportunity to decompress and recharge—given the oft-heard descriptions of academic stress.

Moreover, nearly a quarter of students (24%) talk about going off-campus—despite the wealth of resources and services available on most campuses.

One first-year student majoring in genetics explains: "I wanna explore [college town] more. I feel like you're kind of trapped on campus, just because there's so much to do all the time, that you're always so busy that you don't get to explore, so I'd like to actually, I think, leave campus and see more about the area."

Other students talk about getting farther away from campus. For example, a graduating senior who is heavily involved in Greek life states, "I'd probably take a trip somewhere with a bunch of people . . . kind of like a spring break trip . . . just go somewhere, have some fun, take a break from school and all of our responsibilities."

Interestingly, while numerous and varied campus clubs and organizations are often touted by colleges in admission sessions, fewer than a quarter of students (18%) describe participating in clubs and organizations on campus if given free time. In some instances, students only vaguely mention clubs and organizations, with no reference to specific on-campus groups, suggesting that their intended involvement is superficial rather than deeply meaningful.

Notably, given students' explanations of academic rigor as the major source of mental health stressors on college campuses (as described in chapter 6), we are surprised that fewer than 10% of students talk about using time to get ahead on required reading, study for upcoming exams, or work on papers.

What to make of these findings?

While an abundant amount of money, resources, and planning (and marketing!) are put into "campus life," these opportunities may not be strongly prioritized by students. Indeed, when given unstructured time, it seems that many students would rather take a break from these offerings—relaxing in their dorm rooms by themselves or even separating themselves from campus. While investing in a beautiful new art museum may seem attractive to donors and trustees, administrators may want to consider how students actually use their time on campus and which parts of college life they most value. Those considerations would also be instructive to college leaders as they work to intertwine these valuable opportunities with the academic mission of the overall college experience, so that students can truly make the most of their time on a college campus, rather than valuing the trips elsewhere.

As behooves a serious vocation or sector that aspires to be taken seriously, nearly all institutions of higher education have stated missions. As we peruse the mission statement of the campuses we have studied, we encounter many grand, even grandiose statements of goals (some too long to quote here, or, perhaps, anywhere). As we scan the statements of these ten schools, we also find a wide range of missions, including academic goals, religious or spiritual missions, civic missions, aspirations for leadership, health and well-being, and diversity and inclusivity.

It's of course understandable that colleges proliferate missions. In contemporary jargon and with appropriate buzzwords, they want to attract and please potential "customers." We note with approval (and relief) that most mission statements highlight educational and learning goals—along with a recognition of the desire for personal, social, and healthy growth. Only rarely do the mission statements explicitly highlight what turns out to be most on the minds of most constituencies (and surely on the minds of the student tour guides and the admissions staff who give the information sessions)—athletics, internships, campus centers and dining halls, and careers. In Part IV of this book, we discuss our observations and recommendations for the mission of higher education.

To make this point vivid, consider an experience that turned out to be unexpectedly revealing. A few years before we commenced our study, Howard had the opportunity to eavesdrop on a discussion about the college experience among a dozen undergraduates from elite colleges—six from Harvard, and the remaining six from selective schools in the Northeast United States. The discussion was deliberately designed to be free ranging, to cover a wide variety of topics that occupy the radar screens of college students. Students discussed the stresses of college life, the diversity of the student body, the scramble for leadership roles in campus organizations, and anxiety about the proper summer internships and future job opportunities. After an hour, Howard asked for permission to step out of his role as observer and to make a few remarks.

Howard: "Many thanks for giving me the opportunity to listen to your conversation. I found it interesting and enlightening. And it also helped me to think about a problem that keeps me up at night.

"As it happens, I am a member of the board of trustees of the University of Northern New England [a fictitious institution]. We are having severe financial problems, and we are worried about whether we can admit another class. We really have to save money, and I have been charged with figuring out how.

"In listening to your conversation, I could not help noticing that you never spoke about *anything* having to do with the curriculum, or with the academic mission of your schools. And so, the solution to our financial dilemma is really quite straightforward. We should simply get rid of the faculty, the lecture halls, the seminar rooms, the library, the museums, and the research laboratories. They seem not to be important, and I infer that they would not be missed!"

Clearly, Howard was trying to be provocative. Indeed, an embarrassed silence followed his remarks. And after the session concluded, one of the students, a Harvard sophomore, approached

Howard and asked whether they could meet during his office hours. Days later, when they discussed the issue quite seriously, Howard broke the ice by asking him: "Are you from the *Harvard Crimson* [the school newspaper]?" They both had a good laugh—but the absence of explicit concern with matters academic, on the part of so many students at select four-year colleges, is a matter that we take extremely seriously.

That said, in our view, as we will detail in the later part of this book (chapter 8), most campuses are *far too ambitious—too grandiose—in their respective missions*. Paradoxically, as a result, they achieve far less than they could and should. We speak of rampant *projectitis*—the rapid increase of centers, staff, and initiatives that are created in efforts to help achieve the raft of missions, but which all too often overwhelm and confuse students.

The distinctive concerns we unearthed about students' mental health, lack of a sense of belonging, and confusion with respect to purpose associated with the proliferation of projects, have convinced us of three imperatives: the importance of *more sharply defined* (and accordingly, more limited) *missions*; better *onboarding* of students; and more strategic *intertwining* of activities or aspirations with the academic mission. Taken together, the solution to these challenges should promote a new and much-needed level of trust on campuses—necessary both for the successful undergraduate careers of individual students and for the overall achievement of the fundamental learning goals of colleges, universities, and higher education itself. We revisit these themes throughout the book.

THE TIMING OF OUR STUDY AND THE
INEVITABILITY OF COHORT EFFECTS

As noted, we planned our study in 2012 and collected data over the period of 2013 to 2018. Fortunately, the process of the study unfolded very much as we had anticipated.

But less than two years later, the entire world—and, of course, the stratum of higher education—was disrupted to an unprecedented degree by the COVID-19 pandemic, and the temporary suspension of education on campus in schools everywhere. Nor at the time of this writing (2021) is it at all clear to what extent and in which ways the sector will be reorganized or reconstituted in the near future.

Any study of human beings—be it longitudinal or cross-sectional—will inevitably reflect the time in which it was conducted. Thinking back to the recent past in the United States, students enrolled in 2001 would have been shaken by the attack on the Twin Towers; students enrolled in 2008 would have been affected by the financial crisis. And if we think back to their grandparents' generation, living through the Depression of the 1930s, or the Second World War in the early 1940s, students in those cohorts would have been massively disrupted—and fewer of them would have been enrolled in college.

Our study reflects the circumstances in the middle of the second decade of the twenty-first century—politically, we might call it the period of Obama, or of the dominance of social media, or of the steady rise of global technology companies and the loss of secure jobs—and so inevitably our findings are most deeply rooted in the world of that era. *And yet, we firmly believe that the situation that we described, as well as the trends that we observed, are not restricted to a particular moment in time.* In fact, we believe that the portrait of higher education in these pages—what it aspired to yesterday and what it could achieve tomorrow—is evergreen; and while surface features will undoubtedly change—more online teaching, for example, or perhaps fewer four-year residential schools—the deeper academic, social, and personal themes will continue in broad scope. We would even maintain that our portrait applies not only to nonvocational institutions in the United States, but also to others that have sprung up around the world.

One related point. The pandemic, along with other upheavals around the world, has necessitated nearly every sector of society— from law and medicine to the arts and athletics—to consider which aspects of its work are absolutely central, and which ones are peripheral and could readily be dropped or reworked. In our view, higher education in the United States can and should turn this crisis into an opportunity. Those who care about the sector— all of us involved in such critical reflection—should confirm its core reason for existence. And, accordingly, we should refashion our work to ensure the optimal nurturance of the minds that have been entrusted to us.

GETTING STARTED

With these historical and contemporary trends and considerations in the background, we launched our own study of higher education in the United States. But, as we've stressed, we were

not armed with strong expectations with respect to specific findings and recommendations. Though by no means "blank slates,"
we wanted to listen carefully, probe sensitively, analyze deeply,
and only then come up with conclusions and recommendations.
Indeed, it was only as we moved toward recommendations, that
we realized and fully confronted some of our own strongly held
values and beliefs: higher education should be principally about
the acquisition of new ways of thinking and the possibility of
significant personal transformations—and not primarily about
athletics, club leadership, specific career paths, or other societal
markers of success.

METHODS FOR OUR STUDY OF HIGHER EDUCATION

Over the course of the study, we were often asked—indeed, until this day, we continue to be asked: "What are, or what were, your hypotheses?" When succumbing to the academic's urge to be clever, we quote Sir Isaac Newton, who famously claimed: "Hypotheses non fingo"—loosely, "I don't make any hypotheses." But in fact, that claim has considerable legitimacy. Other than some areas in which we and our colleagues at Project Zero had particular interests (e.g., ethics, civics, digital life, the arts), we determined to cast a wide net. And we feared that if we ourselves introduced particular topics—for example, the cost of higher education, pressures from parents, social tensions on campus, or even the term "liberal arts"—we would inevitably skew the interview, and thus possibly miss more important (but less evident) themes and concerns.

Accordingly, we designed a semi-structured interview questionnaire, consisting of approximately forty open-ended questions. The interview questions were organized into three main sections: academic program, campus life, and conceptions of higher education. Within these areas, we developed more targeted questions through which we hoped to pinpoint specific attitudes and stances.

An example: Toward the middle of the interview, we asked every participant, "If you were in charge of the academic program—the czar—what are three changes that you might make?" In response to this question, participants could proceed in numerous directions. For instance, they might provide a set of reflections about course requirements ("Let's eliminate foreign languages," or "Abolish courses with limited enrollment"); or share a view of specific course content ("More on diversity," or "Knowledge about how to balance a checkbook"); or share thoughts about the inadequacies of advising, housing, or athletic facilities. Some participants stretched the boundaries of the question to discuss yet other considerations, including the location of offices and departments, and even the size of dormitory desks and drawers (yes, we really heard *all* that). In box 3.1 we report some of the responses to the "czar" question.

Using this approach, we ferreted out the kinds of topics that arise naturally in conversations about higher education, as well as those that don't come up often, or those that participants don't mention at all. We avoided constructing a survey with pointed

Box 3.1

"If You Were the Czar . . ."

Christina Smiraglia

If you were the czar—a figure with absolute power—what changes would you make to your college's academic program?

We asked this question of all participants. In response, some immediately say that they would abdicate, while others relish the power. Some praise, more gripe. A surprise: most stakeholders actually want *more* added to the academic program. All sorts of responses emerged, from introducing experiential learning to creating additional support services.

But strikingly, participants in every group frequently suggest adding content about social issues (e.g., race, gender, religion). We hear this from all constituency groups—about half of the faculty, administrators, and trustees; more than one-third (38%) of alumni want additional academic content, followed by 23% of students and 16% of parents. Rarely, do we hear specific comments about free speech, cancel cuture, and political correctness.

Here are a few examples that highlight a desire for academic content about social issues:

I think a really important addition would be . . . at the beginning of the freshman year where students are forced to take a class on one of these issues. Racial diversity, or social diversity, or religious diversity. . . . [This school] has a lot of resources to do that already. But it's very much voluntary for the students to enroll in them. And so, when you have discussions on the LGBTQ community, or sexual awareness, or how to be a bystander, to not be a bystander in the instance of sexual assault, you only have the people who are already aware of those issues that show up. (Student)

I think there are a lot of issues that come up in the world, for example racism. We don't talk about that here. Social equality, we're not talking about that here. Criminal justice system, what's wrong with it here? We incarcerate so many people, why is that? We incarcerate more people than anywhere else in the entire world. So, there are, I guess, these social justice issues, that just never find a place at [this school] in my view. (Faculty member)

However, while participants across constituency groups generally call for adding content about social issues to the academic program, they are *not* as aligned on the other kinds of content they seek. Specifically, different stakeholders have different views about adding content related to job skills, professional fields, and life skills—all areas outside of a traditional academic curriculum. Students and off-campus adults (alumni, parents, and trustees) are generally aligned in wanting to see more of these future-oriented areas added to the academic program, with some variation, as discussed below.

First, the most frequently suggested addition for off-campus adults is job-related skills, such as software training, resume writing, interviewing strategies, and professional internships. For example, one trustee notes:

I think everybody ought to take a sales and marketing course. And in that course should be, 'How do you interview?' There should be a whole back and forth on how do you interview, and what sort of questions are employers asking. . . . Our children should never go to a job interview without being totally prepared for that interview. How do you prepare? What do you do? How do you dress?

In contrast, on-campus adults and—perhaps surprisingly— students rarely suggest adding job-focused content.

Second, on-campus adults rarely mention adding professional fields—like business, engineering, or education—to the academic program, while these are relatively common suggestions from students and off-campus adults. Comments include:

Offer more application-type of classes. For example, [the school] really didn't have an accounting program, or a finance program. I think to really broaden out the program, [the school] would do well at adding some accounting classes, some finance classes and other application-type classes. (Young alum)

It's not to say that what we offer isn't good, or any of those sorts of things, but, you know, engineering is such an enormous part of the world today, and we don't have an engineering school, and I would love for us to be able to. (Trustee)

Finally, students, young alums, and parents frequently suggest adding future-oriented content related to life skills—such as personal finance or mindfulness—and other applied content relevant to the "real world" that is not framed in terms of a career. (Such personally applicable content is actually students' top recommended addition to the academic program.) Suggestions include:

Individual personal finance . . . it's very helpful personally as well as almost any job you're in, you're going to end up looking at financial statements to measure performance at some level for most of the people sometime. Or even to monitor their own income. (Parent)

More life learning classes. As part of maybe a prerequisite or something mandatory, not optional, 'cause as much as I appreciate my college education, none of it really prepared me to become the adult that I am today. . . . I had to learn how to cook on my own. Nobody really taught me how to build up credit. . . . It's a goal of mine to purchase a property, and I have no idea about the housing markets. (Alum)

In contrast, adults in campus leadership roles—trustees, administrators, and faculty—rarely suggest such life skills in their responses, highlighting another misalignment between the higher education consumers and producers.

The "czar question" highlights a widespread hunger among college stakeholders for more engagement with social issues. However, the wide variety of responses overall indicates that institutions have a fair amount of leeway in designing and implementing the curriculum, allowing for different campuses to tailor their academic program to their particular mission and context.

questions in which participants are required to choose among pre-designed options (on which the vast majority of empirical studies of higher education are based); we thought it more important to let participants talk freely, guided as much as possible by carefully crafted questions and well-trained interviewers.[1]

We do not claim that our research methodology should be adopted more broadly—it reflects our own history, interests, and skills (see box 2.1)—but we found it to be an asset. As we indicated, if we had designed our research instruments in light of our own interests, concerns, and hunches, or with an eye toward those questions and concepts already featured in the academic literature or the popular press, we would have missed some of the biggest themes that we uncovered—for example, the mental models of the college experience (described in chapter 5) and the varieties of belonging and alienation (described in chapter 7). And perhaps we would have over-scrutinized issues like political correctness, which loom large in some media, but which we found to be virtually absent on most campuses—unless a controversial speaker happened to have been picketed or even barred from campus a few days before our visit.

Although we lacked *hypotheses*, it turns out that we did have *beliefs*—indeed, strong ones. And, as just noted, these did not emerge clearly and vividly until we had largely finished data collection and were trying to make sense of our findings. To list three strong beliefs:

1. Higher education that is not *avowedly* vocational should be primarily focused on academic learning, not on preparing for

jobs or engaging primarily or extensively in extracurricular activities.

2. All individuals enrolled in higher education should be encouraged to stretch intellectually: to study topics and disciplines and modes of analysis that they may not have not known about, and, armed with these concepts and approaches, to attempt to make sense of many facets of our world.

3. Ethics (including honesty) is at the heart of education, and accordingly, those who engage in academic dishonesty, or who choose to ignore it, are undermining a central pillar of the sector.

SELECTION OF CAMPUSES

Without question, for an in-depth study such as this, we needed to be mindful about our selection of individuals, constituencies, and campuses to visit (the fictional Greenly College visited in chapter 1 constitutes an "ideal type," representing a mixture of the various campuses in our study). Similarly, the four campuses to which we bring recommendations in Part IV draw on conclusions that we reached across the various campuses and constituencies that we studied.

At first, we were inclined to visit campuses that were convenient and similar to those that we knew best—such as the three selective New England campuses on which we had developed the reflection sessions. (See the beginning section of chapter 2.) At the same time, we wanted our findings to have wide impact and applicability; and so, after numerous conversations with many informants, we deliberately chose to study campuses that were quite distinct from one another: differing in size, selectivity, geography, culture, and avowed or apparent mission.

Certainly, a sample of ten schools can't possibly reflect the variety of institutions of higher education in the United States—depending on one's definition and criteria, anywhere from 4,000 to 7,000 institutions. But we believe that our set of ten is about as varied and revealing a sample as we could secure. And because some of our instruments can be used in the future (and we hope that they will be), it would be straightforward to cover sectors that we had to omit—for example, single sex institutions, historically Black colleges, and schools with specific missions (like Saint John's College's focus on great books, or Berea College's work-study amalgam).*

We began by piloting our interview questionnaire at two schools geographically close to Cambridge, Massachusetts: University of New Hampshire in Durham and Tufts University in Medford, Massachusetts. The convenience of these campuses helped us to navigate the complicated logistics involved with a first set of interviews. At these campuses, we had the luxury of interviewing nearly every participant in person. Eventually, as we selected campuses farther away from our home base, we interviewed some participants in person and others, including students, via Skype (or another platform).

These pilot schools also provided instructive contrasts: University of New Hampshire is a public school in a more rural

---

* In fact, we have devised such a survey, and have piloted it on some campuses. For further information see https://www.therealworldofcollege.com/about-survey.

environment, which draws nearly half of its students from its own state; Tufts University, in a more urban environment, attracts students from all around the world. Once we had completed about half of the interviews at each of these schools, we began to think about other schools we should add to our sample—ones where we might encounter different or complementary perspectives about higher education. For example, we wanted to find schools where faculty essentially live on campus in the same setting as the students; schools that focused on teaching (rather than being part of research universities whose full-time faculty are expected to "publish or perish"); schools in different regions of the country; and those that attract students for a variety of reasons, such as religion, sports, selectivity, size, affordability and/or convenience.* And, indeed, we visited many other schools in addition to our ten target schools. For a list of the ten campuses and their features, see appendix A.

We have often compared our process of selecting campuses to that of playing chess. Once we included a school and began interviewing, we thought about the strategy of our "next move"— which next school would help to "round out" our study. Note that we deliberately included one "comparison" school—Olin College

---

* While "selectivity" can be defined in many ways, for the purposes of our study, we grouped the participating schools into three categories (low, medium, and high) according to reported SAT scores of incoming students. As detailed throughout the book, we also use these categories to report our findings. In addition, we created three categories of size based on the number of undergraduates in the student body: small (fewer than 7,000 students), medium (7,000–20,000 students), and large (20,000 or more).

of Engineering—that has a specific vocational goal. Olin gives us information about the ways in which an avowedly vocational school may differ from a traditional college, but may also embrace some of the same means and goals.

At each school, we had to adjust the process of securing permission for participation. At some schools, we received rapid approval from the president, the provost, or the dean of the appropriate division. Other schools asked us to present our case to a variety of groups on campus before confirming participation. In each case, even though we had approval from our own institutional research department, we worked closely with the respective offices of research at each school. It is worth noting that we approached eleven schools; only one school declined to participate.

SELECTION OF CONSTITUENCIES AND INTERVIEW PARTICIPANTS

Every college or university campus houses many different departments focused on academic subjects and/or on student life, as well those supporting the overall institution (such as admissions, development/institutional advancement, and institutional research). Additionally, off campus, many sectors of the society are also concerned about higher education—ranging from political leaders to job recruiters to journalists.

In this study, we sought to understand perspectives of the key stakeholders both on and off campus. Roughly speaking, on each campus, we interviewed about two hundred participants, including fifty first-year students, fifty graduating students, and approximately twenty-five faculty, twenty-five senior administrators, and a smaller number of trustees, parents of current students, and alums who had graduated five to ten years before. We also interviewed each college president and nearly two dozen job recruiters, though the recruiters were not campus specific.

From the initial pilot schools, we learned a great deal about strategies for inviting and recruiting participants for the study. With respect to all ten schools, we carefully and strategically selected faculty and administrators in order to ensure that we spoke with individuals who were knowledgeable about the school (e.g., those who held positions for more than a few years) and those who represented various academic and administrative departments. We used the schools' websites as our primary source, sometimes scanned school newspapers, and gathered background information on each of the targeted individuals. We deliberately did not ask for recommendations from the school; we wanted to ensure that we were not interviewing only those individuals who had been "cherry picked" for a particular reason.*

For most of the other constituencies—students, parents, young alums—we employed an opportunistic approach for recruiting, including posting fliers, sending emails, tabling, and advertising on social media. Overall, we recruited a "convenience sample"; however, we carefully observed and monitored the sample to make sure

---

*To recruit faculty and administrators, we sent invitation letters via email. If we did not hear back after a week, we sent one additional request via email or telephone. On average, we had a 50% positive response rate from faculty and administrators, which ranged from 30% at one school to 89% at another school.

that we included students who reflected the general demography of each school (e.g., gender, students involved with student government, religious organizations, athletics, Greek life).

Importantly, other than asking students where they grew up and the type of high school they went to, we made an explicit decision *not* to ask students specifically for other demographic information in order to protect students from feeling as if they were "checking a box" in our study, and/or to ensure that students did not respond to questions as if they were representing a particular demographic.* When apparently undersubscribed with respect to a given group, we made extra effort—usually successful—to recruit participants from that constituency.

In general, as a group, trustees were difficult to recruit, to schedule, and, in many cases, to reschedule. But with the help of each school president and/or secretary to the board, we secured robust cohorts across the campuses.

INTRODUCING ALIGNMENT

Why did we choose to interview the range of constituencies? Again, this decision draws on one of the conclusions of our earlier studies of the Good Project (see box 2.1). We had discovered that "good work" is much more likely to emerge when the various interested parties in any profession are *well aligned*—when the different stakeholders have similar values and work toward the same goals. Alignment contrasts with a less desirable situation

---

*While we did not ask explicitly for certain demographic information, we made tentative inferences from name, dress, and appearance.

when the various constituencies surrounding a profession have different, even clashing, sets of values—in short, when they are *misaligned*. As we sought to apply the results of our earlier study, this concept of alignment (or misalignment) helped us to make recommendations to individuals, workplaces, and entire fields of work through scholarly and popular articles, as well as through targeted interventions—all in the hope of bringing about stronger and more appropriate alignments across the sector.

As an example, let's consider one question in our interview: "What are your goals for the student college experience?"

In comparing constituencies across schools, we find that most students express goals related to "academics," but these goals are very loosely defined. Interestingly and importantly (especially as it relates to issues of mental health, which we discuss later), half the students who describe these "academic" goals talk about them only in terms of *external markers* of success: securing degrees, high grade point averages, and overall high performance. The other half of students who describe "academic" goals focus broadly on cognition, overall mindset, or specific skill sets. Only a small group of students describe intellectual pursuits, or content knowledge, or powerful concepts or methods from a specific discipline or set of disciplines. As conveyed in the anecdote related earlier by Howard, important concomitants of learning—libraries, museums, research laboratories, specific books, methods, concepts—rarely come up spontaneously. In addition, a majority of students also describe "career" goals for the college experience: setting themselves up to get internships during college and a job after graduation, as well as seeking and engaging in networking opportunities. Fewer students describe "personal" goals: expanding perspectives, becoming independent, and taking risks.

On the other hand, a sizable majority of faculty believe that students should work toward "personal" transformations, while fewer than half of the faculty (as compared to a majority of students) describe "career" goals. Unsurprisingly, faculty agree with most students that goals for college should be "academic," but faculty have a very different conception of that realm; teachers focus on content knowledge, cognition, and academic skills (e.g., critical thinking, developing an argument, writing); rarely do faculty members talk about academic success per se as a goal, if they talk about it at all.

Young alums and parents describe goals in ways more akin to students than to faculty. Nearly half of the young alums and parents focus on career goals—quite possibly, they feel a sense of urgency that other on-campus adults may not prioritize. Few parents and few young alums discuss "academic" goals in terms of content knowledge. Most of these off-campus adults focus on skills that will serve students well beyond college, especially in the workplace.

To be sure, not all parents and young alums take this immediate "return on investment" stance. For example, in one of the schools that we studied, a significant proportion of parents and alums mentioned the centrality of asking big questions and minimized the importance of job-related skills. Of course, we pondered why this might be the case—whether, for example, there was more assiduous onboarding of the academic mission of the school, or more effective intertwining of essential questions across the curriculum and the four years of college (these issues are discussed in Part IV).

It's important to mention that, in the course of the study, we also visited many other campuses—particularly ones that featured programs or approaches that intrigued us. And in several instances, we carried out in-depth case studies of programs that were apparently successful in bridging noticeable misalignment among key constituencies. In Part IV of the book, as we make recommendations to several "ideal type" institutions, we draw on these aligned programs.*

One more point. We have found it helpful to think of alignment and misalignment in a fractal manner. To unpack that description, the most global alignments and misalignments cover the whole sector and its relation to the broader society; in contrast, the most fine-grained alignments and misalignments occur within specific constituencies on specific campuses, or even within the minds of individual subjects. In Part IV, we present both the broadest forms of alignment/misalignment, as well as ones restricted to particular constituencies or to particular campuses.

As we think of various institutions and sectors of a society, it's evident that in general, *alignment is a good thing*. We don't relish the prospect of an institution (like the judiciary) or a profession (like law) being torn apart by massive misalignments. That said, sometimes, *mis*alignments are desirable; they can open one's

---

* See appendix C for a summary of programs.

mind to alternatives, push one to reconcile, or, less frequently, make one dig in one's heels. And hopefully, though only rarely, when entities are in turmoil, misalignments may be needed to set things right.[2]

Again, for much of this book, we put aside "shop talk" of alignments and misalignments. But when we come to reports and recommendations to individual campuses toward the end of the book, as "medical anthropologists" we find it useful to draw—albeit lightly—on the concept of alignments and misalignments that vary in type and breadth.

Whatever our method, our metaphors, our madness, or our mode of reference, we did what we set out to do—we carried out over 2,000 one-hour interviews on ten campuses. That's a lot of words, a lot of pages, and a lot of recording. Wendy conducted perhaps 400 interviews, and Howard conducted perhaps 250 interviews. We have both read more than 2,000 transcripts, sometimes more than once.

Types of Analyses: Nuts and Bolts of Coding

How did we arrive at findings (e.g., ones that reveal alignments or misalignments)?

For a systematic analysis of the data gleaned from each of the interviews, we developed a rigorous coding scheme. This is divided into two major sections.

Section 1: Scoring of Holistic Concepts   The first form of scoring requires a researcher from our team (called a "coder" in the phase of data analysis) to read an entire interview transcript (about ten to twenty single-spaced pages) and to respond to a variety of questions about "holistic" concepts that we developed after reading through all the transcripts. Such holistic concepts can't be reliably inferred unless one has reviewed the entire interview, since we did not ask about these concepts directly. As examples:

- Coders compute "Higher Education Capital" for individuals— the extent to which, in their responses, students reflect the kinds of analytic, connecting, and communicating skills that we believe should be evinced by a successful college student (see discussion in chapter 4).
- Coders assess the "mental models" of how individuals conceptualize the college experience (discussed in chapter 5).
- Coders discern if, and how much, a student (or other constituent) indicates "belonging" or "alienation" to the academic program of the school, to peers, and/or to the institution as a whole (discussed in chapter 7).

In coding these holistic concepts, coders write brief "rationales" for their decisions and provide evidence (e.g., quotes) directly from the transcript to describe and justify their line of thinking and their conclusion.

Section 2: Scoring of Specific Interview Questions In this section, coders must ponder a participant's response to specific questions throughout the interview and categorize the participant's responses.* For example, coders are asked to categorize a participant's response to the direct question: "If you could give one book

---

* See appendix B for the interview questionnaire used with students, as well as an acknowledgment with respect to minor linguistic adjustments for the other constituencies.

to students before they leave college, which book might it be?"
(e.g., coders note title, genre, how the participant knew about this
book, and why they recommended it).

A couple of our questions are rank-order questions (about the
purpose of college, about problems on campus), or single-word
questions (e.g., one adjective to describe students at this school).
Analysis of these data was (thankfully) straightforward.

Needless to say, it is crucial in a study like ours to make sure
that coders achieve reasonable agreement with one another. To
ensure reliability across coders (to make sure that independent
coders interpret the data in the same way), each transcript is
coded (alternatively, co-coded) by two different coders.

The first coder reads the transcript and responds to the holistic
section of the coding scheme; the second coder "shadows" the
coding of the first coder (makes sure that coder 2 agrees with the
initial coding by first reading the entire transcript independently,
and then second reviewing the coding of holistic concepts of the
first coder). The second coder notes any disagreements about the
coding and discusses such disagreements with the first coder, in
order to reach a decision that satisfies both. If the disagreement
is still unresolved after a discussion between coders, these coders ask a third coder to participate in the discussion and to help
resolve the disagreement.

In addition, after reviewing the holistic section of the coding
scheme, the second coder also completes the second half of the
coding scheme—that is, categorizing a participant's specific
responses to particular interview questions. Because this coding requires straightforward categorization, there's no need for

a review by another coder. However, if at a later point (e.g., in analyzing the categorizations for patterns and themes), researchers come across a categorization that is insufficient in some way, researchers can correct the mistake. We use a widely used statistic—Cohen's Kappa—to calculate reliability, consistently achieving over 0.80 reliability (a value above 0.80 is typically considered "excellent").

We have invested a lot of time and resources in our coding—*it represents the crux of our research enterprise.* For an hour-long interview, we estimate that it takes about three hours to code and shadow (1.5 hours to code and 1.5 hours to shadow).

After this "first pass" of rigorous coding, we also carried out detailed "subcoding" of central concepts and interview questions. For instance, once all the coding was completed for each constituency, we could look across a single concept, like "mental models" (see chapter 5) or one question for students, like "What have been your biggest struggles in college?" Reading for one specific question or concept enables coders to categorize unique responses according to the themes that emerge across the board. As an example, with respect to the question "What have been your biggest struggles in college?" coders ultimately created six categories for responses: academics, basic life skills, peer relationships, time management, finances, and miscellaneous items. Even within just one category, such as "academics," we further coded the data (deeper subcoding) into struggles focused on curriculum and pedagogy, or lack of institutional supports (e.g., advising, tutoring, accommodations).

To say that we took the coding seriously is an understatement. In fact, we often had to stop ourselves from "overprocessing" some of the tiny details and to remind ourselves that we also needed to focus on the big picture of what we were finding and what it might mean.

From Words to Numbers

By training and inclination, we lean toward qualitative analysis— searching for the themes and stories that characterize complex human beings involved in complex human activities. (As anthropologists *pro tem*, we seek to capture the culture of a campus and—in the aggregate—of a sector of society.) For example, when we look across our clusters of data, we distinguish between two cohorts: trustees who have a deep and enduring interest in what happens on campus; and trustees who seem to value the prestige of their membership and perhaps the social connections attendant thereto, but who appear to be largely ignorant of what is actually happening on their own campus over time (see box 5.2). Or, to focus on another constituency, we are struck by those students who make it a point to be present during the "club hours" each Wednesday at noon; as well as those who are not even aware that this period exists—and the possible reasons for these contrasting stances. For reaching conclusions, statistical analyses are helpful but are not necessarily definitive.

But we would have been ill-advised—indeed irresponsible, if not delusional—if we had simply read the transcripts and reported our impressions of what we thought that we had heard and what we thought it meant. Accordingly, aided by several skilled research methodologists, we have carried out a variety of analyses; these allow us to make far more powerful and, we believe, more convincing (and, perhaps, more conclusive) assertions about what we have found and what the findings might mean.

To verify our assertions and put specific findings into context of the larger study, we pursued three kinds of analyses:

1. *Text analyses* to explore the similarities and differences of words and phrases within and across campuses (e.g., the frequency and context of the word "help" across constituencies and schools).
2. *Descriptive analyses* from our coding scheme (e.g., the biggest struggle in college as reported by students as compared to the biggest struggle according to parents).
3. *Correlations* between individual factors (e.g., the relation between "mental models" and such variables as school selectivity, gender, size of campus, first-year students, as compared to graduating students).*

Confidentiality

With respect to the ten target schools, as well as the additional campuses that we visited, and with respect to every participant in the study, our agreement was simple and straightforward: We promised to the best of our ability to keep our data confidential.

---

*In this book, all statistical differences described as significant have a p-value of 0.05 or less. In addition, any reported correlations are statistically significant.

In other words, we did not, and will not, share information about whom we interviewed—even in the case of interviewing a participant's spouse at one school or a parent of a student at another. If participants *chose* to share this with their colleagues (or families), that was fine, but we ourselves would not. As soon as participants were interviewed, they were assigned a "participant number"; whole schools were also assigned a number. By using these numbers, as researchers and coders, we would not be in the habit of using a person's name, and if, by accident, anyone spied a folder in our office, or overheard a conversation, that individual would not know to whom, or to what school, we were referring.

Clearly, by the end of our several trips to each campus, we had solid impressions of the culture of each school; and upon completion of our full coding and analysis of every interview at each school, we now know what the data show. We have the ability to do countless comparisons—a good number of which we have actually done—but we have promised to share with the public only data that have been deidentified. Accordingly, in writing this book, we have found ways to compare data from schools by grouping schools in terms of size, type, and selectivity. In this way no specific school is exposed to criticism, or even praise, which may then cause the other schools to wonder where they fall in the queue.

However, on request, we will share—and on some campuses have already shared—school-specific data with the leadership of the ten participating campuses. In chapter 9, we give detailed examples of how such sharing might unfold with respect to four "ideal type" campuses; in chapter 10, we indicate how such sharing might occur with reference to different constituencies. As researchers and writers, we strive to achieve a balance—giving detailed information about our data, without identifying particular persons or institutions.

We have confidence that in the pages that follow we have upheld the promise of confidentiality, while sharing instructive data. We describe promising interventions and recommendations at the end of the book, with the hope of reframing college education for the twenty-first century.

Also, we are relieved—and grateful to the many talented individuals who worked on the project—that confidentiality was respected and that we had no significant (or even minor) mishaps. On a large and complex project like ours, this is a considerable achievement.

THE NAME OF THE PROJECT: AN UNEXPECTED ENIGMA

Our original motivation to preserve and, if possible, to strengthen the "liberal arts" in a form viable for the twenty-first century, led us initially to dub our project "Liberal Arts and Sciences for the 21st Century," or our in-house, abbreviated name, LAS21. This title reflected our own belief (alluded to in the introduction) in a post-secondary education that features broad study, for a productive work and civic life, rather than training for a specific job. Ultimately, our goal for the project was to use the data to make well-informed recommendations that would preserve the heart of this form of education.

But because we did not want to impose our values on others, we never announced this title or used it in public. Indeed, in introducing our study, we asked potential participants if they were willing to speak with us about their views of the "college experience" as part of a study on "higher education in the twenty-first century." Not until one of the last questions of our interview did we ask: "Your school defines itself as a 'Liberal Arts' institution. What does that mean to you?"* Indeed, we deliberately used this phrasing because in our pilot work, direct requests for a definition often yielded embarrassed silences or puzzlement—sometimes even on the part of faculty and administrators on campuses that heralded themselves as "liberal arts" schools.

Though we kept this question as a concluding one throughout the whole study, it became clear early on that most individuals claim not to know what it means (or even to have heard of it) or have a misunderstanding—for example, construing "liberal" as "left leaning" or "free choice" or "what you have to take if you are not admitted into the nursing program or the business program." (For details about how participants responded to the direct question about "liberal arts," see box 3.2.) Only in the final pages of this book do we return explicitly to the phrase "liberal arts." For the most part, throughout this book, we use less evocative but less problematic phrases like "higher education" or "nonvocational higher education."

---

* At Olin College of Engineering (our comparison school), we reworded the question: "Many undergraduate programs focus on the 'Liberal Arts.' What does that mean to you?"

Box 3.2

"What Does 'Liberal Arts and Sciences' Mean to You?"

Christina Smiraglia

Because we wanted to understand perspectives on the liberal arts and sciences, we listened carefully for how participants would talk about this or related concepts during our interviews. Importantly, we deliberately did *not* use the phrase itself in any of our communications about the study. Only at the end of the interview, when there was no chance to "bait the witness," did we explicitly ask participants what the term "liberal arts" meant to them.

The short answer: Disappointingly few of our participants at institutions that describe themselves as foregrounding the liberal arts seem to understand the term in any kind of depth. This finding may not be unexpected for students entering college. But we are surprised and, frankly, disheartened to learn that even faculty and administrators, in addition to graduating students, young alums, parents of college students, and trustees, also have trouble defining the term.

Before delving into our findings, it is important to note what *we* have in mind when we ask about the meaning of liberal arts and sciences. We are not looking for an explicit definition, for even experts invoke a range of criteria. In analyzing what our respondents say, we instead look for one or more of the following indicators as evidence of understanding the liberal arts:

- Working within and across scholarly disciplines
- Spanning the arts, humanities, social sciences, and natural/physical sciences
- Engendering communication skills in various media
- Inculcating critical, discriminatory, and analytical abilities

- Acknowledging the importance of different perspectives
- Tackling big questions, with an eye toward continuing to pursue them
- Nurturing ways to contribute to society as an active, knowledgeable, and reflective citizen

Across the wide range of interview responses, an unfortunate but common theme across students, parents, and alums—and even college administrators, faculty, and trustees—is uncertainty about the definition of the liberal arts. Administrators and faculty, unsurprisingly, are clearer about the concept, but even so, nearly 40% of them deviate from our list of indicators. Students seem to gain clarity across their years in college; more than 60% of first-year students offer ideas that demonstrate confusion, but fewer than 50% of graduating students do so. However, more than 60% of alums and parents are "off"—suggesting that experience in the broader community may not lead to a better understanding of the liberal arts.

Beyond direct admission of not knowing what the term means, participants discuss the following points, which we consider to be off the mark:

- Political liberalism: "I think liberal arts is also a nice way to say that we're very, very liberal. Like politically." (Student)
- A specific major: "The liberal arts major here is the default position for a student who doesn't know what to major in." (Faculty)
- A kind of school, generally of small size: "A small college focus on like the literature, art and science." (Faculty)
- Fine arts: "Openness to all types of art . . . not just painting and stuff like that, but allows the student to be open-minded, maybe you want to, you're a painter or going for painting, but you, you know, it's not just . . . the single, you know, we're all going to do

Realism here. I think it allows for Cubism and . . . Post-modern, all these different . . . types of art." (Young Alum)

- Exclusion of science: "Quote unquote, not science." (Parent)
- Freedom of course selection with little overarching structure: "I would say liberal is freedom, because you're free to pick and you're not limited to picking one thing under one major . . . Liberal arts meaning freedom, you get to choose whatever courses that you would wanna take." (Student)
- Disparate disciplines: "What it means to me . . . the philosophy that you can't intermix . . . excellent science and math with excellent humanities and . . . literature." (Trustee)

So how exactly do participants define the liberal arts when *they* believe that they understand the concept, as nearly half (48%) of all participants think they do?

The most common response overall relates the liberal arts to well-roundedness; this definition is one of the most common responses for each constituency group. Here are some examples of how participants discuss the liberal arts as a well-rounded education:

- Studying a little bit of everything: "Liberal arts means kind of getting a broad knowledge base. I think it's about building this foundational knowledge that you take all these different kinds of classes . . . I think that the core of the liberal arts is to become educated in a variety of different fields." (Student)
- Broadening one's perspectives: "An exposure to a diverse set of perspectives and modes of thought, and . . . you know it's a, it's about gaining perspective on yourself and on humanity, on society." (Administrator)
- Receiving a holistic education: "I think it means getting a holistic education. . . . Not letting a student get totally tunnel visioned into their . . . specific area of interest." (Student)

- Gaining an ability to look at issues through multiple separate lenses: "It's basically a system that teaches you some of the fundamental notions of various other disciplines . . . being part of one discipline doesn't necessarily exclude you from understanding any other disciplines out there. So I think a liberal arts curriculum allows that flexibility for a person trained in one particular discipline to understand perspectives, ideas that come from other disciplines." (Young Alum)

Although the idea of well-roundedness does not encompass the entirety of a liberal arts education, these concepts resonate with the traditional idea of the liberal arts, and they relate to the first two points in our definition above.

Why does this ignorance about the definition and concept of the liberal arts matter? Our findings indicate that a sizable number of students are enrolling in an academic program without realizing what they are supposed to be engaging in. Parents are similarly confused, and thus cannot provide clarity for students. Even after they have arrived on campus, students may find themselves surrounded by faculty and administrators who may not discuss the liberal arts, nor even fully understand the concept. How can we expect students to have a cohesive academic experience or to be full participants in their learning in college if there is so much misunderstanding about this form of education from those directly involved?

Furthermore, although the number of participants who describe the liberal arts as a well-rounded approach is heartening, this conception is incomplete. Without a reasonably capacious understanding of the liberal arts, students—and other stakeholders—cannot understand its value and may uncritically revert to vocational approaches that have a more immediate clear purpose and outcome.

As higher education grapples with decreasing enrollments in liberal arts colleges and majors, as well as with societal skepticism about the utility of a liberal arts education, confusion over the name "liberal arts" may be partly to blame. To be sure, having a clear understanding of the term is less important than valuing and embodying the underlying principles. That said, students—and other stakeholders—can better value and embody the liberal arts if they are intentional about engaging in an explicitly liberal arts education.

MOVING FORWARD

In the next sections of the book, Parts II and III, we report what we found, and, equally intriguing, *what we did not encounter* on our massive listening and conversing enterprise. Given our interest in the tradition of a broad general education—which we describe as higher education in its essence that is not vocational in nature—we begin in chapter 4 with what we regard as the heart of the enterprise: an individual's demonstration of the capacity to attend, analyze, reflect, connect, and communicate effectively—capacities we hope will be enhanced over the course of college. We seek to determine and document how students (and others) on campus conceptualize and address a variety of issues that can arise in the course of conversation on a topic with which a conversant should have some familiarity—in this case, the college experience. Having coined the concept "Higher Education Capital," we introduce the methods that we used to investigate this construct and the sometimes surprising results that emerged.

Complementing our investigation of how students think about and discuss a range of educational topics, in chapter 5, we report on students' own conceptions of the purpose of college. Specifically, we look at various "mental models" of college: Is college simply the next step after high school? Or is it a place to gain credits prior to securing a job? Or an opportunity to explore new disciplines, acquire new ways of thinking, a lifetime opportunity to reconsider one's beliefs, values, and goals—to try out different kinds of thinking, social interactions, or even the kind of person that one is in the process of becoming? Once again, the similarities and differences within and across constituencies, and within and across campuses, are often surprising and, we believe, instructive.

When we began our study, we fully expected to focus on these two features, which we might call *cognitive* or *intellectual* in nature. But—and here emerged an unexpected advantage of a study that was not strongly or pointedly hypothesis-driven—we were not prepared for two mammoth themes that emerged at various points of the study. From the very start of our field work, we were stunned by the centrality of mental health issues across campuses and constituencies. Clearly, we had to examine this phenomenon more carefully, seek to understand it, and, if possible, as clinicians *pro tem*, to offer some helpful recommendations. And then, as the study continued, we were equally surprised to encounter the growing importance of issues of belonging—or, its less happy complement, non-belonging, alienation, anomie. Accordingly, in Part III of the book, we concentrate on these issues, which, though not central to the traditional mission of higher education, are clearly of critical importance in our colleges and universities in our time.

Having laid out as best we can our principal findings in Parts II and III, we relinquish our role of cultural anthropologists. Instead, as aspiring clinicians making the rounds, in Part IV, we offer analyses and recommendations that we hope will prove useful across this vital sector of our society.

II THE INDIVIDUAL LEARNER

Suppose that you are embarking on a long ride on a train. Sitting next to you is a young person, evidently of college age. You begin to chat with this person, and before long, you find yourself in an extended conversation about the person's schooling. The time passes quickly, and after an hour, you realize that you have touched on many topics—the goals of higher education, the factors that contribute to an effective education, the various barriers to such an education—whether due to inadequacies on campus or to challenges that the young person has faced in earlier days. For a change of pace, you also ask that person what changes could be made to improve education, what might be done for fun, as well as the student's personal aspirations for the short and long term.

Suppose, further, it emerged that you had both watched a recently televised political debate between two leading candidates for the upcoming national election. With your fellow traveler, you might discuss the substantive issues the moderator raised, how quickly the candidates tweaked the prompts so that they could highlight what they each really wanted to promulgate, and how the overall performance of each candidate compared with performances in previous debates. Or, for a change of pace, you might begin to discuss the movie one of you had downloaded for your trip—the reviews across different sources, how it might compare to the original novel, or even the funky costume design. Or, for yet another stint, you might reflect on a recent economic downturn or the discovery of a rare well-preserved skeleton from the Paleolithic era.

Regardless of the topic of conversation—movies, politics, discoveries, or schooling—you would likely draw some conclusions about your conversational partner. And even if you have never taken a course in social science—let alone been a member of our research team—you might note the clarifications requested, connections made, analyses deepened, questions or comments about your own remarks. If it did not come up naturally, you might well speculate about which institution (or type of institution) of higher education the student attended, whether the student was a good or indifferent student—indeed, whether the young person seemed to have benefited from a college education, or, less happily, seemed to be in need of one.

Of course, we are putting words and thoughts into your mind. All of us invariably make assumptions about individuals whom we meet—whether those assumptions are made explicitly or implicitly, generously or harshly—and presumably the reverse holds true as well. None of us is immune from being judged. Importantly, we can never assume a quality is lacking, just because it fails to appear in a single encounter; but if, for example, the person has a good sense of humor, or is well read, or deeply reflective, those signs are likely to emerge in the course of an hour's wide-ranging conversation.

To be sure, as researchers, we approached this task of speaking to people much more formally—with a script in mind and with particular topics introduced or listened for. And yet, such a conversation about the college experience is essentially what we carried out with over a thousand students as well as more than a thousand other stakeholders in higher education. What we learned about their thinking processes constitutes the topic of this chapter.

THE CONCEPT

Not only do individuals have different views of the purpose of higher education—for starters, a vocational versus a nonvocational focus—they also hold different perspectives on the most desired outcomes for graduates. Is it most important for students to gain content knowledge in a particular field or familiarity with a broad range of perspectives; to secure a job upon graduation, or to have experienced wide-ranging social and extracurricular experiences with people from different backgrounds?[1] Some authorities also argue that college should have even grander goals—for example, helping young people to develop altruism, appreciate the arts, or become exemplary citizens or even leaders of society.

Reflecting back to the hypothetical conversation with the traveler next to you, we believe that a principal purpose of college is to *create or amplify intellectual capital that ideally should last and be drawn upon for a lifetime.* And so, in speaking to students (as well as other constituencies), we have listened carefully to how they think about things—how they attend, analyze, reflect, develop an argument and prove a point, question or push back when something does not make sense, pull things together, synthesize, communicate effectively—overall, whether they use their minds well. Developing this kind of "capital" should not only be the major goal of academic coursework; metaphorically speaking, it should also be in the air that students breathe on the college campus—pervading the atmosphere and culture that students experience, both in and out of class.

Sometimes students will arrive in college with considerable intellectual capital courtesy of their family, their friends and classmates, their precollegiate education, and/or their previous reading, writing, computing, and conversing. At the same time, this capital (or lack of capital) is not necessarily predetermined by any particular upbringing—parents who may or may not have gone to college, or by matriculation at one kind of a high school as compared to another. Opportunities and encouragement to listen carefully, make connections, reflect, ask critical questions, challenge perspectives—and to activate one's voice—can come from a range of experiences and exposure to individuals and institutions, including engaging in service work in the community, conversations at family dinner, and/or religious traditions. Indeed, in some cultures, students are taught to just listen, and not speak up.* But when this encouragement to develop your mind in certain ways does not occur "naturally"—from one's upbringing or educational background or personal motivation—then the higher educational system, in its broadest sense, needs to provide it. If it fails to do so, in our view, the system has not fulfilled its primary mission. (And of course, whatever our "starting capital," we can all benefit from its enhancement.)

As we launched our study, we were struck by the differences in sophistication of responses by our various participants. Some participants understood our questions, thought carefully about their responses, challenged the assumptions built into certain questions, alluded to other questions, or drew on courses and readings, as well as their own historical, scientific, cultural or humanistic knowledge. In contrast, other participants gave only superficial responses, and most revealingly, rarely evinced a critical attitude toward either the questions or their own responses. Given our interest in education that is not vocational—what we initially labeled "liberal arts and sciences"—we readily infer that the first group of respondents provided evidence of a broad and sophisticated educational stance; in contrast, the latter group gave little, if any, evidence that they have had, or have benefited from, the kinds of education that the bulk of our nonvocational institutions of higher learning claim that they are providing.

Consider, for example, two students, whom we'll call Jackson and Rebecca. Both are about to graduate from their respective four

---

* See "Activating One's Voice . . . Always a Plus?," https://www.thereal worldofcollege.com/blog/activating-ones-voice-always-a-plus.

year-colleges. As part of our standard interview questionnaire, Jackson and Rebecca are asked: "Is it important to go to college?" They answer in revealingly different ways.

Jackson responds:*

I think it's incredibly important. I mean it's important on so many different levels. It's important on a social economic level. It's important on a cultural level, making sure that we raise the educational level in general, which in turn increases participation on a national level really. Especially in a democracy, a representative democracy like we have. We really need a lot of education, and in that sense, a non-educated populist is ignorant and lends itself more towards totalitarian[ism] . . . I mean, that's something that we talked about a lot . . . I should probably stifle myself before I get too excited. And then, also just on personal levels, I mean, we have such a unique culture in the United States, which is so strangely focused on money and material wealth that my time at university has completely changed [me], and has made me look at it from a more, I feel, worldly perspective. . . . I feel that if you don't attend university . . . it prevents you from understanding the world. . . . I cannot remember who originated the quote. I know Eleanor Roosevelt had it, but it's, "Small minds talk about people. Good minds talk about events. Great minds talk about ideas." And that is something that was really drilled in through college, that if you don't go, really you miss it. Unless you're able to travel the world and experience other cultures, you really miss it. Because we grow up in a bubble otherwise.

Rebecca responds:

---

*All quotations and deidentified descriptors of participants in the book are accurate, but we have created pseudonyms to protect the identity of our participants.

That's kind of a loaded question, you know . . . Just because society says so, that it is. I mean, you know, you can't even consider yourself like a, a first-class citizen unless you go to college . . . I do think it's important . . . I'm sure the really good jobs . . . require a two-year degree, or a four-year degree.

Jackson's response connects a point of view to social, historical, cultural considerations—making the point that people need education in order to "understand the world" and to participate in a democratic society. He also spells out implications for society if individuals do not have a higher education—drawing on conversations in school ("we talk about this a lot") and knowledge of influential figures in the United States (Eleanor Roosevelt). In sharp contrast, Rebecca's response lacks detail and elaboration.

To explain such stark differences, we developed the notion of Higher Education Capital (which we abbreviate in house—and often, in what follows—as HEDCAP). This measure denotes the extent to which an individual displays the kind of thinking one would reasonably expect of a graduate of an institution of higher education—a form of education that is *not* focused on one area of expertise and an education that is *not* meant solely to prepare students for specific careers and jobs, typically in a designated sector of the economy. To be sure, grade point averages, academic honors, or jobs secured upon graduation are relevant considerations; but as investigators of the unique benefits of higher education, we are *most* interested in the ways in which students think, reason, and reflect on significant matters. Put succinctly—perhaps overly succinctly—*Higher Education Capital denotes the ability to attend,* *analyze, reflect, connect, and communicate on issues of importance and interest.**

Armed with this rough-and-ready definition, let's return to our hypothetical conversation. If you were sitting on the train next to Jackson and started to talk with him without knowing anything about him, you might make some assumptions—the kind of school he attends, what he studies, whether he applies himself in academics, or does as little as he can get away with. At the same time, if seated next to her, you could make some assumptions about Rebecca. And if you compared your conversations with each of them, you would most likely come to the conclusion that genuine differences exist between them. Perhaps Jackson got more out of his college experience, as he responds to questions with passion, clarity, and thoughtfulness. And, less happily, after an hour, you might lament that for whatever reason, Rebecca seems to lack something that Jackson has in abundance. This is what we call Higher Education Capital: Jackson displays a lot of it, whereas Rebecca exhibits very little.

In all probability (reflecting your own Higher Education Capital), you may well be thinking: Well, let's say that Rebecca had an off day or was simply not interested in speaking to the researcher.

*Two whimsical asides: (1) As a mnemonic for these five indicators, we have relied on "AARCC," which encapsulates key elements of the numerous factors to which we attend in scoring HEDCAP. (2) In the study originally formulated as a study of liberal arts and science (see box 3.2), we coined the concept "LAS Capital" (a phrase we enjoyed voicing for its Marxist economic and literary connotations). But even in-house, we quickly substituted the innocuous "HEDCAP."

Or, alternatively, perhaps Jackson is applying for a prestigious fellowship, so he had recently been coached on how to talk to a stranger about his college experience—and as a result, he comes off as "über-capitalized"; if you had spoken to him two months earlier (or six months later), you might have thought he was more like Rebecca.

And so, it is important to make—indeed to underscore—two points. First of all, we use numerous responses to determine Higher Education Capital, and we *never* depend on a single response. Second, we can never prove that an individual *lacks* Higher Education Capital—all we can demonstrate is that the individual has *not exhibited it* on this particular occasion. But we do assess every respondent on whether they take the interview seriously. Fortunately, we found we could count on the fingers of one hand the number of respondents who did not appear to take the interview seriously.

HOW DO WE SCORE HIGHER EDUCATION CAPITAL?

As stated, it would not be fair, or perhaps even ethical, to base an individual's Higher Education Capital on any single response (or block of text in a transcript). Accordingly, we developed a method to derive scores for each individual.

To assess an individual's HEDCAP, using a single transcription of the interview, we use two separate measures, administered at different times. First, using blind coding (i.e., the coder lacks any identifying information about the participant), we score a partic-ipant's responses to seven specific questions that are distributed across the interview (i.e. each response receives a score). Here are the seven questions:

1. Is it important to go to college? Why or why not (and for whom is it important and for whom is it not important)?
2. If you were in charge of the academic program—the "czar"—what are three changes that you might make?
3. What should you get out of your course of study when you leave here? Do you think there's anything that *everyone* should get out of their college education? For example, specific areas of knowledge or skills everyone should gain?
4. What kinds of ethical dilemmas, if any, do students face on the college campus?
5. Some people say that college should be a transformative experience. Do you agree with this statement? If "yes," in what ways should students be transformed?
6. If you could give one book to students before they leave college, which book might it be? Why?
7. Please rank order the following statements about why it's important to go to college, and explain why you put each in the order you did. Please rank order the choices from 1 to 4 (1 = most important and 4 = least important): To get a job; To gain different perspectives on people, knowledge, and the world; To learn to live independently; To study a particular content area in depth.

Note that all of these questions deal with the college experience per se—invocation of movies, literature, political or scientific matters are "extra credit," so to speak.

Second, after reading the whole interview transcript, the same coder assigns an overall HEDCAP score based on the entire interview—a cumulative or holistic measure. Coders maintain consistent scoring through careful documentation of evidence throughout the transcript and a summary rationale for the overall score.

We always code HEDCAP in these two ways. We seek to ensure that we consider the specific questions that we believe elicit the most HEDCAP, but also to monitor what else may emerge over the course of an hour (in case a participant does not have much to say about the group of targeted questions, but proves to be reflective about other matters that arise).

For each approach—scoring responses to specific interview questions and the scoring the entire interview—participants receive HEDCAP scores from "1" for little to no capital; "2" for some capital; and "3" for a high amount of capital. Because we only score for evidence of HEDCAP, not a lack of evidence—our scoring system starts at "1."

In awarding a Higher Education Capital score, here are the principal considerations that we take into account:*

• Making connections in two senses: (1) between and among topics, issues, questions, and disciplines; (2) responding to what the interviewer says or implies.

---

* In making judgements about HEDCAP, we evaluate the degree to which participants show evidence of these criteria, which (as noted) we conveniently summarize as the abilities to attend, analyze, reflect, connect, and communicate ("AARCC").

- Seeing things from multiple perspectives (e.g., putting oneself in someone else's shoes).
- Noting and explaining complexities of issues and questions (e.g., a response may be "it depends," but with reasoning spelled out).
- Developing an argument and defending it with examples, evidence and details (real and/or hypothetical).
- Articulating the limitations of one's own personal experience or perspective (e.g., acknowledging that there is a larger and more varied world).
- Situating issues in context (e.g., of literature, history, geography, current events).
- Acknowledging that learning is a lifelong endeavor, and that sometimes learning happens in new and uncomfortable situations both inside and outside of the classroom.
- Articulating the value of the above concepts in the learning process (e.g., essentially, why it is important to have the skills listed above).
- Articulating the value of critical thinking, interdisciplinarity, strong communication skills—not just uttering these words, but giving examples and details.

As noted in the previous chapter, for both methods (scoring individual questions and providing a score for an entire interview), we ensure that assessments are consistent across coders (through pilot testing the measures and discussing them in team meetings). As is the case with other holistic concepts (such as mental models, described in chapter 5), if there are any scoring disagreements between two coders, these disagreements are discussed and resolved. On the whole, the two measures—the overall measure and the mean of seven questions—correlate quite well.*

An important caveat: we can't prove that an individual does *not* have ways of thinking and communicating that reflect a liberal arts education; but if such evidence does not emerge in an hour-long, wide-ranging conversation, it is certainly well hidden. And the apparent inability or reluctance to display this kind of sophisticated thinking and communicating will surely handicap the student in the years ahead, in both vocational and personal matters. Furthermore, while the HEDCAP scores of individual participants may sometimes be of interest, as researchers of the sector, we are interested principally in the mean scores at a given college and the extent to which those scores increase (or fail to increase) over the period of students' matriculation.[2]

An important finding: in addition to the exchanges and answers given by our conversant, we will presumably notice the particular words that this person uses. Therefore, we must stress that across student groups and across campuses—despite their enormous differences—we repeatedly encountered the same words and often the very same phrases. In the United States, at the word level, college students sound remarkably similar. (For details, see box 4.1.) This finding is notable because it provides a "level playing field" from which we can interpret data for students across the ten campuses.

---

* In this book, we use just the holistic scores to report HEDCAP data.

Box 4.1

Words Across Students

Our more than 2,000 interviews contain approximately 265,000 participant responses and more than 11 million words. Thanks to current computational resources, we can analyze the words most frequently used by all individuals as well as by particular constituency groups and other clusters. Even within constituencies, we can investigate word usage by first-year students or graduating students, by students of different background (e.g., gender, type of high school).

A surprising discovery—*the words students use across campuses are shockingly similar.* Except for obvious differences (names or people or places), we find almost no differences between campuses based on location, size, selectivity, or other evident variables. No matter where they are housed, students in the US sound alike.

Furthermore, some of the words most frequently used by students surprised us. While we expected that some of the 100 most common words would be words like "class," "campus," and "friends," we did not anticipate that we would find words such as "parents," "health," and "help." In fact, the words "time," and "job," two words in the twenty most common words among students, come well before "professor" or "faculty."

Moreover, the way these words were used also surprised us. As an example, we decided to focus on the word "help": we wanted to document the ways in which students could come to the aid of their fellow students. However, when we examined the context for these words, it turns out that the overwhelming majority of uses of the word "help" were *not* occasions where students helped their peers (or others in need). Rather, usage occurred when *students themselves* were seeking help, or describing others seemingly in the need of help.

There are numerous other examples of surprising connotations. We originally thought "job" would be used to describe the current part-time work of students; but we found that it is more often used to talk about future work (as well as the pressure students feel to have their studies lead directly to a specific job). The word "mission"—though not used frequently among students—is focused on individualized goals—a *personal* mission—rather than a group, class, or *institutional* mission. Moreover, it mostly appears as part of the longer word "admission," and therefore is not included in our calculations. We even found different connotations of the word "academic." While some students used the term to designate knowledge and disciplines, other students used (or stretched) this word to categorize work done to achieve desired grades.

Across every school, we find "I"/"Me" were used much more frequently (11 times) than "We"/"Us."* Furthermore, it is not the case that "We"/"Us" words were used more often at smaller, residential schools, those at which a sense of community might be more evident. We believe that this egocentric focus may be particularly characteristic of US students, and during this period of time.† (Cross-cultural and transhistorical studies could be illuminating with respect to the degree of egocentrism.)

Clearly, we could have spent countless hours just studying the words students use in an interview—not only the frequency and denotation of words, but also location (where certain words are used in an interview), networks of words (how words "hang together" in an interview), as well as emotion (feelings with which words are stated by a participant). That said, the finding that words across students—at different schools and at different stages in the college experience—are more similar than different is notable and important. Indeed, this finding of surprising lexical convergence provided the "equal ground" from which we could analyze and interpret other important concepts and perspectives across students in our study.

---

* See also Robert D. Putnam and Shaylyn Romney Garrett, *The Upswing* (New York: Simon & Schuster, 2020).

† In our study, across campuses, only a small minority of students were international—not enough to allow such a comparison.

MAKING SENSE OF HIGHER EDUCATION CAPITAL

Toward the end of each interview, we ask all participants to rank, in their opinion, four purposes for why it's important to go to college from 1 to 4 (where 1= most important and 4= least important). As noted above, the options are:

- To get a job
- To gain different perspectives on people, knowledge, and the world
- To learn to live independently
- To study a particular content area in depth

We also ask participants to discuss the rationale for their ordering—their thinking with respect to each option and their rationale for judging one particular item as more or less important than the others. This is also one of the seven questions we code for HEDCAP—using the criteria just mentioned. It is important to note that as coders (and researchers), we are not looking for specific responses to this (or any) question—for example, we do not penalize those who prioritize "jobs," nor do we reward those who valorize "different perspectives." Rather, in scoring HEDCAP, we focus on participants' *rationale*—understanding and evaluating *how* respondents think about the items.

Furthermore, for "extra credit," if students indicate that jobs are the most important or second most important reason to go to college, we ask a follow-up question: "Like you, some people list getting a job high on this list, but what if the job students are training for disappears in the future?" (As an aside, perhaps not surprisingly, most students were stunned by the question, and only a handful of students offered a substantive response beyond "I don't know," or "I've never thought about that!")

To return to our two students, Jackson ranks the options as (1) to gain different perspectives on people, knowledge, and the world; (2) to study a particular content area in depth; (3) to learn to live independently; and (4) to get a job.

He describes his rationale:

The first thing that pops into my mind is really that I have changed my views on college from the beginning. Really, [college] was [a] means to [an] end, it was means to a master's program which would eventually land me a job, which would eventually land me a certain salary of a certain amount, allowing me to live comfortably, whatever. Since then, I mean, I have learned that there are far more things that are more important in this world than a job necessarily . . .

So I've had to rank it down at the bottom just because you can get a job without a degree really. I mean you might not get a good job. If you want a really good job and you wanna live comfortably, obviously you should go to a university. But going to a university has allowed me to pursue something that I love and study more in depth which is why I put that much higher.

And learning to live independently, that's a really difficult one . . . I feel like you never really get independence to be honest. And this is maybe more [of a] broad, meta-social concept . . . You're always dependent on someone else to do something else for you even if it's just a favor or if it's making sure that you get paid or it's. . . . No one's an island. . . . We all exist within a framework of some kind of community.

And then to study a particular content area in depth, obviously that's really important. Knowing your major . . . When I started to focus on music, I really learned that that was what I loved.

So, it does allow you to study a particular content area in depth, yes, but getting different perspectives on people, knowledge, and the world, I'd say is the absolute 100% fundamental point of college life and the college experience . . .

And this is gonna sound strange; without a liberal arts education, I think I would've fared much worse to be honest . . . Here, I was able to take a class in women's studies. And whether I took a class on the politics of nuclear physics, and the politics of the usage of nuclear technology, I ended up taking a mythology course and all of this has not only opened my world view, but it's also opened my own study and opened my own content area. So, I really feel that getting that broad liberal arts education was really good for me. I can certainly see where people might prefer to do a more intensive study somewhere else that's more focused on one thing in particular, but having that broad education really just opened my eyes to new perspectives.

It is clear that Jackson carefully reflects on how his views have changed over the course of college—signaling that had he been asked the same questions when he was an incoming student, he might well have responded differently. He also discerns and scrutinizes the complexities in the various items; for example, he questions the meaning of "independence," and he discusses the benefits and drawbacks of a single focus on one particular field. Furthermore, Jackson brings up the importance of a liberal arts and science education on his own—a bonus for our tight-mouthed research team.

On the other hand, Rebecca rank orders the options as (1) to get a job; (2) to study a particular content area in depth; (3) to learn to live independently; and (4) to gain different perspectives on people, knowledge, and the world.

Here is her rationale:

Yeah, that's . . . the biggest reason I think for anybody, to get a job, that's the most important of all, one, yeah of course.

To gain different perspectives on people, knowledge and the world, oh that's, there's a lot I can say about that . . . Absolutely, I don't give a damn, I have respected some people, I can write a book about that.

To learn to live independently . . . the millennial generation . . .

Study a particular content area in depth, well that's kind of interesting actually, I think it's a little more important too, especially in contemporary post–World War II, or especially anything Vietnam or afterwards.

Really to gain different perspectives on people, knowledge and the world. I have enough perspective and knowledge that I don't . . . I have plenty of perspectives on people.

In terms of our rubric, it is clear that Rebecca does not give the question much thought—she does not stretch to see how the items might connect, nor does she expand or explain her own perspectives on why independence is important for the millennial generation, or why the aftermath of World War II or the Vietnam War is particularly important to her. We might even assume that she was a high school student.

Let us emphasize: in scoring Higher Education Capital, we are *not* looking for a "right" or "wrong" response about whether "perspectives" should be more important (or not) than a "job." Rather, we score *how* a participant thinks about a question or a topic and *how* a participant explains this thinking. We note that there are many cases in which a researcher may not personally agree with a certain perspective—say, about a childish book recommendation or trivial suggestions for a putative czar of the academic program—but the particular content of a response does not in itself constitute a reason for a high or low score.*

Consider, for example, two additional students, Charlotte and Mateo.

Charlotte receives a high HEDCAP score (score of 3) for her description of "to get a job" as the most important purpose of college:

There were two things I was thinking about when I put these in order, which is both personally what I feel the value of going to college is, but also society's value. As a result, I decided to put "to get a job" as number one.

I think, ultimately, at the end of the day, like, no matter what you do, you got a piece of paper that will help you get a job. There are so many employers who aren't gonna hire you unless you have a BA or some sort of college degree . . . And I, ultimately, don't think that college has been this amazing experience, learning, source of education for me to succeed in a job. I think I have gained those skills along the way while in college and, maybe, I wouldn't have had access to those skills if I weren't in college. But I feel in terms of the value society places on college, I feel it's always, oh, go to college and then get a good job and get paid well and move up, whatever that means.

I put "to gain different perspectives on people, knowledge, and the world" as number two, because, for me, that's the number one. It may not be the value that society places on it, but, I think, ultimately, even at a school like [this one] . . . it's still one of the few colleges—still one of the few opportunities where you're going to be exposed to a diverse population of people, a diverse number of beliefs. I think, in general, people segregate themselves. I mean just look at studies of the US. Most

---

* From this point on, we refer to "low HEDCAP" as a score of 1, "moderate HEDCAP" as a score of 2, and "high HEDCAP" as a score of 3.

towns are segregated in one way or another, racially, I think, by socio-economic class. Eventually, you're gonna have a job, and chances are, your friends are gonna be through your professional world or through other communities you're a part of, but, oftentimes, those communities are faith-based or based on specific interests you have, so it's a lot of very similar people.

In this response, Charlotte earns a high score (a score of 3) because she considers how her personal values square with society's values (yes, a degree helps one secure jobs). But at the same time, she critiques the social structure of society and the very way in which jobs—as well as religion, and personal interests—tend to "segregate" individuals into silos. Furthermore, she acknowledges that even though college is important for a degree, it is not the answer or "source" to succeed in a job; that only happens through learning that takes place in college (which she would not have had "access to" without college). Charlotte also continues this line of thinking later in the interview (in response to a different question about the academic curriculum):

At the end of the day, is [college] helping you in whatever career you're going into? In a lot of ways, no. Which also begs the question, should the point [of college] be building your skills for a career or building . . . just knowledge in general? I think college is sold as what's necessary to . . . have a job. So, perhaps, it's less of an issue with the college and more an issue of how we look at college, but I think either way there's a disconnect there for a lot of people.

Without having access to any of the thinking of our research team, this student foreshadows the problems we highlight throughout this book and discuss in more depth in the latter chapters of this book.

And in so doing, Charlotte signals multidimensional thinking—suggesting more than one interpretation of the original prompt "to get a job."

On the other hand, the second student, Mateo, receives a low score (a score of 1) for his explanation of why "gaining different perspectives about people, knowledge, and the world" is the most important purpose of college:

Learning other people's perspectives, I feel like that just makes you . . . it just makes you smart to learn from, not just to have your own perspective, your own opinions, but to learn how other people think and why they think [that way] . . . I feel like that will get you just a little bit more ahead.

Mateo does not make a convincing argument about why this option is more important than any of the other options (even though we might endorse the ranking); indeed, he is mainly restating the very sentiment entailed in the prompt. Suppose instead that this student had stretched to include his own explanation of how gaining different perspectives helps someone to become "smart"—and what "smart" in this context actually means—or in what ways different perspectives help someone to get "ahead." In such cases, this response may have earned moderate HEDCAP (a score of 2), rather than low HEDCAP (a score of 1).

In addition, in our comparison of Charlotte's explanation of the importance of "gaining different perspectives" with Mateo's explanation of the same topic, the difference in the quality of analysis, reflection, connection, and communication, should be clear.

WHERE HIGHER EDUCATION CAPITAL COMES
FROM AND WHAT IT MEANS

Understanding the experiences of each of the participants on and off campus has been instrumental in finding patterns in Higher Education Capital across individuals and institutions.

For example, the backgrounds of Jackson and Rebecca reveal some interesting surprises. Jackson is graduating from one of the least selective schools in our sample. As a senior in high school, he had wanted to go to four other schools, but did not get into any of them. Jackson settled on his current school because of its well-regarded music program. Reflecting on his college experience, Jackson has enjoyed his time in college. Not only has he developed a passion for music and been inspired by the faculty in his department; Jackson has also participated in drama club, assumed a role in school government, and made friends and acquaintances through living in the residence halls.

On the other hand, after attending community college, Rebecca attended a medium-selectivity school—citing its geographical location as convenient. She chose history as a major by default, in her words, "because it was the only major that did not require math courses to graduate." In general, her college experience has been bumpy. She was suspended for a period of time (for harassing a course instructor over email), which has caused her to spend more years in school than she wanted.

As noted, after each interview, the researcher (or researchers) jot down impressions. Here are the comments on Rebecca: "This participant struggled to answer a lot of my questions, often saying

'I don't know' or 'That's tough.' I think that she truly does not know that much about [the school] and is not a part of the community . . . She also isn't inclined to think beyond the superficial—there wasn't a lot of effort on her part to answer my questions, which I think might reflect on her tendencies as a student." Notably, the researcher's impressions of Jackson are quite different: "It was the smoothest running Skype interview I've had yet. It's clear that he was taking this conversation very seriously and had a lot of opinions that he was willing to share."

These individual descriptors of Jackson and Rebecca lead us to many important questions: Does the selectivity of an institution predict Higher Education Capital? Does one's choice of major predict Higher Education Capital? With the examples of Jackson and Rebecca in mind, does one's connection to the school—its academics, its student body, its overall mission—tell us anything about Higher Education Capital? Or: does length of one's response, or the richness of one's vocabulary, predict Higher Education Capital?

To be sure, we are interested in these specific questions as well as the individual stories of each student—like that of Jackson and Rebecca (and Charlotte and Mateo). But our primary interest as researchers is whether within an institution there is greater HEDCAP among students after college than before college—suggesting "growth" as a function of the college experience.* Put

---

* As noted, because these data are not longitudinal, we can't demonstrate growth in any particular individual, but we can infer growth by comparing data from the two groups of students.

another way: we all may have assumptions or predictions about the HEDCAP of students at highly selective institutions as compared to those at less selective schools—and whether students at more highly selective schools come in with more HEDCAP than those students at less selective schools. But we are far more interested in whether individual institutions—and the sector as a whole—"move the Higher Education Capital needle" for students in a positive direction.

We have investigated these questions using both qualitative and quantitative analyses.*

On the whole, looking across all students, we find a normal "inverted U-shape" distribution of Higher Education Capital scores. About half of the students have moderate HEDCAP (a score of 2); and the remaining half of students are almost evenly divided by low HEDCAP (score of 1) or high HEDCAP (score of 3).

But just focusing on the overall data from more than a thousand students at two different stages (first-year students and graduating students), across schools that differ in size, selectivity, and focus—does not suffice. We seek to understand some of the important nuances.

Across Time

In general, in comparing two groups of students over the course of college—first-year students and graduating students, we find

---

*We have included data from Olin College of Engineering in the quantitative analyses described in this book. While we designated it as a "comparison" school, data from this school are consistent with data from its peer schools.

Percent of students with each HEDCAP score

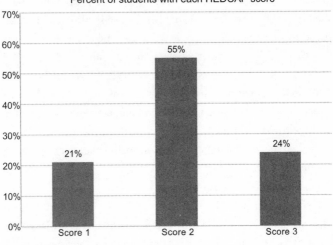

Figure 4.1

that Higher Education Capital increases—certainly good news for this embattled sector of US society. While more than a quarter of first-year students (30%) are scored as having low HEDCAP (a score of 1), this number decreases over time (12% of graduating seniors have a score of 1). We find little difference between first-year students and graduating students who are scored as having moderate HEDCAP (54% of first-year students as compared to 56% of graduating students are scored as a 2). However, while fewer than a quarter of first-year students (16%) are scored as having high HEDCAP (score of 3), the percentage of graduating students with this score doubles over the course of college (32% are scored as a 3). Put succinctly, as we scan the spectrum

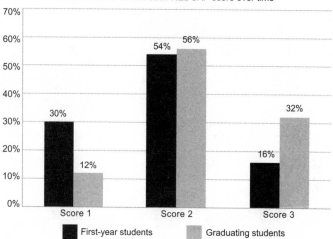

Percent of students with each HEDCAP score over time

Figure 4.2

of first-year students to graduating students, students with low scores of HEDCAP decrease, and students with high scores of HEDCAP increase.

Of course, we need to take into account the fact that some students drop out of school, and it's quite possible that the dropouts are ones that display little to no gain in HEDCAP . . . not every dropout moves to Silicon Valley and starts a successful tech company!

We can also examine Higher Education Capital *after* college with our sample of young alums. Interestingly, and somewhat disturbingly, we find that HEDCAP "growth" does not seem to continue at the same rate after graduation. Specifically, the HEDCAP scores

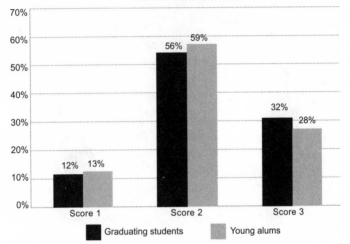

Percent of graduating students and young alums
with each HEDCAP score

Figure 4.3

of young alums are strikingly similar to the HEDCAP scores of graduating students: fewer than a quarter of young alums (13%) are scored as having low HEDCAP (compared to 12% of graduating students); more than half of young alums (59%) are scored as having moderate HEDCAP (compared to 56% of graduating students); and nearly a third of young alums (28%) are scored as having high HEDCAP (compared to 32% of graduating students).

More specifically, at six of our schools—which vary in selectivity and size—HEDCAP scores decrease between graduating students and young alums; at three schools, HEDCAP scores stay consistent, and at only one school do HEDCAP scores increase between these groups.

We cannot overstate this claim, for two reasons. First, the sample size of young alums is far smaller than that of students; and second, because we used an opportunistic approach to interviewing young alums—posting advertisements in school bulletins, websites, and newspapers—we can't be certain that these participants constitute a representative group of young alums. Yet it is most unlikely that we have inadvertently sampled those alums with HEDCAP that is *lower* than that of their fellow alums.

Certainly, we don't want to argue that once students graduate from college, there are no longer opportunities for learning or for increasing one's Higher Education Capital. But at the same time, it is important to highlight the point; not only does college seem to generally "improve" one's HEDCAP, but it might prove to be more effective in increasing HEDCAP than the experience of a first post-college job. And this result could reflect various possibilities, ranging from the fact that those working full time have less time and opportunity to engage in intellectual endeavors, to the possibility—indeed the likelihood—that the ages of 18–25 represent a developmental period when cognitive growth can particularly flourish.[3]

Regarding Higher Education Capital, we might quip "use it or lose it."

Across Institutions

We see clear patterns across selectivity of institutions. In general, the distribution of Higher Education Capital scores—from low to high—reflect the selectivity of the institution. Specifically, low-selectivity schools have the most students (36%) with

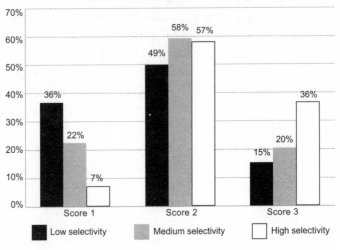

Figure 4.4

low HEDCAP (score of 1), compared to high-selectivity schools with students who have this score (7%). At the same time, high-selectivity schools have the most students (36%) with high HEDCAP (score of 3), as compared to students at low-selectivity schools who have this score (15%). Given these findings, it is unsurprising that students at "medium-selectivity" schools have the most students with moderate HEDCAP (score of 2) and that on the whole, students at these schools have neither the least or the most scores of 1 or 3.

But these cumulative data tell only a part of the important story. Over time, more graduating students at schools in all three categories of selectivity are scored as having high HEDCAP (score of 3) than are first-year students; and fewer students at schools in all three selectivity categories are scored as having low HEDCAP (score of 1).

At the very least, college is doing no harm; and in all probability, the college experience—along with the process of maturation—boosts the amount of Higher Education Capital across the board. Based on these statistics, we can conclude that regardless of selectivity or status, higher education can make a positive impact in increasing or improving one's Higher Education Capital over time.[4]

Furthermore, when we dig deeper to examine trends in particular institutions within each category of selectivity, we notice a few revealing outliers within selectivity groups. For example, one of the least-selective four-year institutions exhibits the most dramatic positive change in HEDCAP. Specifically, within this category of schools, though this school has the most first-year students (62%) with low HEDCAP (score of 1), it also has the fewest graduating students (15%) with this score. This school also shows a steep increase for students with high HEDCAP (score of 3), in comparing first-year students (9%) to graduating students (26%).

By the same token, we also note an outlier for HEDCAP growth in the category of most selective schools. Though this particular school has the most first-year students (17%) with low HEDCAP (score of 1), it also has the fewest graduating students with this score (0%). This school also shows the most dramatic increase for students with high HEDCAP (score of 3), comparing first-year students (23%) to graduating students (56%). We would like to think that this school is doing some things right; and we suspect that other observers would agree.

Unfortunately, and in contrast, at one of the medium-selectivity institutions, we find that the percentage of students with low HEDCAP (score of 1) does not change between first-year students (12%) and graduating students (12%); and there is only a modest increase in those students scored as having high HEDCAP (score of 3) between first-year students (19%) and graduating students (29%).

Clearly, there ought to be specifiable reasons for the dramatic growth in Higher Education Capital in two of our schools, as well as the disappointing stagnation of HEDCAP at one of our schools. In Part IV of this book, we identify specific factors—the nuances of the academic program, campus culture, and/or overall mission of the school—all of which putatively contribute to change (or no change) in Higher Education Capital over the course of college. In particular, we argue for the importance of a clear and explicit focus on academic matters for students—indeed, for every constituency.

Across Disciplines

Overall, we find little to no differences between students who have selected majors in the natural sciences, social sciences, and humanities. In other words, similar to all students in our sample, when we consider the group of students in each major, we find that roughly half of students in the natural sciences (60%), social sciences (51%), and humanities (57%) have moderate HEDCAP (score of 2), while among the other half of students, more students in the natural sciences (24%), social sciences (30%), and humanities (31%) have high HEDCAP, and fewer students in the natural sciences (16%), social sciences (19%), and humanities (12%) have low HEDCAP.

Put differently, it is not the case that students with a declared major in the social sciences have substantially different HEDCAP scores than students who have a declared major in the natural sciences, or the humanities; nor is it the case that students who are about to complete a major in the humanities have noticeably different HEDCAP scores than students who are about to complete a major in the social sciences. HEDCAP seems to be "discipline blind."

Moreover, the growth in Higher Education Capital scores among first-year students (who have declared these majors) and graduating students (who have nearly completed requirements for these majors) proves fairly consistent across all three majors, with one caveat: on average, as a cohort, those students who major in the natural sciences exhibit more overall HEDCAP growth than those who major in the social sciences or humanities (13% of first-year students in the natural sciences have high HEDCAP as compared to 32% of graduating students with this capital).

We posit two explanations for this finding: first, students who are about to *complete* a natural science major may not be representative of all students because of the higher attrition among students in these disciplines; and second, owing to required lab work, students in these majors may take more time to graduate than students in other disciplines.

Interestingly and relatedly, we also find overwhelming consensus in the kind of courses students seem to value (and don't value) across different disciplines and across HEDCAP scores.

Specifically, most students agree that courses in the social sciences are "time well spent," while courses in the natural sciences are "wastes of time." These findings stay consistent across both majors as well as students with varying amounts of Higher Education Capital. In other words, a student with a high HEDCAP (score of 3) does not place significantly more or less value on social science courses than a student with low HEDCAP (score of 1). Across HEDCAP scores, students agree that they value these courses the most because they offer the most relevance to their own lives and contribute to their own personal development. Courses in the natural sciences are more often viewed as "wastes of time," because they tend to be presented in more formulaic and technical terms; students apparently feel a much greater distance between the material covered and their own personal experiences (see box 4.2).

Across Words

We have now compared students at different stages in college, at different types of colleges and in different majors, and even with respect to the type of courses students consider to be valuable (or not). But at the beginning of this chapter, we described the concept of Higher Education Capital—and differences between high and low scores—in light of students' responses to specific questions in the interview, as well as throughout the hour-long conversation.

As noted, we find striking similarities in the words students use across campuses (see box 4.1); but we find significant differences in the *number* of words and overall length of responses across students with varied Higher Education Capital scores. Specifically,

Box 4.2

College Courses: Time Well Spent, or a Waste of Time?

Sophie Blumert

We asked all students to tell us about particular courses that are "time well spent" and those that are "wastes of time."

Students readily name both courses they value and those they do not value; of the participants who were asked, 86% name courses that are time well spent, and 79% name courses that are a waste of time.

In general, students tend to name courses in the social sciences—psychology, political science, and economics—most frequently as "time well spent" (26% of all students), while students tend to name courses in the natural sciences—biology, chemistry, and physics—as a "waste of time" (18% of all students). It seems that students place more value on courses in fields that are new to them, while courses from fields that are more familiar, such as those from high school, are often identified as wastes of time. Perhaps the novelty (or lack thereof) of certain courses might play a role in why students do or don't value them; most students are not exposed to anthropology or sociology in a high school, while many have taken natural science courses before matriculation.

Students also point out that courses such as psychology, sociology, and political science are timelier, connected to everyday life, and more explicitly linked to social issues. In contrast, students seem to feel that natural science courses tend to be more formulaic—removed from the everyday human experience, and much more focused on grades.

There are few other discernible patterns—we looked at gender, year, and school selectivity, but found no other trends. Importantly, we also found no differences across our two holistic measures: Higher Education Capital and mental models (chapter 5). And when students talk about their own majors, they cite both courses that they like and courses they consider a waste of time.

Students give several different explanations for why certain courses are valuable or not.

Level of difficulty: First, we learn that students do not value courses that are too easy or that do not challenge them (19% of all students). Additionally, it is very rare for students to talk about courses being "too difficult" (5%); when they do, it is often related to other factors such as teaching or assessment, rather than purely to course content. Overall, students want to be pushed with college-level content; otherwise, they don't feel like they are learning.

Presence or absence of an experience of "Flow": When material is repetitive and easy, students become bored and soon disengage from their studies.[5] A sense of flow—that treasured space between boredom and anxiety—is crucial to students in both appreciating and retaining what they are learning. Of course, flow may differ from one student to another, making its achievement challenging for instructors.

Relevance of a course to one's life: Students often link a course to what they believe is relevant, or irrelevant, to their academic or personal goals. Approximately 17% of students mention relevance when talking about courses that are time well spent, while 23% of students bring this up when listing courses that are a waste of time. This is also reflected in the aforementioned point regarding social sciences versus natural sciences.

These findings raise important questions for educators: Who determines the relevance, and how? Sometimes, students do not immediately realize the relevance that a course may have in their lives, and faculty may not always know what resonates with students. It's therefore desirable for faculty and students to consult through discussions and consistent feedback about what is "relevant." Faculty should stretch to convey the rationale for the content and style of their course, while students ought to give an involved faculty member the benefit of the doubt.

students with higher HEDCAP use more words than do students with lower HEDCAP. Because by definition, high HEDCAP students express clear and well-developed responses, it is not the case that students with high HEDCAP use more "filler" words (or even that they use more sophisticated vocabularies). Rather, we believe that high HEDCAP responses consist of more words because the students offer more context and more connections in their rationale—regardless of the perspectives.

An example: Though we do not specifically ask students about "social issues"—race, religion, socioeconomic status, gender, and politics—the majority of students across all campuses indicate the salience of these issues throughout the interview (we discuss these social tensions in chapter 7). Students with higher HEDCAP (scores of 3) raise significantly more topics of social issues than do students with lower HEDCAP (scores of 2 or 1); students with moderate HEDCAP (score of 2) raise significantly more topics than those students with low HEDCAP (score of 1). We find that students with higher HEDCAP describe the interrelationship of these issues on campus; in contrast, students with lower HEDCAP are more likely to discuss these topics as isolated issues, if they raise them at all.

There are interesting nuances to this overall finding. A graduating student double majoring in neuroscience and literature with overall *low* HEDCAP describes her perception of high socioeconomic students on campus:

Students [at this school] are primarily very wealthy and also are very smart, so they've had . . . their entire lives, they've never had anything go wrong for them, most of the time, and I think that if any little small thing starts to go wrong for them, then the universe should automatically correct it for them because it's their God-given right to succeed.

Or, consider how a graduating student, a Spanish major who also runs on the school's track team, with overall *high* HEDCAP, explains her view of "affluence" on campus. She believes that the concept of "privilege" can be extrapolated to a general feeling of "inequality," encompassing gender, race, *and* socioeconomic status.

We're a very, very affluent campus . . . early on in my academic career here I took [a] class . . . that really like opened my eyes . . . to issues of racial inequality. Because I think a lot of people tend to think about racism and, and sexism as being things that are, you know, in the past that [are] more or less resolved now, and while . . . I didn't identify as one of those people . . . I was not aware and did not fully recognize how much I still contribute to racism and sexism, you know, like on a subconscious level in my like everyday life or realize how much, like I am privileged in my everyday life because I'm white, because I'm a white woman . . . not from an affluent family but from a . . . a family that never [has to] worry about a roof over my head or where my next meal was gonna come from and it really made me realize how, how privileged I am, but also how . . . how other, how like people of color, people of lower classes, lower socio-economic classes, are like systematically . . . discriminated against in the most mundane ways. . . . There's a faction of students [here] who are very aware and, and we have students of color . . . who really like voice out against that and . . . there have been lots of . . . initiatives for people to share their experiences. . . . But I think as a whole the campus just needs to be more diverse and the administration and classes need to be more open and contributing to that diversity on campus.

Not only does the second student explain the interrelationship among different topics of social issues; she considers her limitations given her own background and also situates this evolving perspective in relation to a feminist course she has taken while in college.

Two other points from this portion of our study: First, throughout our study, few participants cite lessons gleaned from specific courses or readings or substantive conversations encountered in the course of their college experience. We believe colleges can and should do a much better job of helping students to integrate materials and ways of thinking conveyed in their courses to students' life concerns. Second, while we have not asked students explicitly for demographic data (see p.50), we find no major differences in Higher Education Capital score between students across demographies on which we do have some information—including hometown, type of high school (public, private, or charter), or our inferences about gender.

STEPPING BACK

We hope that the various quotations and comments have conveyed the importance of Higher Education Capital, the evidence that we have assembled in ascertaining its presence (or absence), and its relative independence from specific vocabulary or bins of information. But it is also important to indicate *why* we have highlighted it in our study; and also delineate some of the ways in which it resembles, but also differs from, other analyses and measures of the effects of higher education.

To begin with, while we are clearly focused on education that is not exclusively vocational, we began our study with a stated commitment not to develop or mandate a particular curriculum. We do not presuppose particular topics or modes of delivery or examinations. We trust the faculty of institutions of higher education—individually and collectively—to present materials and develop courses that engage and challenge students across a broad number of subjects, and that introduce and model various ways of thinking and performing. HEDCAP can and should be enhanced by a variety of curricular choices and approaches.

Of course, faculty can and should have ways of ascertaining whether the materials from these different curricula and assignments have been covered and mastered. And it is perfectly appropriate when those responsible for education make use of instruments that have been developed by experts in measurement—and these would include the kinds of subject-specific tests developed by the Educational Testing Service or broader instruments like the Collegiate Learning Assessment.

Clearly, our concept of Higher Education Capital differs from achievements in particular subject matters or disciplines—we are not assessing whether students have greater historical knowledge, or deeper insights about personality types as delineated by psychologists, or sharper mathematical acuity, or even the capacity to synthesize information prior to the recommendation of a specific policy. Rather, Higher Education Capital seeks to capture some broad qualities that have been referred to variously as critical thinking, analytic thinking, intellectual depth and breadth, reflective thinking, or even—if more grandly—the goal of a college education.

In our conceptualization, we have benefited from studies of college students undertaken over the decades by psychologist

William Perry.[6] In Perry's deliberately broad formulation, one can classify college students in terms of four, ordered stances toward knowledge:

1. Dualism—issues are seen as either right and wrong.
2. Multiplicity—the world contains ambiguity, uncertainty, and it's difficult to resolve, so all views are deemed as equally plausible.
3. Contextual relativism—the situation is too complex ever to resolve confidently, and one is left struggling among plausible alternatives.
4. Commitment—One has established a set of beliefs—scholarly, moral, spiritual—and one commits oneself to those beliefs, though one remains open to changing one's mind in the face of new evidence or fresh alternatives or arguments.

Perry's own formulation is based significantly on students' wrestling with ethical dilemmas—and the later stances are considered more sophisticated or "developed." Our analytic scheme—built on a wide-ranging but structured conversation—does not deliberately feature such dilemmas. But we are confident that there would be a positive relation between Higher Education Capital on the one hand, and the "higher" Perry stages, on the other.

In sum: where we differ from other assessments of the thinking of college students is in the source of our evidence and the kinds of analyses we have carried out. Instead of free conversation, on the one hand, or a uniform survey on the other, we have a lengthy sample of discourse and conversation on an expansive topic that falls—at least should fall—*squarely in the experience of each of the participants.* Unlike broader measures, like the Collegiate Learning Assessment, we do not focus on the kinds of (admittedly, vital) skills called for within the college classroom, but rather for a broader, more reflective kind of perspective on one's educational and life experiences. And then, rather than a simple holistic score, on the one hand, or a sum of multiple-choice responses on the other, we have two measures—holistic *and* item-specific—that yield the same general picture.

It's legitimate to ask whether the capacities that we are seeking to capture via our concept of Higher Education Capital are genuinely useful—or even demonstrably useful—once one has left college and entered the "real world." It's our firm belief that those who have attained, consolidated, and can continue to draw upon Higher Education Capital will not only possess a capacity that proves useful across the occupational landscape—in securing positions, in advancing to more responsible niches, in working comfortably with others in an organization. (These were all points emphasized by the job recruiters with whom we spoke.) In addition, we believe that this cognitive ensemble should add to quality of life "off the job"—be that time with family, in friendship groups, in hobbies, or even—as conveyed by this chapter's opening anecdote—in one's travels and chance encounters throughout one's life. At present, though we hold it firmly, this conviction remains a promissory note for a positive case on the value of a liberal arts education.[7]

Turning to our notion of "capital," we observe that education—and higher education in particular—is generally (and appropriately) considered a major way to achieve various kinds of capital.

These include economic or financial capital (often the measure of a college's worth is equated with the mean salary of graduates—a criterion about which we remain skeptical); cultural capital (familiarity with and knowledge of historical, humanistic, and artistic materials from the ambient, as well as other, cultures); and social capital (ability to work with and play with individuals from a range of backgrounds, and particularly those with status in the adult world). We do not deplore these alternatives; indeed, we hope that graduates will possess and continue to increase these various forms of capital.[8]

But, at least in principle, these forms of capital could be obtained outside of the halls of higher education—through the luck of one's family's assets or high-quality on-the-job training, trips to cultural centers, or membership in the "right" social clubs, respectively. (These factors often co-occur, as has been amply documented.) The kind of capital we are interested in is "capital of the mind"—the capital that is best, and perhaps only, acquired through careful study across a variety of disciplines calling for a range of performances, and through formal and informal conversations across the day and into the evening with others who are involved in the same general enterprise. That's what we hope college will achieve, and what we have hoped to capture, at least roughly, in our assessment of the capital of higher education.

In the last few decades, general nonvocational education (sometimes using the term that we have proscribed, "liberal arts" education), US style, has been a growth industry in many parts of the world—notably in East Asia and in Eastern Europe.[9] We speculate about one reason for the popularity of this form of higher education: leaders in these countries detect and admire a kind of breadth and sophistication among graduates of such schools that is lacking among graduates in their own vocation-accented institutions of higher education. But this idea remains speculative. Beyond question, those who have had a liberal arts education endorse its long-term dividends and often desire it for their children and grandchildren; but it has proved difficult to demonstrate to skeptics that a broad education (compared to a more targeted, vocationally torqued education) yields preferable "hard outcomes"—which almost always comes down to annual or lifetime income.[10]

CONCLUDING THOUGHTS

Though members of various constituencies certainly don't converge on a single purpose of college, presumably all would prefer that students increase Higher Education Capital over the course of college. We want more individuals who can discuss the political context intelligently, analyze the portrayal of a story in a movie or in a book, draw on data with respect to addressing a health challenge—more students like Jackson, who can articulate the importance of pursuing a broad higher education.

And happily, across all schools in our study, we find that on the whole, more graduating students exhibit Higher Education Capital than first-year students—positive indicators that college *can* make a difference in the intellectual growth of students, regardless of the type of school one attends. And, importantly, this "growth" seemingly occurs across all kinds of students—those of different backgrounds, those who have declared and nearly completed different majors, those from different parts of the country. Moreover, though it is clear that higher selectivity schools are populated by more first-year students with higher HEDCAP and that they have more graduating students with higher HEDCAP, there is generally good news: at *both* the most selective schools *and* the least selective schools, the percentage of students with high HEDCAP nearly doubles, and at the same time, the percentage of students with low HEDCAP decreases by half the number.

Therefore, whether students start college with little or some HEDCAP, we would like to believe that students—as well as their faculty, administrators, parents, trustees, and job recruiters—would concur that HEDCAP is important, and that it can and should be increased. But, as we argue in Part IV of this book, colleges need to make this mission paramount. And particularly with respect to those schools where HEDCAP seems to move little during matriculation, we delineate how this mission can be conveyed in both explicit and implicit ways.

If the ultimate aim of college is to nurture intellectual growth—to increase the likelihood that Higher Education Capital (and other related virtues) will increase over the course of college—we need to understand and be attentive to a variety of considerations: students' views of college, as well as their connection to their studies, to individuals on campus, to the institution that they are attending, and, of course, to their overall well-being.

In the following chapters, we discuss other substantive findings across institutions and constituency groups. Specifically, in chapter 5, we focus on "mental models" for the college experience.

These are the very different and potentially crucial perspectives that individual students exhibit with respect to the reasons for attending college and, relatedly, their aspirations for what might transpire as a consequent of their years spent in institutions of higher education. It turns out that students who view college as an opportunity to learn about various disciplines, meet and engage with different people, "try out" a variety of activities, and "try on" values, beliefs, and identities that have not previously been considered, are more likely to have high Higher Education Capital than those students who view college as an opportunity to build a resume, secure internships and jobs, and interact with others for the purpose of networking. Put succinctly, how one thinks about college seems to affect how much one gains from one's college experience.

5 MENTAL MODELS OF THE COLLEGE EXPERIENCE: LEARNINGS, EARNINGS, AND YEARNINGS

Students arrive on campus with a range of ideas about the purposes of college and what they themselves expect and hope to gain from the experience. On any campus, one student will see college as a means of attaining a high paying job in finance, a second may want to understand how and why cancerous cells emerge and proliferate, a third may want to have fun and join clubs, while a fourth may seek to learn about unfamiliar cultures, religious beliefs, or perspectives about global affairs. Sometimes, students want a combination or all of the above—a desire to experience and achieve *everything* that college has to offer.*

---

* Shades of Eugene Gant's grandiose aspirations in Thomas Wolfe's autobiographical novel *Of Time and the River*.

Given such diverse ambitions and aspirations, almost of necessity, students have or soon develop approaches to college: a mental
framework with which they structure their time to do the kinds
of things they care about most—whether these are extracurricular activities, lab research, test prep, and/or attending career
affairs—or sometimes, ignoring these opportunities, and just
hanging out or watching videos alone or with their peers.

Adopting a phrase commonly used in the cognitive sciences, we
have termed these approaches *mental models*: visions that encompass what college should be about, what it will be like, and how
one might realize that conception. Some students have clear ideas
of what they want and go after it assiduously. Others are open to
many possibilities, or alternatively, are simply passive—treating
the experience as an extension of high school, as a "way station"
onto the next stage of life.

In our interviews with more than a thousand students across
ten campuses, four mental models for college emerged. These
models illuminate how first-year students think about the experience that lies ahead and how, for their part, graduating students
make sense of the whole experience. Accordingly, student mental
models give us a window into the messages and beliefs about college that students bring with them—from their upbringing and
prior schooling. Equally revealing, these mental models indicate
how certain facets of college, such as on-campus or off-campus
experiences, may strengthen these models or, possibly, reshape
one's mindset over the course of college. Indeed, this analytic
scheme also helps us to examine alignment and misalignment
in higher education—how a student's approach to college may

be in (or out of) synch with the overall mission or mental model of the institution, as seen by peers, faculty, other stakeholders, or, indeed, as communicated in the official mission statement.

FOUR MODELS

As we construe them, mental models should be more than just individual goals for the college experience *and* more than what one thinks about the general purpose of college; mental models should serve to guide a student's overall approach to the college experience. Therefore (as we have shown with respect to Higher Education Capital), we categorize a participant's mental model by a close reading and analysis of the entire interview, not just by a single response to a particular question.

We posit four mental models for the college experience:

Inertial: After high school, one goes to college, but does not think much about reasons for being there, or of taking advantage of various opportunities; nor does one exhibit noteworthy aspirations.

Transactional: One goes to college and does what (and *only* what) is required to get a degree and then secure placement in graduate school and/or a job; college is viewed principally, perhaps entirely, as a springboard for future-oriented ambitions. While vocational schools may have other—and perhaps broader—ambitions, at a minimum they constitute a promissory note that graduates will be prepared for specific professions or positions.

Exploratory: One goes to college intentionally to take time to learn about diverse fields of study and to try out new activities—academic, extracurricular, and/or social; one comes to college to "marinate" in new ideas and perspectives; and also to interact with and learn from new acquaintances, especially peers, instructors, or staff from unfamiliar backgrounds and/or demographies.

Transformational: One goes to college to reflect about, and question, one's own values and beliefs, with the expectation, and often, as well, the aspiration that one may change in fundamental ways.

Clearly, these descriptions are what sociologists term "ideal types"—students don't necessarily use these exact words or phrases, nor does every student fit neatly into one of these categories, nor do all students maintain the same stance over the course of college. However, the identification of the prevalent (or primary) mental model is usually evident and uncontroversial.

Consider the following examples.

Inertial: Jeremy is a graduating student at a highly selective school who describes his choice to attend this particular school as simply "they let me in." He admits to being enamored by the "surprising" drinking culture as a first-year student, but now realizes that some of the students who drink their way through college are not so "cool." However, Jeremy mainly focuses on the benefit of the social aspects of college—valuing the "things that I've learned outside of classes" more than any of his academic experiences. Indeed, in discussing his own coursework, Jeremy is apathetic about his own major in science—he only shows interest in the likelihood of gaining employment upon graduation—claiming that he originally declared a major in science because he was fairly interested in this topic in high school. In thinking about changes he would suggest for the academic program at his school, he explains that he wishes that his school would have made it easier for him to satisfy the general education requirements.

While Jeremy believes that he has matured during college—gained independence in terms of living on his own without the daily support of his parents—he does not think that college should be a transformative experience for students. Instead, as he reflects, "I was never, like, super driven to college. It was just kind of like, the next step. And it wasn't a bad next step, but, but it was just kind of like, 'Oh, what do you do after high school? You go to college.'" Furthermore, in giving advice to a hypothetical incoming student, Jeremy characteristically suggests: "Definitely find a friend with a car . . . so you can get off campus and try to do that a lot. I think it really helps stay sane . . ."

Transactional: Elizabeth is a first-year student, intending to be pre-med. As an explanation, she refers to her own immune deficiency disorder that has exposed her to the field of medicine throughout her youth. Elizabeth wants to help treat people, both physically and emotionally. Since high school, this was her "dream school" because of its well-funded science programs and research opportunities. She values a "well-rounded" academic experience because she believes that different courses will help her to communicate better with future patients, write articles for journals, and understand human interactions in the medical arena. Elizabeth views the purpose of college as "giv[ing] you a better world view and it helps you meet people and network so that later on in life you can have a strong career and foundation . . . college is getting you a well-rounded education and also helping you set your aims on a career. So you have to have some direction as to what you're gonna do with your degree in the end."

Exploratory: Azar, a first-year student, chose his particular school because of the financial aid offered, but also because he wanted to live far from the part of the country where he was raised. Unlike his hometown, where "everyone looked like me," he wants to broaden opportunities and meet new people with different backgrounds. Toward this end, even though Azar has only been at school for a few months, he is involved in a variety of campus activities, including ballroom dancing (something he had never tried before), a ping-pong club, and an affinity group for Latino/as (which he is not), which involves social events as well as volunteer activities. Azar recently declared as a communications major (an option for students at this school), because he wanted something "broad" that would help him to understand diverse people and unfamiliar cultures. Azar asserts that he has come to college to "take as many classes as I could . . . learn as much as I could . . . and just kind of like broaden my span of opportunity."

Transformational: Sasha, a first-generation college student from (according to her testimony) an unstable family background, was encouraged by a high school teacher to pursue college. After a few attempts at different schools, Sasha has found her way to a school in which she describes students as "determined." At first, as a college student, she was shy around other people. But once Sasha was "given the opportunity to speak," she realized that she left her "comfort zone," in the company of individuals who were more self-confident and more articulate. She explains, "If you're continuously in the same box, and you continue to follow the label that you're given . . . you just go by what you are told . . . your whole life."

Now, as a graduating student, Sasha is on the debate team and holds a leadership position in student government. Pursuing and paying for formal education has not been easy; as a result of her college experience, Sasha wants to become a social worker to help young people to create "pathways" to college. She says, "That's what I want to do . . . enable other students who are first-generation, like myself, and who feel like they don't have any guidance. I just want to create that pathway, and work with them, 'cause I, that's literally, what changed my life.'" In reflecting on the meaning of college, Sasha concludes: "So, I think school, it, it's not just for academics. It's not just for, 'Let me learn this equation,' or, 'Let me learn how to write properly' . . . You learn how you want to spend the rest of your life. You learn what makes you happy . . . it's very important, because I feel like those are qualities you need to live [a] fulfilling life."

Each of these four stances and responses generates questions that emerge across diverse individuals and disparate campuses.

As examples:

Jeremy ("inertial") indicates that his science major was the easiest pathway to a college degree—he expresses little interest per se in any part of the academic experience. One wonders: do students with certain majors—for example, those in the humanities or in the natural sciences—tend to favor particular mental models?

Elizabeth ("transactional"), at her "dream school," is set with the ambition of becoming a doctor. Do certain types of schools predict particular mental models? Do high school experiences predict certain mental models?

Azar ("exploratory") plunges into different activities on campus, hoping to absorb as much as he can from the overall experience, in the classroom as well as in extracurricular activities. How common is this approach at his school? And what is the most common mental model among more than one thousand students across campuses?

Sasha ("transformational") reflects on her own personal shift over the course of college—coming in as a shy student, but now graduating with passion and a strong sense of self. On the whole, are more graduating students than first-year students categorized as "transformational"? Do mental models stay consistent over the college experience, or over time, do mental models change? And if so, which models and in which ways?

MENTAL MODEL FUNDAMENTALS

In general, across all students in our study we find that nearly half the students (45%) have a transactional mental model. They view college as a necessary next step—*en route* to going to graduate school or getting a job. For these students, the value of a college degree comes down to its instrumentality: what it can help one attain or accomplish in the near, or possibly, in the more distant future, a means to an end.

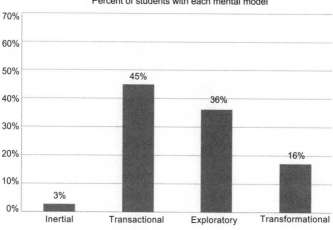

Percent of students with each mental model

Figure 5.1

Approximately a third of students in our sample (36%) are categorized as having an exploratory mental model, while fewer (16%) have a transformational model. We were pleased—and somewhat relieved—to discover that only a very small fraction of the students that we interviewed have an inertial mental model (3%).

As with Higher Education Capital, we can easily present overall data for students, but these statistics only tell part of the story. To understand mental models fully—and the factors that may contribute to the development of the four respective approaches to college—we need to investigate how mental models compare across groups of students at different schools and at different stages in their college experience.

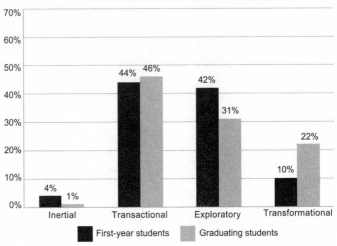

Percent of students with each mental model over time

Figure 5.2

Across Time

In comparing the *overall* groups of first-year students and graduating students, we note *both* consistency *and* shifts across different mental models. For example, the number of students with a transactional mental model essentially does not change over the course of college (44% of first-year students compared to 46% of graduating students); at the same time, students with an exploratory mental model decreases (42% of first-year students compared to 31% of graduating students), and students with a transformational mental model increases (10% of first-year students compared to 22% of graduating students).

Though our study is not longitudinal, these comparisons suggest a range of interesting possibilities. For example, a first-year student who has an exploratory mental model might develop a transactional mental model as graduation and job searching become a vivid reality; or such an exploratory student might develop a transformational mental model as a result of eye- or mind-opening courses and deepening relationships with professors and/or peers.

One additional note: though the number of students with inertial mental models is very small overall, the number of students with this approach also decreases over the course of college (4% of first-year students compared to 1% of graduating students). It seems that inertia does not translate easily into a degree.

Across Institutions

Overall, as we compare schools and groups of schools, we find clear patterns among student mental models.

For example, in general, our *low-selectivity* schools have the most students with a transactional mental model (57%), compared to students at the high-selectivity schools with this mental model (26%). And, at the same time, and perhaps not surprisingly, our *high-selectivity* schools have the most students with exploratory (51%) and transformational (22%) mental models; in contrast, fewer students at the low-selectivity schools exhibit these mental models (26% exploratory and 14% transformational).

It is notable that at the "medium-selectivity" schools—schools that are neither the most nor the least selective—we find that student mental models are more similar to those of the low-selectivity

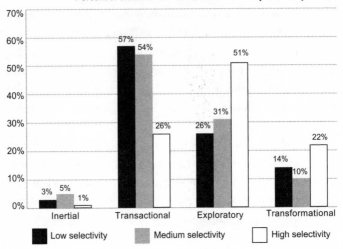

Figure 5.3

schools, rather than to those of the high-selectivity schools. In other words, more students at these schools have transactional mental models (54%) and fewer have transformational mental models (10%)—indeed, we find even fewer students with transformational approaches than those at the low-selectivity schools.[1]*

However, within these categories of selectivity, we see a couple of notable outliers. For example, one of the low-selectivity schools has significantly *fewer students with transactional mental models*

---

* Note that only a handful of schools in the country admit fewer than 20% of applicants.

(43%) than its peer schools (each with 61% and 67% students with transactional models), and *more students with exploratory mental models* (37%), compared to the other schools in this category (19% and 21% students with exploratory models). Similarly, one of the medium-selectivity school stands out for having *fewer students with a transactional mental model* (46%) than its peer schools (58% and 57% students with transactional models) and *more students with a transformational mental model* (18%) than its peer schools (8% and 7% students with transformational models).

These outliers raise searching questions about how particular institutions may contribute to the expression and development of a specific mental model for their students. Importantly, across *all* students we find no significant correlations with the kind of high school they attended—public school, private school, or charter school—and concomitant mental models. This factor strengthens our conviction that institutional culture—from first exposure during the admissions process to the final strides across the platform at graduation—can have a significant impact on the way in which individuals understand the college experience. (For recommendations to specific schools with respect to mental models, see Part IV, particularly chapter 9.)

Digging deeper, we ask: Are there any correlations between students' mental models *over the course of college* across schools that differ in selectivity?

Here, we note two important findings.

First, *at every school in our study*—across all three categories of selectivity—the number of students with a transformational model increases.* To be sure, increases between first year and graduating year are more dramatic at some schools than at other schools, but there are no clear patterns across selectivity categories.

Second, at all of the low-selectivity schools, the number of students with transactional mental models *decreases* over the course of college; while at all of the high-selectivity schools, the number of students with transactional mental models *increases* over the course of college.

At the medium-selectivity schools—unlike the high-selectivity schools and low-selectivity schools—we find different interactions between students' mental models over the course of college. Specifically, at two of the schools, the number of students with a transactional mental model only *slightly decreases* over the course of college, while at one of the schools, the number of students with a transactional mental model *dramatically increases* (41% of first-year students have a transactional mental model, compared to 71% of graduating students with this mental model).

These findings prompt important considerations. For instance, we wonder whether some campuses particularly stress the end goal of careers; or whether, as the end of college draws near, the parents of students at these schools begin applying pressure about the next steps. Or, we muse, perhaps knowledge of

---

* It is of course possible for students to discover the transformative power of higher education before it's too late. See "Taking Advantage of College (Before It's Too Late)," https://www.therealworldofcollege.com/blog/taking-advantage-of-college-before-its-too-late.

the lucrative career opportunities available to graduates of these high-selectivity campuses nudges their ambivalent peers toward a more transactional stance. Focusing on the contrasting pattern, we wonder whether a college education at a less selective school opens up the student's mind to conceptions and patterns that had not previously been entertained; if so, this positive catalyst constitutes a strong argument for directing resources to less-resourced schools (see box 5.1) for students' thinking about financial issues. (To be sure, the different "starting points" for each school must be acknowledged.) In Part IV of this book, we discuss these possibilities—along with recommendations for how best to confront the concomitant challenges.

IMPACT OF MENTAL MODELS ON THE COLLEGE EXPERIENCE

You might be wondering if it *really* matters whether a student approaches college with a transactional, exploratory, or transformational mental model (perhaps we can agree that no one should aspire toward an inertial mental model)—and if so, *how* it matters. In other words, do mental models have an impact on the college experience? And if so, are any positive or negative consequences—or outcomes—associated with particular mental models?

Here are some results that we find intriguing.

Notably, we find a direct relationship between mental models and Higher Education Capital (the topic of chapter 4)—briefly, the ability to attend, analyze, reflect, connect, and communicate on issues of interest and importance.

Box 5.1

Looking Beyond the Sticker Price: Concerns about Money

Sophie Blumert

We have seen hundreds of headlines related to the steady rise in college tuition over several decades.* But do these headlines accurately reflect the financial challenges that college students face on a daily basis? Do students even worry about finances when they are in college?

In our study we purposefully did not bring up finances or the cost of college during the interview—as with other topics of interest, we wanted to see if it would come up spontaneously.

To our surprise, money and finance appear not to be a major source of stress or concern for students in college. Though over 90% of students bring up the topic of money in relation to the college experience, it is not of "high importance" to the majority of students. In some cases, students only make only one passing comment; and few students talk about finances consistently throughout the course of the interview. Even for those more preoccupied about finances, their concerns are not all focused on tuition costs.

(It's important to acknowledge that we collected these data during a period of reasonable economic stability—2012–2018. For succeeding generations of students, the conversation surrounding college tuition might change significantly.)

What did we find?[†] In general, relatively few students describe finances as highly important to them. We coded participants'

---

* For more context on these data, see Ron Lieber, *The Price You Pay for College* (New York: Harper, 2021).

[†] We acknowledge Jeff Robinson for his contributions to coding and analyzing these data.

comments about finances throughout the whole transcript into three levels of importance, and only 18% of students are categorized as "high importance" in this regard. Another 30% are categorized as "medium importance." Even when asked specifically about their struggle in college, most students do not mention monetary matters.

As for students who emphasize financial issues, their concerns fall into two broad categories: current financial challenges; and future financial challenges.

While not an immediate stressor, tuition appears as an *undercurrent*—an influencing factor in decisions that students (and/or their parents) make in regard to their college experience. Instead of accepting as a given the high sticker price of college, students made deliberate decisions, whether by choice or out of necessity, to offset the cost of their education. Approximately one-third (33%) of our sample of students mention that they chose their college for financial reasons. A similar proportion (29%) are working on- or off-campus jobs. A quarter (24%) report that they receive some form of financial aid. And another third (33%) are commuting to campus, thereby saving costs on room and board. Most of these decisions were made before students matriculated but have a lasting impact on their college experience. Few students articulate any stress about not being able to afford college at all, but they do describe the measures they took to alleviate some of the financial burden of pursuing a higher degree.

Notably, the current financial struggles students describe stem from tensions they feel with respect to socioeconomic divides on campus. Most of the students who bring up these tensions are at highly selective campuses, which are costly. However, these schools generally have the resources to provide aid to students in lower income brackets; accordingly, the disparities between the "haves" and "have-nots" may be much more salient on these campuses. Students from lower socioeconomic backgrounds explain that they are unable to participate in certain social activities because they do not have the disposable income that their friends of higher socioeconomic status have; they feel that their struggles are not well understood or ignored; more often than not, feelings of isolation and disillusionment ensue.

One student explains her struggles:

There is socioeconomic diversity, but no one talks about it. People just assume that everyone's from at least an upper-middle-class status . . . and those assumptions can be difficult to undermine. When those aren't real . . . people don't get it. Like, I have a work study job. People have asked me why I have a work study job. Wouldn't I rather have the free time? And I'm like, "No, I actually need a work study job." Or like I don't go home for Thanksgiving generally, because the plane tickets are really expensive. People ask me about that too.

Students are also thinking about the *future*—the types of jobs they want, with the promise of financial stability, and even social mobility. First-year and graduating students differ significantly. Few first-year students are highly concerned about their finances (12%), while graduating students are more worried (24%). Tuition may be more of an abstract concept for first-year students, but for graduating students it is a daunting (and all too real) figure.

Students are more concerned with day-to-day costs of individual purchases than with the large-ticket item of their college education. To our surprise, it sometimes proved difficult to persuade students to participate in our study, even when we offered them $50 for an hour of their time (which would come to $100,000 a year).* This perhaps unexpected phenomenon suggests that students are focused on their immediate financial needs—especially those that are more pressing and more concrete.

---

* For further reflections on this economically surprising result, see "Why So Many Students Spurn $50/Hour ($100k/Year)," https://www.therealworldofcollege.com/blog/why-so-many-students-spurn.

Students' financial needs and decisions are sometimes tied to their overall conception of the college experience. As noted earlier, almost half of the students in our study are categorized as having a transactional mental model. In many cases, this means that students approach college with the goal of securing a desirable career. Students choose majors that they believe are more "practical;" they actively seek out internship opportunities and extracurricular activities on campus that they can put on their resume; and they are highly preoccupied by academic success—grades and GPA that they believe would set them apart from their peers in the future.

One student describes his professional drive:

Well, the way I look at college is very academic-based because I was very . . . I [have a] pretty solid plan of what I want to do after college, I know I want to go to med school, I know I want to get into a dermatology residency, so the way I look at college is to give the best I can, like get as involved as . . . much as possible, get the best grades I can and just try to do what I can to get on to my next step.

Views of Other Stakeholders

Perhaps unsurprisingly, adult constituencies view the issue of college finances quite differently. While only a fifth of students in our sample are highly concerned about finances, more than a quarter (27%) of on-campus and off-campus adults are extremely concerned about students' financial issues. We note an important difference across campuses.

At the high-selectivity campuses, faculty often seem disconnected from the day-to-day challenges that students face—they talk about the intricacies of financial aid and the increasingly high sticker price of private colleges. Very few acknowledge the challenges that students at their own campuses face regarding socioeconomic tensions. Additionally, adults at these schools are prone to anecdotes—they reference the experiences of a few students rather than considering the larger population. And perhaps most importantly, faculty and administrators at these schools are not able, or at least not inclined, to make the time to listen to their students' struggles beyond academics. They rely instead on their knowledge of such struggles from the news, and, on occasion, the experiences of one or two students.

In contrast, faculty and administrators at low-selectivity institutions tend to be more aware of the day-to-day difficulties students face. In particular, faculty at one of our campuses are highly attuned to their students' financial situations. These teachers are committed to their mission, regularly set up meetings with students, and strive to create a sense of community and belonging. As a result of this intentional practice of fostering personal connections, and perhaps as well owing to signals from the school's leadership, the faculty and administrators at this school are able to give us much more detail and texture to the financial experiences of students.

Shifting to off-campus adults, approximately a quarter of alumni, parents, and trustees are highly concerned about students' finances. But in contrast to those on campus, these adults are more worried about a return on investment—they want to be sure that the experience of the current generation will be "worth it." This stance is not dissimilar from students' concerns about future jobs and careers, but still does not acknowledge the challenges that many students face while on campus.

In sum, while we do not hear as much from students about finances as we might have expected, it remains a throughline in our study—whether through lifestyle choices, social issues such as socioeconomic status, or future careers. While adults both on and off campus are concerned about finances, the issues they foreground differ from those of concern to students. A modest amount of discussion of these different perspectives might bring about better alignment—and perhaps suggest approaches that could prove helpful to all constituencies.

Specifically, we find that students with high HEDCAP (score of 3) are more likely to be transformational and exploratory; while students with low HEDCAP (score of 1) are more likely to be transactional or inertial. Furthermore, we also find a significant difference in HEDCAP scores between students with an exploratory mental model and those with a transformational mental model. The implication: students with a transformational mental model are most likely—compared to students with the other mental models—to display high HEDCAP (score of 3).

Clearly, it is not the case that all students who have transformational mental models have high HEDCAP; nor can we prove that having a transformational mental model will necessarily lead to developing high HEDCAP. But at the same time, it is understandable that students who approach the college experience with exploratory and transformational mental models—those oriented toward discovery and reflection—are more likely than their peers to develop new ways of thinking and communicating, and more sophisticated viewpoints over the course of college. In contrast, those students who fail to ponder the purposes of college or those who don't have any reason to go to college are less likely to garner HEDCAP. Put bluntly, mental models seem to matter for the development of Higher Education Capital.

This finding signals good news: While some students come to college with a transformational mental model, and some students come to college with high HEDCAP (score of 3), we find that on the whole, the number of students who have a transformational mental model *and* high HEDCAP (score of 3) increases over the course of college. Specifically, of those first-year students with high HEDCAP (score of 3), a third (30%) have a transformational model, compared to graduating students with high HEDCAP (score of 3), nearly a half (49%) have a transformational model. (This finding is similar across schools that differ in selectivity.) Again, longitudinal data would be highly desirable; but in its absence, we believe quite firmly that the experiences of specific students at specific colleges at specific historical moments can make meaningful differences. If not, if Higher Education Capital does not budge—were it not for housing or socializing purposes—we might as well shut down these institutions.

Interestingly, we find no major differences in mental models across students who major in humanities, social science, or natural science.

TERMINOLOGY AND INTERPRETATION

As researchers, we strive to be careful in how we apply our terminology and how we make sense of what we hear and observe. Even though we develop measures and models to describe our analyses, we always remind each other that we don't want to squint to make a categorization work, and, equally, we don't want to fool ourselves. To interpret our findings, we investigate and take into account the settings and backgrounds of people and institutions: context matters.

As an example, consider a student who approaches the college experience with a primary focus on getting a high-paying job in finance; indeed, this student structures nearly every aspect of the college experience so that it culminates in this desired outcome.

This student will be categorized as having a transactional mental model. But there may be two very different scenarios.

In scenario 1, the student may have attended an elite high school and now attends a highly selective college known to place students in these jobs; in scenario 2, the student might be a first-generation student, attending a low-selectivity school—one who had never heard of economics, but succeeds in landing the job at an investment bank. In the second case, the transactional mental model takes on a different meaning, what we have referred to as an example of "transactional in order to be transformational." While we hear such stories at nearly every school, the majority of the latter set of students attend the low- and medium-selectivity institutions. Those students at the high-selectivity schools who talk about social mobility—the opportunity for college to change the course of their lives—most often reference how their own low socioeconomic background influences their approach to college. This revelation is especially poignant given that we deliberately do not ask students about socioeconomic factors at any point (in conversation or on a survey form). The fact that this information nonetheless emerges in self-report underscores its importance to their overall experience.

Therefore, while approximately half of the students across the study are categorized as having a transactional mental model, it is important to acknowledge that not all students approach the putative "transaction" in the same way.

Some students in our study focus narrowly on one particular academic discipline with the goal of graduate school or a specific job in the future. One first-year student planning to go to medical school after college explains: "Like for me, chemistry, that's my major . . . it's obviously sometimes boring to just do science all the time, but at the same time, I don't want to have to focus on things that won't really be important for my future." Another student talks about English as a way to solidifying a job: "So for here [at this college] it's just really to get my first reading, to feel things out to decide where, you know, if I have a . . . shot in the publishing industry . . . If I can build a sort of reputation for myself—being published . . . [in a] a literary journal. For the next four years, those will be my goals."

Other students with a transactional frame of mind specifically focus on building their resumes—networking in and out of class, participating in clubs to secure leadership positions, and achieving high grades in order to become "marketable" in the job search. For instance, a student majoring in neuroscience explains that the most important goals of college are "getting the diploma, building up as much of a stacked resume as possible, getting out with the best start I can, into real life. Some people, you know, think of college as like the best years of their life, but that's not the way I look at it. It's a stepping-stone to get to better things. If you're looking at college as like the best years of your life, you're doing it wrong."

In general, at the more selective campuses we find that the students with a transactional mental model are likely to approach college with these perspectives. Specifically, most students at these schools tend to aspire to particular types of graduate programs and careers that require a strong academic background and resume (e.g., medical school, law school, jobs in the financial sector).

However, especially at the low-selectivity schools, students are more likely to focus on the practical steps of "getting through college"—graduating on time and earning enough credits to graduate or to transfer in order to graduate—some for jobs, but others for social mobility.

A student majoring in anthropology with a minor in museum studies reflects:

I'm in my first quarter as a freshman and it's already stressing me out like thinking about . . . these gen eds . . . I have to get these gen eds out of the way so I can focus on my degree in anthropology. . . . how long is this gonna take to get rid of all these gen eds and satisfy all these requirements before I can actually focus on what I really want to study. And that kind of worries me sometimes because . . . the pressure of graduating in 4 years with an undergraduate degree is a really big one. Like I don't want to be in college for 5 years working on an undergraduate degree.

At the same time, this student acknowledges that college entails hard work, and this is why she is at her school, to take advantage of engaging in academic work: "That . . . transition was kind of difficult at first but like I realize that I'm here for the purpose of an education, so I've gotten used to that . . . but I mean this freedom has also given me . . . responsibility . . . to do as best I can . . . in every class here . . . I'm so lucky to be here. . . . I want to do as best I can, get my undergraduate degree and then go on to get my master's, [and] later, [my] doctorate."

Another graduating student majoring in English explains that he chose his school for "diversity of interests (such as environmental studies, art, and creative writing)," "open-mindedness of opinions," and "people who were interested in all sorts of things."

As he puts it: "Honestly . . . I need to survive. . . . I'm just so overwhelmed with the homework and the papers, and now as a senior thinking about post-college, and where am I going to live, and money . . . And I really am just doing the bare minimum to actually get through my classes, finding out what I really need to do to get the grade . . . I feel like it really just has been, especially since sophomore year, just to survive until graduation, and to really figure out how am I going to support myself after college."

It is important to note that students with transactional mental models at the less selective schools *also* talk about the importance of jobs (not just getting through college). However, these students tend to focus on the general notion of getting a job, rather than a specific job or career path. And furthermore, when they do talk about specific jobs and careers, most of these jobs and careers don't require mastery of a particular academic discipline.

BEYOND "PURE" MENTAL MODELS: PARALLEL, BLENDED, AND CONFLICTING

To this point, we have focused on the majority of students who apparently approach college with a single, steady approach. But sometimes, we find exceptions—those individuals who seem to embody more than one mental model: for example, some of the students with transactional mental models, like those just described, who need to be hyperfocused on getting the degree, with the hope of eventually approaching future school, work, and life in more exploratory and transformational ways.

In selected cases, students approach college with two mental models, but these seem to remain separate, distinct, in the individual's mind. We call these *parallel* mental models—the two approaches exist simultaneously but essentially independently—leading such students to compartmentalize their goals, courses, and activities throughout the college experience. In still other cases, students approach college with mental models that interact with each other. We call these *blended* mental models.*

Consider Heather, a first-year student at a small, medium-selectivity school. She chose her school because it will enable her to "get some mastery in some particular field so [she] can have an employable plan," suggesting a transactional mental model. However, at the same time, Heather reflects that "in terms of growth as a person . . . it's very, very difficult to replicate the experience of college in any other medium"—thereby acknowledging that the college experience can be transformational. Even in her first year, Heather talks about how college has "definitely challenged the way I think," citing conversations with friends that occur outside the classroom: "They're great for just helping us really identify what our beliefs are."

In general, Heather describes college as an opportunity that "gives me a different lens on a lot of issues that I previously thought I had a concrete understanding of." This mindset leads Heather to approach social experiences with an openness to introspection and transformation—a stark contrast to her rather

---

* For this argument and these examples, we acknowledge the contributions of researchers Sophie Blumert and Jeff Robinson.

constrained view of academic goals. With these parallel mental models, Heather approaches the academic and social realms with two different points of view. She manages to maintain—or, perhaps, to juggle—a pair of mental models for college by keeping her idealistic and practical views separate.

In a contrasting case, Marlowe is about to graduate from a medium-sized, less selective, public institution. Marlowe readily discusses the challenges he faces coming from a "low-income neighborhood" and describes his goals for college as "getting out of poverty . . . [and] being an example to [the] younger ones in my family." When not in class, Marlowe spends most of his time carrying out multiple part-time jobs and taking care of family members. In this sense, Marlowe is a prototypical transactional student.

Despite these demanding responsibilities, Marlowe seems driven to complete his degree because he believes its receipt will change his life. As he puts it, "to be educated . . . it's not just schooling, it's . . . gaining knowledge . . . Education will be the only thing that will help me, you know, enrich my life and get out of the socioeconomic class that I'm in." Marlowe values the social interactions that take place at college, even on a campus where the overwhelming majority of students commute. Whereas Marlowe has the transactional aim of completing his credits as quickly as possible, he also seeks to establish meaningful relationships with his peers and also with faculty members. Through these relationships, he signals that college can and should be transformative: "I'm forming myself as a person . . . I think I finally get where my ideas are and who I want to be, and what I want to be."

Both Heather and Marlowe exhibit indicators of both transactional *and* transformational mental models. Heather's mental models (parallel) seem to be traveling on quite separate tracks, while Marlowe's mental models (blended) seem to interact, if not merge. In Marlowe's case, transformation only becomes a possibility because of his transactional mindset with respect to securing a higher education degree.

Sometimes, as in the case of Marlowe, blended mental models enrich the student experience and/or give students goals to which they aspire for the future. However, students can also have *conflicting* mental models about college—approaches that bring about difficult, even wrenching decisions for students, especially with respect to priorities or to the structuring of time.

For example, Allison, a graduating student from a high-selectivity school, reveals an inner conflict. On the one hand, her natural inclination is to be exploratory in college; but, on the other, she reveals a concomitant desire to be transactional, because she believes that such an approach will set her up for success in the future. These conflicting mental models are compounded by the pressure she feels to be transactional in light of her peers at school and the overall school culture.

Allison describes her own exploratory approach: "I kind of am the type of person who likes to . . . explore and take classes because I like learning . . . I had no idea what I wanted to do . . . as a result, like my entire college experience was me like jumping back and forth and never really growing too much in one area 'cause it was mainly me like exploring myself."

However, being exploratory threatens her ambition to be successful: "Most people who are successful are the ones who . . . know what they want the whole time . . . so you know how they kind of tell you to explore in the beginning, you're kind of like anxious to get on the track already."

As a result of this inner conflict, Allison seems disappointed by the overall college experience, expressing a feeling of being "lost": "Well, I guess, I [was] really lost [and] . . . I wasn't sure what I was gonna do when I got to college, which I think gave me like a pretty severe handicap . . . which is kind of a little bit annoying about college. I think the people who did best in college were the people who knew what they wanted from the start . . . from the beginning, like know exactly you wanted to work at this lab and like over the four years you would like rise. . . . And I had no idea what I wanted to do."*

As an additional example, Tim, a graduating student at one of the least selective schools, also navigates conflicting exploratory and transactional mental models.

On the one hand, Tim believes that college should be about learning and finding one's passion: "I feel like college should be seen as like 'I really am passionate about this and I want to learn

---

*Compare David Epstein's *Range: Why Generalists Triumph in a Specialized World* (New York: Riverhead Books, 2019), which defends broad exploration across numerous pursuits, with Malcolm Gladwell's *Outliers: The Story of Success* (New York: Little, Brown, 2008), which highlights deliberate practice for thousands of hours in a single activity, like playing chess or practicing the violin.

from people who know more about this to extend my knowledge and make me better at it.'"

With this view, Tim advises incoming students: "Stop looking beyond graduation while you're here . . . just find something [your] passionate [about]. Stop worrying about the 8:00 a.m.s and [stop] worry[ing] about how difficult the teacher's gonna be and just take the class because it's something you want to take and it's something you wanna [learn]."

But Tim regrets that this strategy was something he could *not* himself enact because of his own financial constraints. Reflecting on his own experience, he discusses the need to stay vigilantly focused on a discipline. In fact, he questions his own decision to take electives he thought he was interested in: "I should have spent the last two years at a community college just getting these electives done." Once I decided [on] my major, then [I would] spend the real cash to come somewhere [like this]."

As evidenced by these and some other students in our study, navigating college with more than one mental model can certainly be challenging, especially when the goals of the models come into direct conflict. But we find that those students who embody "pure," or even "parallel" or "blended" mental models also need continually to monitor their approach within the context of their overall institution and their peers.

MENTAL MODELS CAN CLASH WITH OTHER VALUES

In the best of all possible worlds, students' mental models will remain open to new possibilities, and those models will be supported and encouraged by the institution. But sometimes that is not the case—indeed, students' models may clash with those of their fellow students and, perhaps, those with the overall institution.

Clashing with the Institution

At times, students' mental models appear to be misaligned with the priorities and values of the institution and of other key constituencies in the sector. Colleges and universities implicitly and explicitly send messages to the community through a range of media—campus tours and information sessions, marketing materials, as well as decisions about hiring for academic and administrative departments, and investments in new campus facilities and programs.

As an example, recall the campus tour at hypothetical Greenly College, described in the first few pages of this book. The first three areas highlighted on campus were the dining hall, theater, and athletic center. The academic programs came later. At schools that we actually studied in depth, we were also struck by the implicit message—that students will be, and even *should* be, more concerned with the nonacademic campus amenities than with the academic opportunities.

A computer science major who took a gap year before starting college conveyed his own frustration with how money is allocated on his campus and the message it accordingly (if perhaps unwittingly or unintentionally) sends about the value of particular disciplines and majors: "At this school in particular, it's pretty lopsided, sorta like there's a lot of business majors, engineering majors, especially now that they both got brand new buildings, multimillion-dollar buildings. So, I feel that is the majority, and then the rest of us are in the less cool buildings."

Picking up on these signals, some students complain about the relentless emphasis on internships, jobs, and networking opportunities—palpable from the very beginning of their experience on campus. Others lament that, though they may enter college with a diverse set of interests, by graduation, they find themselves focusing on a narrow set of job and career prospects. This "funnel effect"—as we have termed it in earlier studies—can be shaped and perpetuated by the institution, through its invitations to specific firms to come to campus, timing of recruitment activities, overall achievement-driven culture, and lack of guidance and support for those students who display deep passion for fields in which the immediate job may not be obvious or even evident.[2] In other words: rather than tempering the overwhelming influence of a competitive job market and the widespread perception that a degree constitutes the royal road to specific jobs and/or lifestyles, institutions may in fact reinforce these beliefs.

Accordingly, the same computer science student who commented about the allocation of resources on campus explains: "The career services is relentlessly emailing us, 'Prepare your resume. Prepare this, prepare that.' They highly recommend that students take a course on how to do an interview, and stuff like that . . . Even in my classes, teachers talking about the major and stuff, 'What prospective jobs do you have?' When you're undecided and you're deciding a major, they give you a list of prospective jobs that each major has to offer post-graduation. I just feel like that's the main focus."

We are well aware that, in assuming this stance, colleges are responding to a reality of the current marketplace—one that grew increasingly vivid in the decade of the 2010s, even before the onset of the COVID-19 pandemic. And yet, we must ask: do colleges *have to accept* the dominant narrative in the culture, or should they be presenting—and perhaps even foregrounding—alternative visions?[3] And we can add, with particular positions and the job market so frequently disrupted and far from predictable, is the focus on employment a fool's errand?

Clashing with Other Students

Sometimes, over the course of college, as students identify their own interests and passions, get to know their peers in deeper ways, and experience campus life in its fullness, these students come to realize that they have values that differ from those of most peers. It is also possible that, in the first year of college, some students simply assume that others are like them, owing to superficial similarities in background, appearance, or tastes. Later they find that this is not true.

Consider Alex, a graduating student at a high-selectivity college, a double major in literature and neuroscience. He comes from a rural area in the United States, where he graduated from a high school without having received useful advice about the college experience. Half the students from his graduating high school class went to college, while many of the others went into the military. Of those who went to college, he estimates that half went to a community college. He came to college with the belief that "[college is] important [because] searching for knowledge is the number one goal in life, and this is just like the most noble thing you could do."

But over time, Alex finds that his "noble" ambitions are at odds with those of other students. He says, "Everyone here has pretty much the same goals . . . the same career goals of just making a lot of money." Specifically, he reports that within the neuroscience department, "I'm the only person I know . . . that's not trying to go to med school. Everyone is very pre-med or just pre-tech, pre-finance, very career oriented and genuinely don't care that much about the major that they're doing a lot of the time."

On the cusp of graduation, Alex reflects: "I wish somebody had told me more about [this] when I came in . . . [I] generally bec[ame] disillusioned over time with how and why people come into college, and how they deal with their classes, and why they take their classes, and what their career goals are, and realizing that so few people, especially here, are interested academically in what they're doing in any way."

In our terms, Alex's mental model for college is misaligned with the models of those around him. He approaches college with an "exploratory" mindset—that college is an opportunity to immerse oneself in different fields and to "search for knowledge." This mindset clashes with the prevailing transactional mode: according to that currently seductive stance, the goal of college is to get a degree and network with influential people in order to build a resume for a future job or career. In a nutshell, Alex feels alienated: from the academic realm, from peers around him, and from the overall institution he attends (these three varieties of alienation are delineated in chapter 7).

Though we certainly don't want to advocate for feelings of alienation or loneliness per se among students, it is clear that Alex experienced considerable personal growth through the college experience. This form of self-discovery is evident in his articulation of the yawning distance between his own goals as contrasted with the ambitions and motivations of many others on campus. Though he may be "disillusioned" by his experience, he has stayed true to his values, rather than compromising on these values in order to fit in. Sometimes, as we have posited, *misalignment can be positive*, a sign of growth.

Thus far, we have focused on students—their mental models for college—along with instances when these mental models might generate conflicts within their own minds, or in light of signals from peers, and/or signals from the encompassing institution. But, importantly, we have also learned about the alignments and misalignments between and among constituencies—how other groups both on and off campus view and approach college—considerations that can clearly impact the student experience.

MENTAL MODELS OF OTHER CONSTITUENCIES

On-Campus Adults

Faculty and administrators Across our study, in sharp contrast to the student mental models that we have documented, on-campus adults (faculty and administrators) are overwhelmingly categorized as having a transformational mental model for the college experience. In fact, *at nearly every school* we studied, approximately three quarters of the on-campus adults (78%) are categorized in this way. In contrast, fewer than a quarter of these on-campus adults are categorized as having exploratory (13%) or transactional (9%) mental models.

This misalignment between students and their faculty is notable and poses significant challenges. While students sometimes feel that their interests and needs are not being met, faculty do not believe that they should focus on practical applications of learning: instead they should inspire their students to seek knowledge and to develop new ways of thinking. We find this misalignment at both our high-selectivity schools and our low-selectivity schools.

For example, a professor of art history at a high-selectivity school describes the challenge of upholding a transformational mental model of the college experience, while encountering students who approach college with transactional goals: "[College isn't] about passive consumption. It's not just about getting good grades. It's not just about ticking certain answers in boxes, satisfying certain needs, but it is about measuring oneself against the material that's on offer, and maturing as a result. I am sure it's about many, many more things than that as well. And I'm not sure if that model is necessarily one that students have in the forefronts of their minds when they are thinking about going to university. But I certainly think that that is one of the things that we can offer."

A history professor at a less selective school expresses his frustration in light of pressures to focus on transferability, applicability, and employability—rather than giving rein to his own desire

to transform ways of thinking: "It's incumbent upon us to demonstrate the practicality of degrees, in terms of getting a job. As if
everything is ultimately about just giving you a set of skills that
will make you more marketable when looking for a job."

He navigates this dilemma carefully in order to "appease" both
his own goals and those of his students:

And so, for instance I often explain to my students, most of whom are not
gonna become history majors, right? Or, are not going to become history
professors, or go on to higher education. . . . We talk about developing
skills like, you know, analytical skills, reading comprehension skills, writing skills . . . the ability to think creatively to solve problems in the sense
that historians solve problems, right? We collect evidence and then try to
establish cause and effect and so forth . . . And then to think about . . .
how does that actually apply in other fields that you might find yourself in
down the road, you know? Career-wise, for instance, but also as a citizen
in this country, taking an interest in what's happening politically and so
forth, and thinking about how all these things interconnect.

In order to stay faithful to his own values and mental models for
the college experience, this professor delicately balances his own
perhaps idealistic mental model for the college experience with
the predominant mental models of his students—in an effort to
convince students that his course honors both aspirations.

We are not surprised by this result. Certainly, adults who devote
their working lives to educating the next generations should want
to feel that they are making a genuine, perhaps even measurable
difference. But those of us who have embraced these views need
to reflect on *why* we have been less successful and *what we might
do* to achieve greater success—a task we take on in our concluding
chapters.

While students and on-campus adults are misaligned in terms of mental models for the college experience, in general, we find that students and off-campus adults (parents, alums, and trustees) are more closely aligned. This finding seems to be a counterintuitive. After all, students spend far more time with on-campus adults than with off-campus adults (and one would hope that faculty and administrators know the students more intimately than do alums or trustees—since most students don't even know what a "trustee" does!). However, we find some revealing differences between off-campus constituencies.

Off-Campus Adults

Parents   Overall, across all ten schools, parents represent a fairly even divide among those with transactional (35%), exploratory (39%), and transformational (26%) approaches.* For us, this result is intriguing. Asked to predict how parents will think about college, a healthy majority of students, faculty, and administrators say that *all* parents will care most about whether it will help their children secure a job. Indeed, it's possible that students (and in turn, faculty and administrators) "blame" parents for the pressure that students feel to do well in college to get a job or get in to graduate school, or—perhaps more likely—that parents may not be aware of the messages they inadvertently send about the purpose of college (e.g., calling a dean to complain about a grade, repeatedly asking students about internship possibilities). But in fact, we find a more nuanced response among those who, in many cases, bear the financial burden of higher education.

---

* In this summary, we don't include job recruiters.

Similar to the mental models of students, we note revealing trends across schools. At the more selective schools, fewer than 20% of the parents are categorized as having transactional mental models. In contrast, at the less selective campuses, more than 50% of the parents are categorized as having transactional mental models. In fact, at one school, *all* of the parents (100%) were categorized as having transactional mental models. This result is important. It suggests, though it certainly does not prove, that the college experience could be more liberating for many students in more selective schools, and more constricting in the less selective schools. Alternatively, the result indicates that the "mission messages" sent at less selective schools have a more formidable challenge: to provide an alternative to the (understandable) parental preoccupation with "return on investment."

To be sure: we understand and are not the least surprised by the pressure—or obligation—some parents express for their children to secure employment as a result of college. Yet, at the same time, we note and lament that a sole focus on transaction can diminish the likelihood that students will develop blended or even parallel mental models—the opportunity to approach college with the possibilities of exploratory or even transformational mental models (and concomitant experiences). Undoubtedly, many parents assume that majoring in literature or philosophy is a luxury, while a major in computer science is a necessity. But here we are focused on schools that are not strictly vocational—that have elected to describe themselves as part of the broader educational tradition (sometimes invoking the phrase "liberal arts," more often stressing breadth as well as depth). In all such schools, in addition to any transactional goals, all students should also be encouraged to take advantage of the special opportunity college provides to think in new ways. And in pursuing this loftier aspiration, we strongly believe that students will attain Higher Education Capital that will be of use in whatever career they pursue, and will in addition, give them a much fuller life.

Trustees   Overall, the trustees interviewed across our study exhibit a range of mental models. While nearly half are categorized as having a transactional mental model (45%), approximately one third have an exploratory mental model (36%), and fewer than a quarter have a transformational mental model (19%). Similar to parents, trustees differ across schools; but unlike the case with parents, there are not clear patterns of mental models across selectivity of institutions. For example, at one of the most selective schools, not a single trustee was categorized as having a transactional mental model; but at a different high-selectivity school, nearly three quarters of the trustees (70%) were categorized as having a transactional mental model. In point of fact, two medium-selectivity schools have the highest percentage of trustees with a transformational mental model (50% and 40%). (See box 5.2 for more details on differences between trustees.)

Young alums   Though they have arguably the least direct influence on current students, young alums provide a window into how one views the college experience in light of the next stage of life—whether that means graduate school, a full-time work environment, and/or community and family life.

Young alums exhibit mental models similar to others who are off campus. Approximately a third of young alums have a

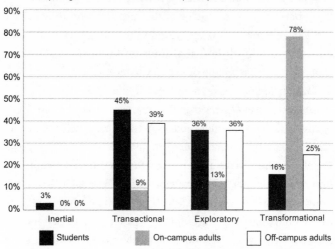

Comparing constituencies: Percent of participants with each mental model

Figure 5.4

transactional mental model (38%), a third have an exploratory mental model (34%), and slightly less than a third have a transformational mental model (27%). Young alums were the only off-campus adult constituency that included individuals who were categorized as inertial, but this is such a small number that we can disregard it (1%). Furthermore, like parents, and unlike trustees, the mental models of young alums reflect patterns according to selectivity of schools. To be specific: the highest percentage of transactional models in alums come from the less selective institutions, and the highest percentage of transformational models in alums come from the more selective institutions.

Box 5.2

Trustees: Can They Transcend Transactionality?

Sophie Blumert

While students often do not know anything about trustees, and faculty have mixed feelings about them, trustees are key decision makers in higher education.* These individuals have a fiduciary responsibility to the school (and the state); they are responsible for the "bottom line." It is important for us to understand their perspective, and though this proved challenging at times, it also turned out to be revealing.

Though students across all campuses are quite similar (they use the same words, discuss similar issues, and express similar struggles), trustees prove to be a much more varied and eclectic group—trustees get appointed to boards in several ways and come from a variety of backgrounds, sectors, and levels of experience.

Notwithstanding their many revealing differences, most trustees have one notable commonality: *they are focused on the job market.*[†] Across the eighty-five trustees we interviewed, almost half (45%) are coded as having a transactional mental model of the college experience. More pointedly, trustees are focused on marketability. They do not necessarily talk about specific professions or graduate programs, as students do. Instead, they emphasize the importance of gaining the *right* skills, the *right* knowledge, and the

---

*We acknowledge Thomas Dougherty's contributions to coding and analyzing the data for this constituency.

[†] See also Michael Hansen, "The U.S. Education System Isn't Giving Students What Employers Need," *Harvard Business Review*, May 18, 2021, https://hbr.org/2021/05/the-u-s-education-system-isnt-giving -students-what-employers-need.

right experience in order for students to get the job they want, no matter what that job might be. While this finding is not wholly surprising, and we might have expected trustees to think this way, it is quite different from how transactional students perceive the purpose of college.

When we express this point in economic terms, the difference becomes clear. Students see themselves as the consumer, paying for an education that will give them experience and knowledge in return. Trustees see students as the product, something to "market" to job recruiters, hiring managers, or admissions officers to improve the reputation of the institution. This divergence in perspective represents a misalignment about whom higher education is meant to benefit. Transactional students view education as a payoff to their own careers; transactional trustees highlight the benefit to the reputation of the college.

As we see it, both of these mindsets are flawed: they cause tensions as the priorities of different constituencies begin to compete with each other. Many students, as well as numerous faculty, notice when new, state-of-the-art gyms are built while other academic buildings have not been updated in decades; many feel devalued when financial resources are allocated to majors or fields deemed more lucrative and hirable; many are confused when once-public resources become privatized; and many wonder why hiring for new teaching positions and resources for teacher training continues to decline.

Overall, these decisions indicate to students and faculty that trustees are more interested in investing in buildings and image than in personnel and academic entities. Ultimately, when college is seen as a simple transaction, it starts to function more as a business than as an institution of learning—and this, we contend, does a disservice to all stakeholders.

However, it is also important to note some differences in trustee mental models—sometimes with regard to school selectivity.

Though approximately half of the trustees in our sample are coded as having a transactional mental model, individuals exhibiting this perspective are not evenly spread across institutions; most tend to come from low-selectivity schools. Trustees that are categorized as having an exploratory approach make up approximately one-third of the sample and tend to come from high-selectivity schools. A relatively small number of trustees (approximately one-fifth) are categorized as having a transformational mental model—and interestingly, these tend to come from medium-selectively schools. Given our limited sample, we hesitate to make too much of this trend; still, it prompts us to wonder how these trustees differ from each other, and why school selectivity might be a factor.

The trustees with exploratory mental models, it turns out, are much like the students with exploratory approaches to college. They believe in living in the present; namely, that the college experience is about absorbing as much academic content as one can, getting involved in extracurricular activities, meeting new people, and not worrying too much about the details of one's future. This perspective mirrors the mindset of students with an exploratory mental model; jobs, careers, and life after college are a distant concern. It is possible that, coming from high-selectivity settings (with more resources and name recognition), trustees might not be preoccupied thinking about students' prospects; they may assume that the brand, with its implied high-quality education, will carry them far.

Trustees with transformational mental models (about one-fifth of the sample) have ambitious goals for the students that they serve. But, importantly, these are not focused on jobs; instead, such trustees talk about the importance of intellectual transformations and engaged citizenship.

Trustees who have a transformational approach most often come from schools with a clearly defined and well-adopted mission, whether that mission is academics, social justice, or religion.

This may well have been the missing piece for trustees who have a transactional mental model. Without a strong mission, trustees may not know where to direct their financial priorities. An institutional mission is not—or should not be—just a statement that lives on a college website; in the best instance, it is the driving force of what the institution believes it can achieve, and, through their fiduciary responsibilities, what trustees have the ability to carry out.

Trustees are given quite a bit of financial and decision-making responsibility, but without a mission that places academics front and center, it is easy to lose sight of the long-term goal. In our view, trustees should push for decisions that serve the institutional mission: one focused on the development of students, academics, and lifelong learning, rather than chiefly on marketability. And, to borrow another economic metaphor, we hope that these decisions will "trickle down" to impact the experiences and mindsets of students so that their college experience can feature exploration and enable a transformative experience.

CONCLUDING THOUGHTS

Our investigation of mental models—across different constituencies, schools, students, and even within one student's mind—reveals important alignments and misalignments with respect to how individuals view the college experience. (Here, we invoke the fractal metaphor introduced earlier; misalignments can range from tensions within a single student's mind to tensions between the higher education sector, on the one hand, and pressures from the broader society, on the other.) Our investigation demonstrates the degree to which these models are supported—or challenged—by peers and others around them: by the explicit and implicit institutional mission(s); and by wider national and even global portrayals of, and aspirations for, higher education. Indeed, it seems that at many institutions, the students—who come to college with transactional motivations—and the faculty—who come to the work with a transformational stance—are (perhaps unwittingly) working at cross-purposes.

What's the impact of such a misalignment? Do students feel lost or alienated, as a result? Might they be so disappointed that they give up, especially when considering the "value proposition" of the college experience? Or could the misalignment sometimes serve to motivate students to persist, faculty to rework their approaches, leaders to rethink how they conceive of their institution and how they communicate their vision or their mission to others?

Stepping momentarily into the role of clinician, we urge leaders, administrators, and faculty on campus to be cognizant of the various mental models and of the frequently misaligned views—and we also urge them to avoid facile assumptions about what students—and trustees—desire from the college experience. Not only do students differ across schools, but they may change over the course of the college years, arriving with one mental model, and leaving with a different one.

In reading this chapter, you have likely discerned that we favor the exploratory and transformational mental models for college. Certainly, while we understand that jobs, careers, and financial stability are important, we do not believe that students should be going to a nonvocational college for the sole purpose of getting the degree and/or to move on to the next step in the occupational terrain—especially since that terrain is more than likely to be subject to frequent disruption. College should provide what is likely a once-in-a-lifetime opportunity to think in different ways, to acquire new knowledge, to try on and try out diverse perspectives, to rethink one's fundamental aspirations and values, and to become aware of individual strengths and weaknesses. Years spent in college should increase Higher Education Capital. Moreover, irrespective of our own values, our data show that students with exploratory and transformational mental models, compared to students with transactional mental models, are more likely to benefit from the overall college experience—as manifested by their demonstration of significantly higher scores of Higher Education Capital.

Without doubt, the COVID-19 pandemic has raised searching questions for institutions of higher education and for its several key stakeholders. Should the college experience (especially if remote) focus sharply on the transactional benefits of a degree? Or should college confirm or reconfirm the core mission of transforming the minds of students? Put bluntly, is the principal purpose of college about earning or learning?

As elaborated upon in the later portion of this book (Part IV), we believe that even in times of challenge—whether by virtue of COVID-19, the rise of online learning options, or some other significant disruption—the sector needs to double down on what we deem as its principal missions of exploration and transformation. Whether in the United States or elsewhere, institutions of higher education should help students explore unfamiliar (as well as familiar) scholarly disciplines and ways of conceptualization; interact with those who are different in one or another significant respect; discover personal strengths and weaknesses; and gain in independence, both in terms of living on one's own, and in formulating and cogently articulating points of view and perspectives based on accumulating knowledge and experience.

Up until this point in our narrative, we have focused on *what we had initially thought* would be the thrust of our study: (1) how students and other constituents think about the college experience (mental models), and (2) whether college itself affects significantly how students think and express themselves with respect to issues of consequence (Higher Education Capital). But as we have signaled in earlier pages, students' own concerns at this time are strongly focused on their own psychological well-being—mental health, rather than mental models—and on inclusion in the community, rather than thinking only or principally about their learning and their future. Accordingly, much of our study has necessarily, and appropriately, come to focus on these issues of well-being on the campus. Indeed, these constitute the topics of the next part of the book.

III THE CAMPUS CULTURE

We originally undertook this study so as to improve our understanding of the various current perspectives toward higher education: we were particularly interested in what is and should be learned in college, and in the kinds of formative experiences students should have both in and out of the classroom. Once armed with this understanding, we had two aims: (1) to help students acquire a broad education and (2) to help this form of education thrive under dramatically changed or ever-changing circumstances.

That said, to make informed recommendations to individual campuses and to the sector as a whole, we needed to investigate not only the opportunities for learning but also the challenges students face in various spheres of their lives. We knew we could not resolve all the challenges with which students contend—ranging from financial struggles to excessive drinking. But we sought to understand the "lived circumstances" of students—again in the hope of increasing the likelihood that higher education's core promises could be fulfilled.

To tweak one of our governing metaphors: In observing the "cultures" of various campuses, we wanted to listen to the "vital signs" that indicate the health of a college—the state of its essential "organs." However, to our surprise, we soon detected challenges that can undermine vitality—specifically: pervasive problems of mental health. While we had not anticipated that mental health would be a major topic of this book (and we have no special expertise in that area)—it is essential that we address it. If students are preoccupied and distracted by overwhelming personal issues—whatever the problems might be—it is very difficult for them to focus on learning, let alone on a possible transformation of their minds.

BACKGROUND

If, in 2012, you had asked us to itemize the biggest problems on the college campus, we might have cited alcohol, sexual misconduct, or possibly free speech issues. It's unlikely that mental health would have made the short list. In fact, the prominence—indeed, dominance—of this issue constitutes one of the major surprises of our study.

But now, nearly a decade later, along with informed members of the public, we can confirm what those who spend time on campuses have known for the better part of a decade: challenges of mental health constitute one of the biggest problems on campus. It's an issue of overriding importance.

Indeed, at the beginning of the study, we heard a lot about alcohol and safety concerns. But over and over again, mental health came up as a source of many problems for students—oftentimes more than any of the other concerns. (And toward the end of study, we began to hear as well about mental health challenges for faculty and other adults on campus.) As a result, early in our data collection, we asked participants to describe problems—*any* problems they perceived as issues on campus. Because we found that students repeatedly named the same problems across campuses, after posing this open-ended question, we added an immediate follow-up. We asked respondents to rank five major problems in terms of their relative severity—namely:

- Academic dishonesty (e.g., plagiarism, cheating)
- Mental health (e.g., stress, anxiety, depression, eating disorders)
- Relationships with peers (friendships and romantic relationships)
- Alcohol and substance abuse
- Safety issues (e.g., violence, sexual misconduct)

In doing so, we wanted to understand how individuals thought about the relative potency and urgency of each problem.

Now, as we are writing this book, issues of mental health have been so widely reported in newspapers, journals of education, and more popular books that this finding is no longer shocking— for some, it may even seem like yesterday's news. But the high frequency of concern across all participants, stakeholders, and schools is important—indeed, we consider it a major headline. Furthermore, the ways in which participants describe the problems are sometimes surprising (because issues of mental health are so often misunderstood); and the search for helpful interventions is pressing.

MENTAL HEALTH: NUTS AND BOLTS

Across all participants, nearly half (44%) rank mental health as *the most important* problem on campus—one of the few agreements among all participants. Put another way, each constituency group in our study—first-year students, graduating students, faculty, administrators, parents, trustees, young alums—ranks mental health as the biggest problem on the college campus. This alignment—among students at different stages, faculty and administrators who are on campus, as well as trustees, young alums, and parents who are off campus—is notable; indeed, *it does not obtain with respect to any of the more than three dozen other questions in our interview protocol.**

To underscore the point: participants at all types of campuses—ranging in size, selectivity, and geography—perceive mental health as the biggest problem confronted by students. That is, across small, remote, residential campuses as well as large, urban, commuter campuses, the most selective campuses as well as the least selective campuses, the concern for mental health is

---

* In this summary, we don't include job recruiters.

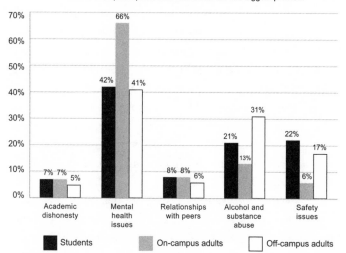

Percent of all participants who rank items as "the biggest problem"

Figure 6.1

It is important to note that more on-campus adults (66%) rank mental health as the most important issue on campus, as compared to students (42%) and off-campus adults (41%). We believe that this difference may be due to the administrators interviewed who were specifically in "student life" positions, including mental health directors and counselors, who know about mental health issues firsthand.

consistent and regnant. Speculation that this is particularly an urban problem, or a problem at selective schools, or only a concern of residential campus, or only prevalent in certain demographic categories, is not borne out.

In addition to the ranking, without any prompting, approximately 20% of our students (that is, one out of every five students), testify and explain that they struggle with their own mental health issues. Furthermore, more than a third of all student participants (38%) discuss the prevalence of mental health on campus. This finding suggests that participants do not just rank mental health as the biggest problem because they themselves confront it; they also see it as a widespread problem for others and for the larger campus community. As an interesting and revealing contrast: though participants also describe academic dishonesty as widespread on campus, this issue was consistently ranked as the *least* important problem students confront. More on this—to us discouraging—finding in Part IV (see box 10.2).*

Such widespread consensus suggests that there are few, if any, differences in how participants with various backgrounds might rank mental health. For example, we find no significant gender differences, nor do we find any significant differences in the responses of students who come from different types of high schools (public, private, or charter schools). However, we note an increased awareness about mental health issues over the course of the college experience: whereas first-year students (35%) see mental health as the biggest problem on campus, this percentage significantly increases among graduating students (50%). Implication: whether students are thinking about their own personal issues or not, as they spend more time in college, they develop increasing alertness to and/or concerns about the issue of mental health for their respective campus communities and, presumably, the well-being of their peers.

---

* Many sources have reported increased cheating during the COVID-19 pandemic.

These overall data are revealing. Unlike the national polls and individual school surveys on which much current understanding is based, we do *not* ask participants to respond directly to questions about their own mental health.[1] Rather, we seek to understand "why" participants think that mental health is the biggest problem on campus. To be clear, our intention is *not* to diagnose particular ailments, nor to collect statistics about the prevalence of specific conditions, such as depression or suicidal tendencies. Some individuals volunteered information about their own mental health issues, but these respondents might have shared even more if we had posed the question directly. Instead, our data are illuminating because we ask participants for *their own reasoning* about mental health issues—regardless of whether the rationales arise from their own experiences and/or their observations of others.

FACTORS CONTRIBUTING TO MENTAL HEALTH PROBLEMS

Whenever we present these findings, we are asked *why now?* Why is it that individuals seem to be reporting more concern about their own mental health, and the mental health of others, than ever before? We are predictably queried whether the problems have worsened over time, and/or whether students are finally openly admitting to problems that have always existed, perhaps beneath the surface. And we have also been asked whether reported differences could be due to different mortality rates for children across the decades, to larger and increasingly diverse demographics on campus, to greater pressures in high school, to child rearing that spoils children, to greater dependence on therapy and drugs in the precollege years—and, more recently (after our study was completed), to anxiety about the COVID-19 pandemic. No doubt readers of this book could readily come up with other hypotheses and speculations.[2]

But at this point, no firm answers exist—and indeed the question may be impossible to answer, because of so-called cohort effects. That is, we can't assume that students in 1950 are the same as students in 1985, or in 2020, and so such comparisons are necessarily speculative—if not odious. But, having listened carefully to several hundred respondents talk about their rationales, and then having sought to ascertain patterns across schools and constituencies, we can make educated inferences about what has become so challenging for young people in college. And herein lies one value of our approach.

Indeed, our data suggest a quite distinct perspective on the prevalence of mental health issues on the college campus. While some hypothesize that students are "overly coddled," or that social media have caused students to feel more loneliness and social anxiety, the majority of students in our study describe an overwhelming pressure to do well, as opposed to just "do okay"— indeed, to build a perfect resume—as the primary source of mental health distress.

Academic Rigor: The Most Commonly Cited Cause

Across all students in our study, the most common explanation (52% of all student-reported causes) about why mental health is the most important problem on campus is *academic rigor*—the "pressure" of academics. Indeed, we also find that students describe this pressure as what "keeps them up at night" (see box 6.1). But what exactly is the pressure? Is it about learning difficult content? Or preparing for exams or writing papers? Or building a favorable transcript to get a job or get into graduate school? Or (reminiscent of response options on school admissions exams) "all of the above"?

Perhaps not surprisingly at this moment in history, when students discuss academic pressure as a cause of mental health, the most frequent explanation focuses on *achieving external measures of success*—securing a high grade-point average, or "doing well" on an assignment or an exam (51%). For example, a first-year student majoring in communications explains: "I know a lot of kids who . . . get super stressed out over grades and they get really anxious about it . . . like intense people make like, 'You have to have a good GPA, you have to have As and stuff.' And so, like people get really stressed out over that." A graduating student in the midst of applying to graduate programs describes needing to perform: "I think, you just want to have a good grade in the class because it's one step forward to your degree, right? It's one step forward to being [on] the honor roll . . . Am I gonna graduate? Am I gonna graduate with honors? And like, you know, like, will I get into a good graduate school?"

Interestingly and importantly, these concerns with the external markers of success are the most common descriptors for academic rigor at *every* campus—from most to least selective. For example, of the three schools with the most students who comment on external measures of success, two schools are high-selectivity campuses in

Box 6.1

What Keeps You Up at Night: The 3 a.m. Worries

Katie Abramowitz

In our study, we aimed to uncover the sources of worry and concern for undergraduate students. We approached the topic from different angles, such as asking participants to describe their own "biggest struggle" and to rank the most vexing problems at their respective schools.

Toward the end of each interview, we sought to get at the issue of stress in another way through a potentially revealing question: "In thinking about your work and this school, what kinds of things, if any, keep you up at night?" We wanted to understand what kinds of concerns weigh on students so much that they can't fall asleep. (We also posed this question—appropriately worded—to the other constituencies in our study.)

More than half of all students (53%) indicate that academic stressors keep them up at night. For the most part, these responses have nothing to do with actual academic content or material that students learned in class. Of those who describe academic stressors, the two biggest categories of concern are time management and workload issues (as they relate to academic responsibilities), as well as pressure around grades, success, and performance. Often, these categories are connected; students express anxiety about workload because they want to do well (and feel the need to do well), and they are preoccupied with achieving high markers of success. Most students do not articulate where exactly these pressures come from (e.g., parents, peers, internalized standards); when asked explicitly, the majority of students in our study refer to these stressors in explaining mental health challenges on campus. These anxiety-provoking conditions seem to derive from a combination of upbringing, peers, and campus culture, as well as the transactional expectations for college (including future aspirations) that all too often weigh on students.

For example, one student expresses concern about completing assignments and meeting deadlines: "I'm always worried I'm forgetting an assignment . . . I'll be laying in bed at 3 a.m. and I'm like, 'Did I forget something?' 'Did my professor say something, and I forgot to write it down?' Because they don't put their PowerPoints online, so I can't check. So I think just like sometimes making sure that I've got everything managed. And most of the time I'll have things done over a week in advance, but I'm just a worrier. So I will worry anyways."

A graduating senior speaks specifically to the pressure to succeed—in terms of securing high grades and an overall high grade point average: "I have a 4.0 GPA and I got a B minus on my English paper. . . . I want to be perfect when I graduate. So, again, that brings me back to this whole idea of not being good enough . . . things like that keep me up." This student suggests that a single grade often has the power to keep her awake in anguish.

As we hear their responses, when it comes to "academics," students seem to be more concerned with managing performance and success than with the substance of what they are learning.

Importantly, students at both ends of the college experience describe these concerns, although the level of pressure seems to decrease—more first-year students (58%) than graduating students (48%) describe these academic pressures as keeping them up at night.

Furthermore, while we did not explicitly ask about mental health (only asking students what kept them up at night), nearly a fifth of students (17%) raise mental health issues in relation to these academic concerns. Words like "anxiety," "stress," and "worry" are used unsparingly with regard to academic performance.

One first-year student responds, "Dealing with tests, readings, and stuff. And sometimes you get pressure, if you're studying very late at night, it's even harder to fall asleep, like if you're studying until 12, 1, or 2, it's hard to fall asleep. You're anxious, you're nervous, 'cause there is a lot of pressure, especially if a class has only given you two midterms, then if you don't do well on one . . . even if you do better on the final . . . that one counts so much. . . . The pressure really gets to you."

While a majority of students describe academic stressors, a noteworthy number also raise concern about post-graduate plans. More than a quarter of all students (27%) express concern about their future "next steps"—specifically, jobs and graduate school. Indeed, this constitutes the second largest category that students cite as what keeps their minds churning at night.

A neuroscience major states, "My future . . . actually being able to do well enough here to go on. It's not even a job, I would say. It's just like my next step in my education. . . . Getting into med school. . . . I guess if you have a plan to go to a certain graduate school and you don't do well enough in college to move on, then you've lost the value of your time here."

These two categories—academic stressors and future plans— are inextricably linked for many students: thoughts about keeping up with academic work often spiral into thoughts about the future. In several responses about middle-of-the-night worries, academic performance is directly related to post-graduate life. Such students feel as if their entire future success could hinge on their GPA. These worries are common across *all students* in our study.

One student discusses academic pressure as it relates to life beyond college: "I think my future . . . I just really wanna succeed and be perfect in a lot of ways. And that can really stress you out at night, especially when you're trying to go to bed. Yeah, so I think a focus on success, and no matter how much I wanna be okay with the unknown, it still scares me sometimes."

> Given how we have phrased the question, we noted that several students talked about their own sleep issues. Available evidence signals the importance of sufficient sleep—particularly uninterrupted sleep at night. While sufficient sleep in itself will not eliminate pressure on students, it may help them deal with the challenges that they face.[3]

our sample (67% and 60%), and the other school is one of the low-selectivity campuses in our sample (63%). On the other hand, of the three schools with the fewest students who comment about external measures of success, two schools are medium-selectivity campuses (45% and 40%) and the other school is one of the high-selectivity campuses in our sample (45%). In other words, student stress with respect to academic rigor pervades *every* campus, regardless of its selectivity. Therefore, we can't—and shouldn't—presume that students at the most selective institutions feel more pressure than do students at other schools—nor that the faculty at these selective institutions apply more pressure than faculty at other schools. Students at *all* schools report stress with respect to "doing well."

The same pattern holds true for most of the other major categories of academic rigor which students describe. For example, among students who talk about academic rigor, the second most frequent category is managing academic workload (21%)—both in terms of managing the work across an entire course load and just in an individual course. One student, aspiring to become an elementary school teacher, comments "I started having a little bit of anxiety from . . . the amount of workload that I had, and I felt like, everything was just, like, bundling up, so I would say that is the biggest issue." A second student, majoring in natural science, says: "You know, sometimes school can be overwhelming. I feel like I am drowning. I don't know if that is in the 'anxiety department' but it's like, sometimes it becomes very stressful."

Again, and notably, the school with the *most* students who comment on workload (33%) is one of the high-selectivity schools in our sample, whereas the school with the second most students who comment (32%) is one of the low-selectivity schools in our study. Moreover, of the two schools with students who comment the *least* about workload, one is a medium-selectivity school (4%), and the other is one of the low-selectivity schools in our sample (15%). Clearly, we can't simply assume that the students with the most problems managing workload are the commuting students who often need to balance academic workload with off-campus responsibilities—such as taking care of families or juggling jobs while trying to find some free hours for study. Though these demands or constraints might be challenging for some students most of the time, or for many students some of the time, it is not necessarily what these students see or cite as the primary or most frequent cause of mental health issues.

In light of a third category of student comments about academic rigor, we are again motivated to check our assumptions. We refer here to compensating for, or overcoming, lack of preparation—not feeling ready for college-level work, or experiencing general difficulty with academics. A first-year student double majoring in biology and Spanish says: "I feel like a lot of people, when they come to [school], they don't understand how demanding the academics are and get stressed out pretty easily." Another student specifically describes readiness issues related to the transition to college: "Stress, because [first-year students who] are not fully transitioned, start stressing out . . . they start getting anxiety because, you know, they're too scared to ask for help from anyone."

Yet another surprise: One might predict that students who complain (or blame) lack of preparation for academic work may not have experienced high-quality secondary education—and that they are thus more likely to attend a college that is less selective. (Presumably it would be more difficult—though it's clearly possible—to gain admission to a moderately selective or highly selective college without a good high school education.) But, in fact, we find a different pattern: the two schools with the most students who comment about lack of preparation are a medium-selectivity school (20%) and a high-selectivity school (14%)—and not one of the low-selectivity schools. In contrast, of the two schools with the fewest students who describe lack of preparation, one of them is a high-selectivity campus (7%) the other is a low-selectivity campus (5%) in our study.

However, we encounter a perhaps more expected result when students describe the fourth most common category of reasons for experiencing stress: the drive to satisfy internal standards of perfection. As one graduating student majoring in international relations explains: "I think the type of student that goes to [this school] is probably someone who's an overachiever, and anxiety-driven. So I think it's definitely . . . a problem that some people have to get really worked up about the work they have to do." A first-year student says: "And I do see a lot of stress. I just have noticed it in a few of my close friends. . . . They've been really, really stressed to the point where I have been concerned, and I talk to them about it. I think especially at [this school] where people really wanna do well, and not necessarily even in terms of grades. . . . They really wanna be the best, and they are kind of perfectionists, it becomes a problem."

Unlike the other categories, the most comments relating to perfectionism come from students at the high-selectivity schools. At least two possibilities arise: (1) students with a strong sense of "internal perfectionism" are attracted to a particular type of school and student body, and/or (2) students who attend these schools develop a heightened internal drive over the course of the college experience. The former reason seems more likely. Some students explicitly discuss the "high school effect," in which even to get into these highly selective colleges and universities, you need to be flawless: "A lot of people here, I feel like they have a lot of pressure. Like, in high school they had a lot of pressure to do well, and they've kind of carried that over into college, and feel like . . . they need to be meeting impossible standards. And, they feel a lot of stress over that still. I think if you're pursuing a higher education, that there's like a certain level of perfectionism that a lot of people are dealing with."

However, when we look closely at these three schools with the most students who comment about perfectionism, we notice a big difference. One of the schools has far more students who comment (35%) in contrast to the peer schools (each at 13%). Students at this "perfectionist" school are notably overzealous about their academic work, as well as their commitments to extracurricular

Percent of students who describe the "top four" causes of academic pressure

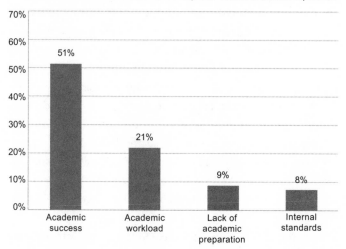

Figure 6.2

Of the student comments about academic pressure, 11% are miscellaneous and represent a range of many other categories.

activities on campus. A first-year student who describes the student body as "busy" talks about this "über" passion at his school: "And it's hard because everybody here wants to do as much as they possibly can, and people don't know in general how to say no . . . And people care a lot about their academics, but the amount of cocurricular obligations that people sign themselves [up for], or extracurricular obligations that people sign themselves up for is unparalleled. It's ridiculous."

We would not have predicted that comments about academic rigor as the most common cause of mental health would have emerged equally from all different types of schools. (If you are skeptical, ask a friend to predict the results of our study.) For example, one might have hypothesized that students at the more selective schools would talk more about striving for academic success, while students at the less selective schools would be more likely to lament lack of academic preparation. Moreover, our predictions might also have been far from the actual state of affairs—that students at the more selective schools actually discuss lack of preparation, and that students at the less selective schools are stressed about academic success, not just matriculation and graduation. Put another way, one already familiar to readers, students across disparate campuses turn out to be more alike than different.

Time for a different perspective. On measures from a variety of studies, students nowadays are being asked to do much *less* than they once were—reading, writing assignments, and tests are all on the decline.[4] Also, thanks to grade inflation, many campuses have a high number of "A" students. A well-known study, by Richard Arum and Josipa Roksa in *Academically Adrift*, presents a disturbing picture of meager student learning across the collegiate spectrum. Notwithstanding the pressures and the presumably well-intentioned efforts of faculty and administrators, it has proved difficult to demonstrate powerful effects of learning in college. Experiencing stress does not seem to produce more effective learning. Indeed, it may even prevent learning—a challenge that the entire sector needs to confront.

So, the question arises: Why, on the one hand, are students worried about success and perfection, and on the other hand, apparently learning less and having less ambitious learning aspirations? Herein lies one of our major contentions: If students are coming to college simply to get a degree and build a resume in order to move on to the next stage in life, they may come with inappropriate or inadequate expectations—feeling overwhelmed in facing the central educational mission of college, which entails more than just "checking the boxes." Certainly, many students come to college with sufficient skills and knowledge to "do well"; but students *also* need to come prepared to do more than develop a "successful" portfolio, if they are to engage deeply in the hard work that (in the eyes of faculty) is required to explore the intellectual landscape and to transform one's mind.

We believe that our joint recommendations of *onboarding* and *intertwining* (detailed in the concluding chapters of the book) can help to assuage this disturbing situation—and, if we are fortunate, increase the probability that higher education can achieve what we deem to be its central mission. Put succinctly, we'd like students to see growth and learning as their goal, rather than getting a high grade.

Other Likely Sources of Mental Health Issues

Aside from academic rigor, students cite two other major causes of mental health complaints on the college campus: social relations (13%) and school culture (13%). At least at times, these are presumably connected.

Students across all schools designate friendship issues as a source of stress—mainly, making new friends, as well as managing difficult friendship dynamics between and among individuals

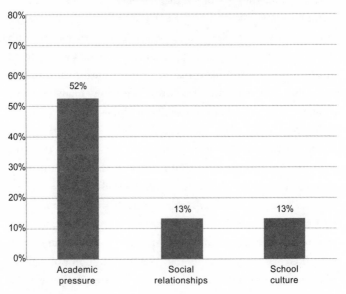

Percent of students who describe the "top three"
causes of mental health distress

Figure 6.3
Of the student comments about mental health distress, 22% are miscellaneous and represent a range of many other categories.

and groups, including social cliques. Some students specifically
link feelings of loneliness with mental health issues. One graduating senior majoring in linguistics and computer science at a
high-selectivity school states: "I've also felt pretty depressed in
some periods since I came here. Like in the very beginning . . . I
didn't view anyone as a real friend, and I was feeling kind of alone.
I wasn't used to it, and I kind of felt depressed. I think many . . . I

feel many people feel that way too . . . sometimes it's just you feel like people here cannot understand you and you feel alone. You feel lonely. I feel it's an issue."

Other students describe "cutthroat social environments" or an unhealthy school culture—students feel as though they are in constant competition with others for friendships, romantic relationships, or body image, as well as grades, academic kudos, or general academic performance. Students also describe being "on" all the time—needing to be your best at all times in all realms—in order to keep up with or even surpass peers. A graduating student on the varsity soccer team explains: "You constantly feel a little bit of stress to keep becoming a better person inside and outside of the classroom." Another student gives a chilling account of the culture at her school as she perceives it:

I think the atmosphere of competition and so much pressure to perform to be the best really, probably is the driving factor behind a lot of mental issues. And I suspect that if you did a psychological evaluation of every [school] student, that there would be almost a scary number of issues, whether it was anxiety or stress or depression. But it's just not a place where people feel like they can talk about it with other people, because it would be admitting weaknesses.

MENTAL HEALTH AND MENTAL MODELS

It's important to consider whether a particular approach to college relates to concern about mental health. As noted: across all students, mental health is most commonly identified as the biggest concern on the college campus. That said, we find that students who rank mental health as the biggest problem (in comparison to the other problems we presented) are significantly more likely to have a transformational mental model than to have a transactional mental model.

There may be a couple of explanations for this finding. To begin with, it is entirely possible that students with a transformational mental model reflect more about their surrounding community and have a particular sensitivity to the people and issues around them; or that they ask—indeed, demand—more of themselves. It's also possible that students with a transactional mental model may have already adapted to the pressures they and others confront—presumably developing strategies and mechanisms for coping with these stresses—or, less happily, that they are simply oblivious to the experiences of others.

We must point out, however, that we find no significant differences between students with an exploratory mental model and students with a transactional mental model in terms of the salience of mental health as a problem on campus.

You might also be wondering whether the students who generally describe academic rigor as a leading cause of mental health distress are more likely to have a transactional approach to college. Interestingly, we do not find this to be the case for the overall category of "academic rigor." However, we do find that those students who specifically describe the particular pressure of "academic success" are more likely to have a transactional mental model than a transformational model. Again, we do not find any significant differences between students with an exploratory mental model and those with a transactional mental model with respect to this rationale for mental health concerns.

For further findings about the causes for mental health issues, see box 6.2.

Views of Other Constituencies

As we have already noted, on average, *all other constituency groups*—on-campus adults and off-campus adults—rank mental health as the biggest problem on the college campus. However, the stakeholders do not necessarily agree on the causes. In fact, had we been asked to predict who said what and why, we might, once again, have been surprised by the findings.

Counter to what we might have expected, we find that faculty—presumably the group of individuals with the most regular contact with students—seem to have views about mental health issues that are farthest from those of students. In offering their perspectives, faculty focus most commonly on time management issues (30%)—balancing multiple responsibilities with academic work. And here is where the less selective schools do differ from the more selective schools.

Specifically, faculty and administrators at the low-selectivity schools focus on time management issues—such as juggling responsibilities outside of school. In contrast, faculty and administrators at high-selectivity campuses refer instead to the challenge of balancing extracurricular activities with academic work. For example, a faculty member at a low-selectivity school explains, "Stress, which can present itself in so many ways. . . . It's trying to juggle a lot of things. . . . If you're a very bright student, it's because you have to work and you have a family or you have . . . children too and you've gotta try and get all these things going

Box 6.2

Less Frequent Reasons for Mental Health Issues on Campus

In addition to the reasons cited in this chapter, students mention several other causes for concerns about mental health: they raise issues regarding general time management (10%), finance and worries about future work (9%), particular school traits such as size or location (6%), preexisting mental health conditions (3%), and parental pressure (1%). For the most part, the students' comments about these topics, much like those about academic rigor, come from students at all schools, not just particular schools or certain types of schools. As an example, students who are most likely to comment about financial pressures or anxiety regarding future work come from a medium-selectivity school (17%), a low-selectivity school (16%), and a high-selectivity school (13%). Again, it's presumptive to assume that we know the problems of students (as they perceive and describe them) before we actually listen to their words.*

These less frequently described causes of mental health among students turn out to be revealing—because they are the kind of causes about which we thought we would hear, more than others. Notably, not only do these topics appear to be less on the minds of students across our study; we rarely heard mention of deeply troubled backgrounds, unsettling uses of social media, and the condition of "FOMO," or "fear of missing out," often linked by pundits to the use (or overuse) of social media platforms.

---

* Since we are not trained mental health professionals, we report what we've learned from the interviews and refrain from speculating about deeper psychodynamic or cultural factors.

> Though in some cases mental health issues on the college campus presumably carry over from high school, we rarely hear explicitly about the college admission process—undoubtedly very much part of the fearsome pressure high school students experience. Two possibilities spring to mind: (1) either these formative influences, like high school or parents, seem to lie in the distant past for college students (especially for graduating students), or (2) these perennial pressures are so interwoven in their own approaches and daily lives that they don't identify and describe them as independent "causes." One must wonder whether students actually think about where the pressure began, or whether the pressure has just become a part of who they are. And of course, we need to acknowledge that perhaps some of the reasons for mental health complaints may simply not be evident to the students themselves.

while you're trying to improve your life to be able to help everybody else. . . . It's the stress '. . . I didn't have time to study, professor, because I've got all this going on in my life.'"

On the other hand, an English professor at a high-selectivity school worries about students being stretched too thin because they try to do too much *on campus*:

The sets of behaviors that got you into this place, that you did in high school, if you keep doing them while you're here, [they] will kill you because we are complicit as an institution in getting you to overcommit to doing things that are not academic. It's one of the ways in which you get into [school]. You're in too many clubs . . . And I ask them, "In order to get in here, in a place like this, what do you have to do?" And they all have it right. "Be in a lot of clubs, be important officers in all those clubs, take leadership roles, etc. in a lot of them. Not just one, but a lot of them."

I said, "Okay. You're absolutely right. You can't do that here." But students try. They try, and then what happens is they get into really difficult straits.

In addition, in contrast to the picture emanating from students, faculty views tend to vary significantly by school. Unlike students across our study, "not all faculty are alike." For example, at two schools (one highly selective, one moderately selective), faculty focus on parental pressure as a cause of mental health, whereas those comments rarely appear at other schools. At one high-selectivity school, faculty focus on a particular cause that we rarely hear from any other school, or even from any other constituency group. At this school, perhaps an outlier, the supportive culture on campus specifically around mental health—in the form of resources and outreach to students—seems actually to attract *more* students with mental issues to campus (or is more likely to encourage students to name and to seek aid for their stress).

An administrator from this school puts it this way:

Students say this when they come, they say that one of the things they're attracted to is [our] support for mental health . . . In fact, if we don't provide accommodations quickly or to their liking, if we don't provide it quickly enough, they will complain . . . I'm not saying that it's a problem because I don't like doing it or I'm uncomfortable with it, to me it's actually kinda fun to see how I can adapt . . . how do I adjust to a student, how do I anticipate a student who may not even know that they have a learning disability, or who doesn't even know that depression is not caused by them, not like this failing, you have to kind of hide and get over, it's actually a problem to solve if you're gonna succeed in college.

Furthermore, across schools, fewer faculty (28%) than students (38%) underscore the prevalence of mental health challenges on campus. When they do speak about mental health issues, faculty tend to focus on a single student, sometimes sharing ambivalence about the role faculty should (or should not) play in helping such afflicted students.

A humanities professor states: "I think sometimes we promise too much. Students always are complaining about being overstressed, and I don't know whether they actually are or not. That's really not the point. It's not for me to judge, frankly. But the problem comes when we are asked really to be what we're not, which is health professionals. I have a PhD in English. That's my expertise."

Though she cares about her students and wants to be helpful, this professor concludes: "It seem[s] to me that we have allowed some folks to be here . . . [and] this experience is really not that productive [for them]. They need to take some time out. They're bright, they're interested, but stuff is just getting in the way, and they need to take some time out."

In contrast, among other constituencies, we find that the perspectives of parents and young alums are aligned with the perspectives of students—and this despite the fact that they are geographically more distant from the students than are the faculty. It is understandable that young alums would have the most intimate knowledge about these topics; but on the whole, it is notable that parents seem to be more in tune with students than are the faculty. We speculate that many if not most students still turn to their parents for help, because they don't feel comfortable talking with faculty and/or because faculty are not comfortable talking with students about these issues. Commentators, observers—and also you, readers—are likely to differ dramatically on whether parents' *greater knowledge* about issues of stress constitute part of the problem, part of the solution, or some kind of amalgam.

At the same time, putting on our anthropologist hats, we must remember that (as discussed in chapter 5) when students are asked to predict how parents choose the most important reason to go to college, the majority of students say that their parents would rank "to get a job" as the top reason (even though when we asked parents, they themselves did not always designate this ranking). Clearly, students feel the spoken—or perhaps the tacit pressure from parents to "do well"—whether this comes from their own parents or from the broader competitive environment.

To be sure, many parents may not recognize the implicit messages they may inadvertently send to students—though a few parents in our study unabashedly describe the pressure they intend to place on students. For example, one parent in our study admits:

I think that [students] should have pressure on them. Other parents may see that differently, so mental health, I'd say technically is bad, stress is good. . . .'Cause in the real world you'll have pressure. So, in, in my house . . . you will be studying for the SAT for about four months before the SAT. You will take a full length SAT a minimum of once a month—the whole four-hour deal . . . every day of . . . that four months you're going to be testing, texting me the words that you study today, or what you finished in your module, or what you were working on. And there are going to be some timed pressures in the real world as well, you know when the boss comes and says, "I need X by one o'clock" and it's 11:30 and you didn't even know about it until now. That's real.

To sum up a vital and troubling concern: Mental health issues pervade higher education. This state of affairs looms large—despite the fact that on most measures, students are typically being asked to do less in the academic sphere and are often excused or even rewarded for poor performances. While we might wish this problem (and no doubt its multifarious causes) to go away, it won't; and schools (and students and parents) must cope as best they can. The challenge is to figure out the supportive contributions that can be made by all the relevant constituencies—and this includes the conditions and pressures of the broader society, which go beyond the capabilities of any particular sector and any particular study.

We are not and cannot claim to be experts on the mental health situation—a state of affairs that might even be considered a crisis. Moreover, it would be a mistake to assume that mental health pressures are unique to educational settings—even before COVID-19, there have been considerable and perhaps greater stresses on health in the United States and elsewhere.[5] And so it is deceptive to suggest that even with the best mental health facilities, schools will on their own be able to turn the dial back significantly. Moreover, even the best mental health facilities at schools are still not enough to meet the needs of students—students at every campus in our study complain about wait times or limited services, regardless of how many services are offered (and also regardless of the extent that these services have been enhanced over the last several years).

That said, we have been impressed by a number of approaches that colleges can take to alleviate the stresses that so many of their students feel—and that they observe in their classmates. For example, in addition to robust mental health facilities, we have become familiar with other models, such as peer counseling and peer education programs to bridge the need for more "listeners" and also to create more awareness for resources on campus and reduce stigma associated with mental health issues. Some of these mental health centers also facilitate affinity groups to help students across campus connect with each other. Other schools have also developed programs to facilitate deeper connections between students and faculty. One of the large schools in our study organized small, voluntary groups of students assigned to one mentor—hoping that students would forge meaningful relationships with adults on campus. Furthermore, several institutions enlist campus-wide support from The JED Foundation, a national organization that works with schools to develop a holistic approach to addressing mental health issues across each institution—including the counseling center, finance and operations, and faculty departments.

One further comment. Throughout we have used the phrase "mental health," which has become the common term bandied about campuses in the opening decades of the twenty-first century. But based on our respondents' testimony, we could have substituted the words "stress" or "anxiety," because they were often invoked as well.[6] Clearly, "mental health" is a broad term, one that evokes more serious conditions, such as depression or suicidal tendencies—and these were characterizations that we did not hear very often. Accordingly, for much of our account in this chapter, one could safely use the more focused descriptions.

Next, we turn to another set of disturbing findings—ones that colleges may be better equipped to address.

As conveyed in the opening pages of this book, in-person visits to all of the campuses provided an invaluable opportunity to observe and experience campus culture. We learned about how students spent time and with whom they interacted, as well as the "vibe" around campus—especially palpable during a campus debate about divestment, within days of the 2016 presidential election, or hours before (or after) a game with a traditional football or basketball rivalry. Even on more ordinary days (such as the ones that we described), we might note the stillness of the library or the hubbub at the campus center, and whether students appeared to be studying alone or engaging with classmates in a review of key ideas. These observations set helpful contexts for our interviews with students who often talk about their place in the campus community—how they feel in their classes, relate to professors, get along with peers, and/or identify with the overall institution.

In the fall of 2015, during an interview with a senior administrator at one school, we learned about an important and surprising finding in real time. Just before our interview, she had received results of a school-specific survey. The survey revealed that despite several new initiatives to support students over the course of college, an overwhelming number of students indicated that they felt they did not "belong."[1]

This administrator processed the results with us:

It was pretty staggering . . . A lot of the students struggle to feel like they belong here . . . There's lots of strangers around here, and they've come from a high school where they probably knew most of everybody, and they come here and they don't know hardly anybody . . . nobody in their classes. So we're trying to figure out ways to . . . help them feel like they belong . . . Something that I don't think we've talked about or thought about as much . . . [is] . . . how do students—how do they feel like they belong on campus? How do we make them feel like this is their place and that they can succeed here, and they can graduate from here?

Her first instinct was to develop a plan—to put together a "belonging" committee, one composed of students, faculty, and administrators from across the school—to allocate resources for more advising staff, to consider how residential life can enhance campus living, to increase awareness about mental health services, and the like.

But as researchers trying to understand the topography of the sector, we wanted to know more about what exactly this concept "belonging" means to students: for example, to whom and to what they feel as if they belong, or, less happily, do not belong. We'd wondered whether some, or perhaps many, students actually feel alienated. This interview may have been the first time we heard the formal term "belonging" invoked as part of the lingo of "student affairs." But the concept was not new to us.* Indeed, many if not most students had talked about such issues in the course of our interviews over the years.[2]

Needless to say, once we had returned to our offices in Cambridge, we developed a plan with our research team to investigate "belonging" and "alienation" more directly in our visits and analyses across students and campuses.

BELONGING AND ALIENATION: NUTS AND BOLTS

Similar to our analysis of Higher Education Capital and mental models, we approached "belonging" and "alienation" as holistic concepts that emerge—or do not emerge—over the course of hour-long interviews. Because we did not ask students specifically about their sense of belonging or alienation, our research

---

* "Belonging," first outlined as a motivational theory by Abraham Maslow in his hierarchy of needs (in "A Theory of Human Motivation," *Psychological Review* 50, no. 4 [1943]), and then by Roy F. Baumeister and Mark R. Leary (in "The Need to Belong: Desire for Interpersonal Attachments as a Fundamental Human Motivation," *Psychological Bulletin* 117, no. 3 [1995]: 497–529), has since been investigated by numerous researchers in several contexts. More recently, scholars have focused on "belonging" in K–12 education and higher education, investigating the relationship of belonging and demographic identifiers, among other aspects of school culture.

team coded every interview in its entirety; this review sought to determine the degree to which each individual presented evidence for belonging, alienation, or a mix of belonging and alienation.

In the course of this review of transcripts, we analyzed student descriptions of feeling respected, valued, and included by faculty, peers, and the overall institution, both in the classroom and on campus generally; we also sought all descriptions of feeling involved and engaged with others and campus activities.[3] At the same time, we looked as well for comments in which students describe a *lack* of such connectedness. Sometimes, students use the explicit words "belonging" and "alienation," but often students use associated words, such as "fitting in," "connected" (or "disconnected"), and "accepted." Other students do not invoke these words or synonyms directly but touch on related topics in substantive ways.

Ultimately, after a review of literature on the topic of belonging, we developed our own measures. Traditionally scholars have considered "belonging" as a single construct, focused on social relationships in educational settings. But in the spirit of more recent scholars, we were interested in capturing belonging to (and alienation from) multiple entities.[4] Drawing on a range of conceptualizations of belonging, we developed a scoring measure that includes a five-point scale ranging from "strong belonging" to "strong alienation" with respect to three separate areas. Our operational definitions of belonging emerged from our initial scan of the data.

Academic: Motivation, achievement, and mastery of academic work; feeling supported by campus adults to pursue academic

work; respected and challenged academically; having owner-
ship of one's field of study.

Peer: Meaningful connections with other students, evidence of
fitting in to a larger social community.

Institutional: Affiliation and connectedness to the institution, as
well as to the university's overall mission; being invested in the
institution; feeling in sympathy with a "school spirit."

To flesh out the concept of belonging, let's consider Sarah, a
student who attends a medium-selectivity school. Though she
describes herself as generally "comfortable" in her dorm and with
her selection of psychology as a major, throughout the interview
she reflects on her own complicated relationship to the aforementioned entities.

As an individual learner, Sarah questions whether she belongs
to the *academics* at her school, despite a professor's encouragement and support:

English [title of course] was the worst experience of my life only because
I stressed too much . . . I cried because so much blood, sweat, and tears
went into that class. I questioned myself and I even asked a student, do I
even belong here? . . . [My professor initially] was very abrasive and very
bossy [but then], I had a conversation with him probably I think two weeks
ago and . . . he was like, "Why do you question yourself when you write?"
And I told him, "I don't know." I said "I don't think it's good enough." He
[said], "That's your problem." He said: "You're a great writer . . . just don't
second guess yourself in anything in life."

With respect to her own *peers*, Sarah gives a mixed picture of feeling connected to a small group of friends, but not to the larger
school community: "And I feel like for a lot of people, like college

can be a process of assimilation. You kinda like change your-self . . . or you are influenced by the people around you, and things like that. It just happened that I fell into a very, very small niche at [school] . . . after finding out that I wasn't really fitting in with the rest of the community . . . I don't fit in with the main crowd, so I have to find like my own little, small crowd."

Turning to the dimension of institutional belonging, Sarah is quite negative about the administration at her school, considering whether her mission is actually aligned with that of the *institution*: "I think that they're kind of just like messed up and like the whole corporate sense of college. I don't know if they genuinely have our best interests at heart. I think that college is just a big disgusting business sometimes. I've seen lots of people, oh gosh, like have tons of issues graduating because they're missing like one credit . . . . It's disgusting. And it's just, I don't, honestly the administra-tion here, it's so frustrating."

Many of our students share these nuanced feelings of belong-ing to and alienation from three separate entities. To be sure, some students might express universally positive feelings with respect to belonging to academics, peers, and institutions—while others may exhibit negative feelings, even alienation from all three areas. But most students present a more mixed picture—voicing belonging to one area, alienation from a second area, and a balance of both belonging and alienation in regard to a third area. (It is important to note that expressions of both belonging and alienation are distinct from assuming inherently a neutral stance. In the latter case, students fail to indicate how an experi-ence or perspective affects their own experience—and thus do not receive any score from our coders.) Despite these complexities, across our study, we find an abundance of evidence that allows us to evaluate and score nearly all of the students (more than 90% of the sample).

Let's unpack these layers.

BELONGING

We were pleased—and, truth be told, somewhat relieved—to discover that on the whole, many more students talk about belonging than alienation. Specifically, more than three-quarters of the students in our study (84%) discuss belonging in a somewhat benign way—nearly half of these students discuss belonging to all three areas (43%), while fewer of these students express belonging to two areas (30%), or just one area (27%).

The finding that the majority of students—approximately three out of every four—feel that they belong *in some fashion* is reassuring; but that still leaves many students—indeed, way too many—who feel adrift. In any event, to understand the full landscape, we need to take a closer look at the patterns across students and institutions.

Across Institutions

Across all schools, we find that students at high-selectivity schools indicate more belonging to all three areas—academic, peer, and institution—than students at medium- and low-selectivity schools; and, for the most part, students at medium-selectivity schools indicate slightly more belonging than students at low-selectivity

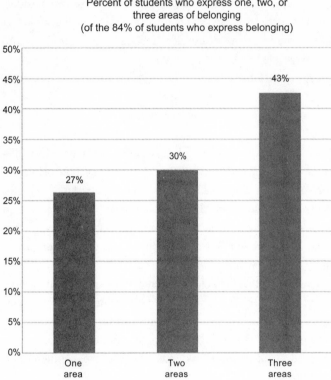

Percent of students who express one, two, or
three areas of belonging
(of the 84% of students who express belonging)

Figure 7.1

schools. Therefore, in general, the amount of belonging among students at certain schools mirrors the selectivity grouping of schools—students at the more selective schools express more belonging, students at the less selective schools express less belonging, and students at the medium-selectivity schools express belonging in the middle of these groups.*

Indeed, one might assume that there is not a big difference between indications of belonging between low-selectivity schools and medium-selectivity schools. Here, it is important to point to noticeable "outliers" for the belonging findings for this group of schools. Specifically, at one of the low-selectivity schools, students show a similar level of academic belonging (75%) to students at the high-selectivity schools, while students at the other two low-selectivity schools express significantly lower academic belonging (51% and 56%, respectively). Furthermore, at one of the low-selectivity schools, students show a similar level of peer (70%) and institutional (74%) belonging to students at the high-selectivity schools, while students at the other two low-selectivity schools express significantly lower belonging to peers (31% and 51%, respectively) and to the institution (38% and 55%, respectively).

As with all of our findings, it is important to highlight these differences; we seek to understand the factors that may differentiate institutions from their peer schools. In these cases, we suspect two important ingredients: close proximity of students to campus

---

*There is one exception: slightly more students at low-selectivity schools indicate more academic belonging (66%) than students at medium-selectivity schools (62%).

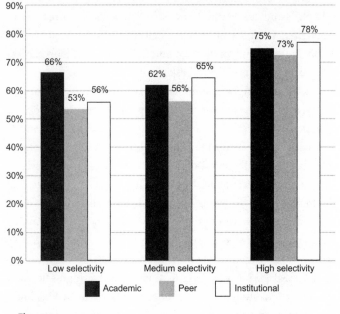

Percent of students with each area of belonging across selectivity
(Categories are not mutually exclusive and do not total 100%)

Figure 7.2

(to explain high expressions of belonging to peers and institution); second, a school's proactive and salient *onboarding* approach at the beginning of the first year, which helps students feel that they belong to the academic program (we illustrate onboarding throughout Part IV of this book).

Furthermore, looking more closely at how students within each selectivity group express belonging, we find that, in general, students express consistent amounts of belonging to each of the three spheres—academics, peers, and overall institution. That is, within each selectivity group, students feel similar amounts of belonging to academics as they feel with respect to peers and to the overarching institution. There is one exception: at the low-selectivity schools, students indicate noticeably more belonging to academics than to their peers or to their institution. A possible explanation: because more students at these schools commute to campus, they feel less connected to peers and institutions, and more connected to the academics—their main reason for coming to campus.

Across Time

In comparing first-year students to graduating students, we find what at first might seem like a counterintuitive finding: overall, the feeling of belonging appears to *decrease* over the course of college. However, across all students, the most notable decline is in expressions of belonging to peers (68% of first-year students compared to 57% of graduating students) and to the overall institution (71% of first-year students compared to 63% of graduating students), *not* to academics (68% of both first-year students and graduating students).

Why should graduating students who have been enrolled for 4–6 years (or 2–3 years in the case of community college students) feel *less connected* to peers and/or the institution than do their first-year counterparts?

There may be several explanations. Consider, for example, the kinds of orientation programs provided before school begins—some institutions offer opportunities for incoming students to

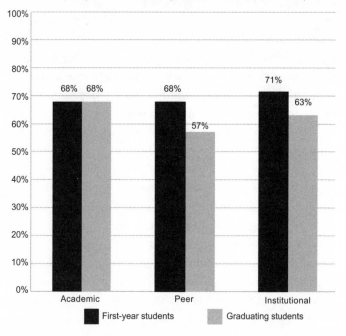

Percent of students with each area of belonging over time
(Categories are not mutually exclusive and do not total 100%)

Figure 7.3

bond with selected peers and faculty in service activities or on camping trips. At least one of the schools participating in our study added a residential requirement for sophomores in order to facilitate deeper connections among peers. In contrast, perhaps graduating students have the proverbial "foot out the door" and are ready to move on.[5]

It is also possible that, over the course of college, as students further identify their own interests and passions, get to know their peers in deeper ways, and experience campus life in a more rounded way, they come to realize that their own emerging values and sense of purpose may differ from those of their peers, and possibly as well from their faculty and administrators (think back to Alex described in chapter 5). Put sharply, they genuinely "don't belong" on their campus.

As for patterns at particular institutions over the course of college, we note the following unexpected contrast. On the one hand, students at high-selectivity schools express more belonging than students at the medium- or low-selectivity schools. But at the same time, compared to students at low-selectivity schools, those at the high-selectivity schools experience a larger decline in belonging to peers and to the institution over time. We should note that the decline in a sense of belonging over the course of college has been reported elsewhere.[6]

Across Students

Sometimes, the non-differences we find in our data are just as or even more interesting than the differences we discern. In general, we find no significant gender differences in how students describe belonging, nor do we find any significant differences between students who major in the humanities, the natural sciences, or the social sciences.

However, we *do* find significant correlations among students with varying amounts of Higher Education Capital (discussed in chapter 4) and different mental models for the college experience (discussed in chapter 5).

Higher Education Capital   In general, students with high HED-CAP (score of 3) and moderate HEDCAP (score of 2) are significantly more likely than those with low HEDCAP (score of 1) to indicate belonging. In addition, those with high HEDCAP (score of 3) are significantly more likely to express belonging than those with moderate HEDCAP (score of 2).

Mental models   We also find significant correlations among belonging and mental models. Specifically, students with exploratory and transformational mental models are more likely to indicate belonging than those with transactional mental models; and students with transformational mental models are significantly more likely to express belonging than those with exploratory mental models.

Given so few differences in general, we note the importance of those we *do* discern—with respect to how students think about the college experience, and what they might be getting from it. Our data indicate that when students view college as more than a means to an end—as an opportunity to focus on learning and transforming the mind—they are better poised to make the most of it.

ALIENATION

Even though a reassuring majority of students indicate a sense of belonging, one-third of students (31%) also express some form of alienation. With several millions of students enrolled in institutions of higher education, we need to be very concerned with the absolute large numbers of students reporting some sense of alienation (in absolute terms, we would speculate clearly over one million); we should strive to understand exactly *from whom* and *from what* they feel most alienated if we are to have a reasonable chance of addressing these concerns appropriately. We also need to consider the possibility that our estimates of belonging may be on the high side; if students feel that they do not belong, they may well be reluctant to participate in a research project (it is of course also possible that students participated in the interview so that they could complain or gripe to a sympathetic ear).

In general, our major findings about alienation are the inverse of our findings about belonging. You might think that this is self-evident; but because we separately categorize those students who discuss a mix of alienation and belonging to each of the three areas, it is not a foregone conclusion that those who don't express belonging will express alienation.

Of the students who signal a lack of belonging, roughly half (56%) indicate alienation from one area—either academics, or peers, or institution; the emphasis is on a lack of connection to peers, as opposed to academics or the institution. A third of students who describe alienation (31%) from two spheres—most commonly indicate alienation from both peers and the institution, as opposed to academics. A smaller number of students (13%) cite alienation from all three areas. In other words, students feel the least amount of alienation from academics—possibly good news, given our perspective on the principal purpose of college. (However, wearing less-rose-colored glasses, we might also conclude

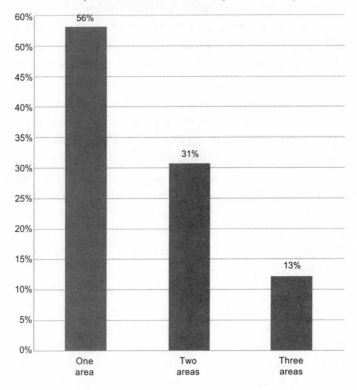

Percent of students who express one,
two, or three areas of alienation
(Of the 31% of students who express alienation)

Figure 7.4

that students don't value academics as much as they do peers, for example, and so, accordingly, are less prone to think of themselves as "alienated" from their studies.)

Across Institutions and Time

Just as students at the higher-selectivity schools express more belonging than students at the lower-selectivity schools, students at the lower-selectivity schools express more alienation than students at the higher-selectivity schools. Of the students who express alienation at the least selective schools, most express concern for a lack of connection to peers (32%) and institution (28%), as opposed to academics (14%).

Furthermore, while belonging decreases over the course of college, alienation increases—less at the high-selectivity schools, and more at the low-selectivity schools. The biggest increase in alienation among first-year students and graduating students is from the institution—notably, more students feel alienated from their overall campus than from academics or peers.

Across Students

If we seek to help these alienated students, we need to know more about *who* they are and *why* they may experience such alienation. Upon closer examination, once again, there appear to be no obvious patterns across demographic traits for those students who present feelings of alienation—no significant differences across gender or disciplines.

Indeed, there is only one major difference: as noted, students who attend a nonresidential campus are more likely to indicate alienation than those students who attend a residential campus. And, of course, the explanation of this finding appears straightforward, since nonresidential students almost invariably have a more transactional relationship to their institution. However, even on the residential campuses, we don't necessarily always know which students actually live on campus (e.g., in a dorm, or other form of campus housing) and which students live in off-campus apartments or homes.

Nonetheless, we can speculate about patterns. On most residential campuses, students tend to live in campus housing during their first and possibly their second year; but after that some of these students find their own housing (two of the campuses in our study require on-campus housing for the entire college experience; at these schools, this is most commonly four years). The importance of these living experiences, even if for just one or two years, should be underscored. As discussed with respect to our findings on belonging, the experience of living on campus with other students not only gives students time to get to know each other and to bond; it also affords the convenience of academic resources—professors and staff, services, and buildings—and institutional spaces to gather, whether this occurs in a laboratory, at the gym, or around a dining table.*

---

*Needless to say, to overcome the challenges of COVID-19, institutions have used different approaches (i.e., online events and gatherings) to foster a sense of belonging.

As with forms of belonging, we do find significant differences in expressions of alienation among students with varying amounts of Higher Education Capital and mental models.

Higher Education Capital   We find that students with a low HEDCAP score (score of 1) are significantly more likely—almost twice as likely—to indicate alienation than those students with higher HEDCAP scores (scores of 2 or 3). In contrast with our findings on belonging, we find few, if any, differences between students with moderate HEDCAP (score of 2) and students with high HEDCAP (score of 3).

Mental models   Students with a transactional mental model are significantly more likely to indicate alienation from each of the three spheres than those students with an exploratory mental model or a transformational mental model. Accordingly, such a finding suggests that students with a transactional mental model are not only more likely to feel alienated from academics (which may logically make the most sense), but that students with a transactional mental model also feel more alienated from peers and the overall institution than do students with exploratory and transformational mental models. In fact, in most cases, students with a transactional mental model are almost twice as likely to indicate alienation.

Here longitudinal data would be valuable, indeed invaluable. We would like to know whether students' (arguably prior) mental model of college helps to determine feelings of belonging and alienation; or whether, in contrast, the students' mental models are at least in part a reflection *a posteriori* of their own feelings of belonging or alienation on the particular campus on which they find themselves. Or, possibly, both patterns might be discernible.

ALIENATION AND MENTAL HEALTH ISSUES

What of the relation among belonging, alienation, and mental health concerns? Surprisingly, and quite counterintuitively, we also find no significant correlation between indicating any type of alienation (academic, peer, and/or institutional) and ranking mental health as the most important problem (or not ranking mental health as the most important problem). Moreover, we find no significant correlations between indicating a form of alienation and self-identifying with issues of mental health (those who report that they themselves are struggling).

Consistent with our overall student findings, roughly a fifth of students who indicate a sense of alienation also identify experiencing a mental health issue themselves. This reflects our general finding (roughly 20% of all students self-identify as having some mental health issue). Expressed differently, there are no significant correlations between feelings of alienation and feelings or perspectives about mental health. Thus, it may well be that quite different interventions are needed in order to address alienation than are needed to address that seemingly more delicate—and presumably more crucial—issue of mental health. Here, we await the insights of professionals who deal with these issues on a regular basis and who report their findings and impressions.

"FITTING IN": THE RELATIONSHIP OF DIVERSITY
TO BELONGING AND ALIENATION

At this time, it is almost impossible to speak about higher education—or education at all—without addressing the topic of diversity. Indeed, the majority of individuals *across every constituency group* in our study use the word "diversity" without prompting. (See box 7.1.) And yet there is a striking lack of clarity about its specific value to higher education—or indeed, even precisely what is meant by this term. While some individuals focus on diversity of thoughts and ideas, others consider its importance in terms of the wide range of academic disciplines, and others highlight demographic differences.

Across our study, approximately 60% of individuals talk about diversity in terms of demographic differences (race, gender, socio-economic status, religion, and sexual orientation)—with the largest proportion of individuals (75%) coming from the school that features an extremely diverse population, and the smallest proportion of individuals (40%) coming from the school that features a far less diverse student body.* On the whole, more faculty and administrators talk about diversity than any other group (though trustees are not far behind); among students, more graduating students than first-year students talk about diversity. It is quite possible that over the course of college, students increasingly recognize the importance of the topic.

---

* Statistics as reported by the schools.

Box 7.1

In a Word: The Adjective Question

Sophie Blumert

If you could describe the students at your school in one word . . .

Sometimes, in an hour-long discussion or interview, a single word can be powerful: it can signal a lot about one's perspective. As a warm-up question, we asked participants: "If you were to describe the students in this school in just one adjective, what would it be?"

A large proportion of participants use what we think of as non-substantive adjectives—ones that do not denote any particular meaning, or that fail to offer any insight into differing student populations. This category includes words such as "nice," "friendly," "genuine," "endearing," and "kind." While these words are quite positive, and we are happy to hear that participants have favorable perceptions of students, they tell us little about the culture of the school.

We did hear quite a bit about students' level of motivation. Most commonly, the words "ambitious" and "driven" are used to describe students' commitment to their goals (though we also heard the opposite: "lazy," "unmotivated," etc.). Though these adjectives are mentioned across constituencies and across schools, we note some clear qualitative differences. In particular, participants from high-selectivity schools describe the pressure that students put on themselves to succeed—to get the best grades, to participate in the most activities, and eventually to obtain the highest paying jobs.

One student describes this pressure:

So in that way it's just like the atmosphere here . . . it's very, like a lot of pressure, a lot of tension, really just, you know, a high stress environment . . . I

---

always feel like there's a grind, and, you know, it's never like you just sort of like get a moment to enjoy what you've accomplished. It's more like, okay, well what else do I need to get done?

Conversely, at low-selectivity schools, participants describe a sense of ambition and drive that is quite different:

Ambitious because . . . everyone's here to, like I said before, to move on to the next level . . . and you have to have a certain amount of ambition to want to do that. And they overcome some really serious hardships. I mean . . . you know, we have students who are homeless, we have students who . . . [wonder] am I gonna eat my next meal or am I gonna buy a [public transportation pass] to go to class? Uh, so, when you look at it from that perspective, you know, having to deal with those realities, that's, there's some drive there.

One type of ambition or drive is not necessarily better or worse than another; but the choice of vocabulary provides insight into the types of challenges that students face while in college—words about students' motivations reveal aspects of the atmospheres on different campuses.

The adjective that comes up the *most frequently* gives us critical insight into what participants value. A large proportion of our participants choose a word to describe *differences* between students. In particular, across all constituencies in our sample—both on and off campus—respondents overwhelmingly use the term "diverse" to describe the student body; this lexical choice accounts for nearly a fifth (17%) of all of the adjectives suggested, and at five of the ten schools in our sample it is the top adjective. Given that there are hundreds if not thousands of possible descriptors, this convergence is remarkable.

Most participants use the term "diverse" in one of two ways: (1) to describe demographic diversity, or (2) to describe different interests (e.g., various fields of study and extracurricular activities). Of the participants who choose "diverse" as their adjective, nearly three-quarters (72%) define it as ethnic and cultural diversity.

Across all of the schools, students use the adjective "diverse" in approximately one-third of responses. However, we note clear differences across schools. In general, participants at high-selectivity schools use the word "diverse" less often than those at less selective institutions. In some cases, these students at the high-selectivity schools describe the opposite, using words such as "white," "homogeneous," or "rich," to denote a distinct *lack* of cultural diversity among the student body.

Moreover, in cases where students from high-selectivity schools use the adjective "diverse," they most often talk about a diversity of interests. Additionally, some students at these schools opt for a different term entirely when talking about this difference: "quirky." While these two adjectives seem to denote similar concepts, there appears to be a difference in how participants feel when describing them; "diversity" tends to have a more positive connotation, whereas "quirky" leans neutral or perhaps a bit negative. As one typical student puts it:

I hate this word, but like, quirky. . . . Because everybody that I've met at [school] has like, very different passions. . . . Like, everybody's from like, very different backgrounds so when you put us all together, it's a very weird mix of people.

Adult constituencies also use the term "diverse" in high frequencies (25% of on-campus adults, and 47% of off-campus adults). As with students, the majority of adult constituencies use the term to describe cultural and ethnic diversity; furthermore, participants from higher selectivity schools speak more about intellectual diversity (if they talked about diversity at all).

To be sure, one word scarcely suffices to describe college students. But the frequency of the term "diverse" gives us a sneak

> peek into a revealing finding of our study: the value that a great many participants place on exposure to difference and diversity. And while the definitions of "diverse" do not always align, the value that all constituencies place on it seems to be similar; participants agree that diversity is a key aspect of the college experience today.

Students talk about diversity in both positive and negative ways. On the one hand, they value opportunities to get to know people with different backgrounds, become familiar with varying perspectives, and participate in new activities; but they also acknowledge and sometimes complain about the *lack of diversity* on their particular campus. Again, in sharp contrast from messages conveyed on some public or social media, not a single student in our study maintained that there was too much diversity.

At the same time and notably, a large majority of students across all schools describe experiences, issues, and perspectives related to different social groups on campus *on their own*—without any explicit questions or probes. These comments mostly focus on demography—specifically on race and gender, with less discussion about religion, socioeconomic status, or sexual orientation. Specifically, across all campuses, two-thirds of students talk about race (64%), nearly half the students talk about gender (46%), and about a quarter of students discuss socioeconomic status (31%), religion (27%), and sexual orientation (23%). And while some students focus on positive experiences that give them exposure to individuals who are different (in terms of demographic differences), students also describe a lot of problems on campus with

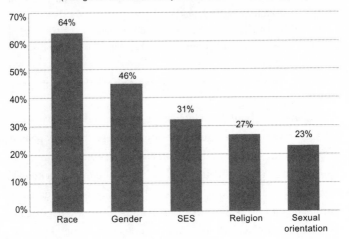

Percent of students who describe social issues
(Categories are not mutually exclusive and do not total 100%)

Figure 7.5

respect to these social groups. In general, students believe that these problems are mostly caused by a lack of tolerance and empathy for difference, as well as the use of "exclusive language" by others on campus.*

Within this context, we achieve some understanding of how and why students express feelings of alienation—especially to peers and to the overall institution. In general, students complain

---

*We should note that these data came from interviews in the period 2012–2018, well before the captured-on-video murder of George Floyd in the spring of 2020 and the greatly increased attention thereafter to the Black Lives Matter movement.

that others do not truly understand them, and as a result, they separate—or silo—into groups of students that are most like them.* Students with complaints also believe that their peers don't know how to conduct productive conversations about issues of race (as well as issues about ethnicity, immigration, stereotyping, and allied concepts), which often leads to frustration, rather than to an enhanced perspective among peers. Some students also talk about blatant discrimination, intolerance, and general insensitivity, aimed especially at minority groups.†

A first-year student explains:

I guess I'm just going to say like the Black students, we feel that some people here don't really fully understand what it means to be like a person of color in general, like everything that you have to go through . . . And definitely, there are people here who understand. But yeah, it's just like sometimes you feel like you don't really fit in. And honestly, sometimes, there's like a Black student union lounge, and that's kind of a . . . people will find that upsetting because they . . . well, it is kind of exclusive, but I guess we kind of have to explain that people of color need a space to just to air out their feelings and stuff . . . It's not exclusive at all. But if there's just like a kind of stigma towards the lounge that people like, "No, it's only for Black people!" We're like, "No, anybody can come."

A graduating student who ran for student body president comments:

---

*There is of course a massive literature on this topic.

†At the time of our interviews, the notion of "DEI" (diversity, equity, and inclusion) and the concept of critical race theory were not commonly mentioned expcitly, but clearly, the informants were touching on these sensitive issues.

But the Black student community [at this school] isn't really integrated with the other parts of the school. They don't feel as comfortable talking about, in talking with white students about race and things like that. And that, I think, is a big thing that [this school] really needs to work on . . . because to me, the measure of diversity isn't the number of different races and ethnicities and religions that you have on a campus; it's how much they interact and learn from one another.

At the same time, a large proportion of students discuss problems focused on gender—an equally salient topic but one that may not have as many diverse connotations. The vast majority of students talk about the prevalence of sexual assault and harassment on campus, contributing to a fear for safety, particularly for female students. At residential campuses, students also discuss the role of Greek life and athletics—most often, they believe, not handled appropriately by the institution, including the lack of clear communication about details and resolutions of reported troubling events.

Furthermore, while students discuss issues of socioeconomic status less frequently than they cite race and gender, we find interesting differences between students in discussion of this topic. For example, at higher-selectivity schools, students focus on a lack of socioeconomic diversity, leading to a deep divide between the "haves" and the "have-nots." In general, the have-nots feel that they are not understood and thus are excluded from participation in activities. On the other hand, students at the less selective schools talk about the impact of financial challenges on their academic and college life—living at home to save money, working full or part time in addition to taking classes, and even selecting a school on the basis of affordability.[7]

A graduating student summarizes:

But I guess like in any school where you have . . . when you necessarily have to accept a certain number of students who can pay the full tuition, you know, who are just like very, very wealthy. Um, I feel like there are just these like really stubborn pockets of people who remain so defensive about what, like, when people, you know, call out inequality or call out their privilege or they maybe, you know, [they are] unconsciously hurting someone else, or discriminating against someone else and they're just like so aggressively, um, defensive and not listening. So, but I think that's everywhere and that's some, those are, that's just something that I'm going to encounter for the rest of my life.

Importantly, students not only observe these issues; nearly half of the students (45%) also talk about the way in which the problems directly impact their experience. And while students recognize that sometimes their peers and administrators work to address the range of issues, they desire more and improved efforts from the institution—improved communications (e.g., more transparency, inclusive language), policy changes (e.g., recruiting and admitting more diverse students, hiring and retaining more diverse faculty), and also more classes and content that address social issues— some students even suggest more required courses (see box 3.1).

However, we note that while students suggest *more* classes focused on these issues, at every school in our study, there are probably dozens if not hundreds of courses that touch on these issues. If the valorization of diversity is part of the mission of an institution—indeed of the sector of higher education—it needs to be intentionally and explicitly and carefully *intertwined* into the academic curriculum. The connections between academics and institutional life needs to become crystal clear for all. Some recommendations about how to do this are presented in the next section (Part IV) of this book.

One question that we cannot address directly—nor statistically—is the relationship between student demographics, on the one hand, and issues of mental health and belonging, on the other. That is because of our decision—explained in Part I, chapter 3—not to request information about race or ethnicity. Of course, on an informal basis, we noticed various demographic features, and we also have available the publicly shared statistics collected by each of our ten schools on the demography of their students. We feel fully confident in saying that mental health issues and concerns cut across the various constituencies; as for feelings of alienation, or lack of belonging, these, too, are not demographic specific, though they may well be significantly greater among students and groups that feel outside the traditional (and/ or the current) mainstream of American society.

That said, across our study, we find important correlations with regard to the ways in which students think about the college experience. Put succinctly, those students who have exploratory and transformational mental models describe a greater sense of academic belonging than those students with a transactional or inertial mental model. Furthermore, students who have a transformational mental model are more likely to indicate and discuss mental health as the biggest problem on campus. Indeed, these two findings may be interrelated: if students are more connected to their peers and their school, they may have—or may *feel* that they have—more of an understanding about the personal struggles of many on campus.

CONCLUDING THOUGHTS: TOWARD RECOMMENDATIONS

Initially, as researchers, we wanted to study the "health" of an education in the liberal arts and sciences at a time where the quality—and even the legitimacy—of that form of education was being challenged. To put it mildly, we were unprepared for the salience of mental health issues across campuses, and the increasing concern with issues of belonging and alienation. Our research methods have allowed us to pick apart these main findings, identify the chief themes and complaints, and, in many cases, demonstrate the surprising similarities across constituencies and campuses.

What is to be done? Clearly, as educational diagnosticians without psychiatric training or degrees, we are not in a position to address directly mental health concerns or feelings of alienation. We are impressed with burgeoning efforts across campuses to deal with these critical issues (see Part IV)—such as the addition of mental health experts and the training of peer counselors; creating support groups for those experiencing specific symptoms, ranging from stress and anxiety to depression and, in the most extreme instance, to avowedly destructive behaviors like self-injury or suicidal attempts; and seeking to support students who experience loneliness and isolation, which may impact their senses of belonging.

At the same time, colleges need as well to address issues of belonging and alienation directly: first, by understanding the full picture (rather than just relying on a single statistic, or a single umbrella term); and second, not just adding more projects, initiatives, and committees focused on "belonging." Indeed, in our observations, no department on campus undergoes more rapid shift in personnel and activities than the office in charge of student affairs; and this disturbing trend may reflect that the challenges—the roaring train of local and society-wide events— overwhelm the expertise. When Howard was invited many years ago to join the board of trustees of a college, he was asked to head the Committee on Student Life. He initially demurred, saying that he knew little about the topic. Pressed, he agreed to serve, think- ing that "Student Life" was a backwater, of little importance. He soon learned that in many ways it was—and remains—*the* central entity on a college campus.

In Parts II and III of this book, we have focused on our find- ings and observations with respect to two large spheres: (1) the Learner—the cognitive minds of students—through the lens of Higher Education Capital as well as the perspective of the four mental models of the college experience; and (2) Campus culture—the emotional and social facets of students, from the vantage point of two vital issues, namely, the challenges to men- tal health and the incidence of belonging and of alienation. We've presented many findings—some quite predictable, others far less so; and as appropriate and as possible, we've reflected on the causes and the possible meanings of some of these findings.

Throughout the presentation thus far, we've been the research- ers: first and foremost, as aspiring anthropologists, seeking to convey the cultures of specific campuses and, more broadly, the culture of higher education in the United States in the second decade of the twenty-first century; second, as appropriate, as qual- itative and quantitative social scientists, presenting categories and concepts that seem apt, and then carrying out and reporting key comparisons across campuses, constituencies, and other relevant groups.

As researchers, we had been critical of those books on higher education where the analysis and the prescription came before, or even instead of, the collection of relevant data. We firmly believe that knowledge and understanding must come first.

And yet, at the end of the day, as with many of our fellow authors, our goal has been to help improve the quality of higher education in the United States (and, if possible, elsewhere) today—both the experiences of students and other constituencies, and the outcomes in terms of academic achievement, intellectual growth, personal well-being, and meaningful membership in civil society.

Accordingly, in the remaining parts of the book, we relinquish the cloaks of anthropologists of education. Insofar as useful, we don the garb of clinicians—chiefly, reactivating our earlier metaphor, as clinicians with knowledge of the educational landscape who have diagnosed problems on campuses in the United States and are ready, when asked, to present some recommendations and prescriptions.

IV WHAT'S TO BE DONE

College presents a unique opportunity to learn, to explore, to prepare for the future, for the long haul, for a lifetime. Exploration
is crucial if one wants to learn how to think—to try out various
curricular and extracurricular pathways, to reflect on different
aspects of the world. Equally valuable—indeed, invaluable—is the
possibility for transformation: transformation in how you think
about the world, in your relations to other people (both those
whom you have known and those whom you are meeting for the
first time), and in your own personality, as well as your aspirations
and means for attaining such significant changes.

To be sure: working at a job, traveling to and living in new
destinations, or doing military or public service can yield significant rewards. But at the end of adolescence and the beginning of

adulthood, no other experiences can compete with several years in college. To be an inertial college student is tragic because it is in effect the loss of a once-in-a-lifetime opportunity; to be transactional is generally shortsighted. (As we noted earlier, when asked what they would do if their first job disappeared after three years, many students had never even considered that possibility.) Whatever its flaws, the four-year (and even the two-year) nonvocational higher education experience has much to recommend it.

But these laudatory goals of exploration and transformation are difficult or even impossible to achieve if students have significant mental health problems, if they feel alienated, or if they feel that the overriding purpose of college is to get their first job. The "earning over learning" state of mind can exacerbate the pressure, anxiety, and sense of inadequacy that so many students described to us.

Accordingly, though college was not created primarily for clinical or therapeutic purposes or for bonding, it's essential for all colleges to do what they can to ensure their students are healthy, eager to learn, and supported by peers and teachers, along with the institution per se. Indeed, imagine a situation where students believe that they are welcome, that they belong, that they are not having to serve many competing masters, and don't feel pressed to get only straight As. Under those favorable circumstances, the students' mental health stresses will be reduced, and they will be better prepared for the rewards that college can *uniquely* provide—an increase in Higher Education Capital, the opportunities to explore, and, possibly, to be transformed.

In the previous parts of the book, we have for the most part focused on our findings about the student experience, and appropriately so—students are the central concern of college. From here on, we institute two changes.

First, as indicated at the end of the last chapter, we shed the garb of the anthropologist and take on the role of clinician. In that capacity, we have a set of recommendations.

Second, we broaden our lens. While continuing to keep the student at the forefront of our attention, we also speak directly and make recommendations to the range of constituencies that we have studied; and we address as well the spectrum of colleges and universities in the United States (and, as appropriate, in other parts of the world).

These recommendations are based on two sources: (1) our detailed study of ten schools; and (2) our associated initiative called Aligned Programs for the 21st Century (ALPS). In that initiative, at several institutions of higher education, we identified and investigated programs that we felt were successful in aligning constituencies around strongly held and strongly communicated missions. (For details, see appendix C.)

But before activating these shifts in focus, we need to highlight a set of issues that struck us from early on in our study and have remained front and center in our thinking.

We have identified a trio of related problems: *mission sprawl*, *projectitis*, and *misalignment*. Though they each have distinctive features, these problematic phenomena are related to one another and merit discussion together. They feed into one another; and they need to be identified, confronted, and ameliorated before we—and institutions—can focus fully on what we regard as the central goals and challenges of nonvocational higher education.

Mission sprawl   Nearly all institutions of higher education—including the ones we studied—have a mission statement, usually publicly available. Not surprisingly, these mission statements differ from one another; and as with businesses and other organizations, there is no need for mission statements in any one sector to essentially duplicate one another.

But the chief problem with collegiate mission statements is not variation; *it is the multiplicity of missions within specific campuses.* Most schools say—occasionally literally, more often in effect—that they are trying to be *all things to all people*. The word cloud reproduced on p. 241 lists the words that are featured in the mission statements of our ten schools. In most cases, the actual mission statements touched on numerous separate issues; and if one reads further through catalogs and other publications, it is a rare school that has a single major mission and adheres to that mission indeed as well as in word.

As for such rare schools: in our visits to campuses across the land, we were struck by those schools that essentially have a single message—whether academic, religious, spiritual, communal—that all students are aware of and that come up spontaneously, regularly, and appropriately. We did not study a military academy or a medical or premedical school—but a single message, similarly expressed, is what we would have expected to encounter regularly on such campuses . . . to everyone's benefit. And quite possibly, we might have encountered such a focused mission at a single-sex school or a historically Black institution or a "great books" college, though we were unable to include any of these in our campus visits.

Figure 8.1

Projectitis   We've coined the term "projectitis" to describe a frequent and distinctly unhelpful ramification of mission sprawl. On campus after campus, we find a multitude of extracurricular or cocurricular activities—some initiated by students, some initiated by faculty and staff, yet others due to endowments or historical precedent, or newly acquired funds or current or erstwhile buzzwords. To be clear, the creation of what Alexis de Tocqueville called "voluntary associations" can be meritorious; but on a college campus, projectitis often exacerbates the problem identified in mission sprawl. Most individuals on campus do not know and do not care about the full range of possibilities offered; what the school highlights in its mission statement or its publications and web presence may well not be on the radar screen of other constituents; and, unfortunately, what students need or want or should (in our view) have available is often invisible, or is sidelined, or is overwhelmed by other "glitzier" entities on campus.

No single project is necessarily bad; and on occasion, it is salutary to launch new initiatives to meet newly identified priorities; but projects, centers, and initiatives need to be curated over time and pruned or eliminated when no longer helpful (especially when new ones are created). Keystone programs should be vetted by the community; they should reflect what the school truly values, embody how the institution operates, and be effective in demonstrable ways. Beware of "creeping" or even "rampant projectitis"!

Alignments and misalignments   As described in chapter 2, growing out of our study of "good work" (box 2.1), a guiding concept for our study has been alignment. As we discovered in that earlier investigation, sectors of society (ranging from professions to institutions) are more likely to function smoothly and successfully when the various constituents concur broadly about the goals of the enterprise; how best to achieve these goals; signs of success, or, alas, signs of failure.

Throughout the book, we have highlighted misalignments within constituencies (e.g., when some students feel that they belong to the academic but not the peer culture, while others feel alienated from the academic culture but identify with their peers).

And we have noted analogous misalignments across constituencies: A recurring example: the difference between the views of on-campus adults, on the one hand, and those of students and off-campus adults, on the other (see, e.g., chapters 5 and 6). Such misalignments can create confusion, engender misunderstandings, and institute "repair strategies" that may or may not be effective.

At the same time, alignment can also uncover pressing needs for an institution or sector. For example, while participants across our study express a range of ideas about changes they would recommend for the academic program (see box 3.1), we find a surprising alignment among constituency groups: the need to address social issues which affect students of different backgrounds and demographies. In this case, while new opportunities can be created, it's possible—and more likely—that existing courses, centers, clubs, and activities already exist, and simply need to be reframed and introduced explicitly to students (thereby avoiding "projectitis"). In our terms, this alignment underscores the need for colleges to onboard students explicitly and vividly to a variety of disciplinary lenses (e.g., sociological, economic, political, psychological) to explore these topics, and to effectively intertwine social issues with the academic program, in order to provide an integrated experience for students.

Of course, it's not possible to align everything; and sometimes misalignments can be stimulating and even productive. That said, in what follows, we address suggestions to a small set of paradigmatic campuses (chapter 9) and to the range of constituencies that have a stake in the success of higher education (chapter 10). In each case, as appropriate, we present our suggestions as ways to bridge misalignments and to strengthen potential alignments.

SPECIFIC CURRICULAR IMPLICATIONS: HANDS OFF

As dedicated educators, we have our own favorite courses, curricula, and concentrations. But in these pages, we avoid making targeted suggestions about what to teach or how to teach it. Exploration and transformation can come about—or be thwarted—in multiple ways. Moreover, and importantly, we believe strongly in faculty governance of the curriculum. That is, choices about what is appropriate for a specific school at a specific time in history are best made by the teachers, preceptors, and academic leaders who are close to the ground. (Of course, other constituencies should be informed about the curriculum, and choices should be justified, but we are extremely wary of intrusion by trustees or governmental agencies on these issues.)

It's important that courses and programs of study are clearly and carefully explained, expectations spelled out, and student progress monitored regularly. We strongly encourage the launching (if not the proliferation) of common courses taken by the full range of students; the avoidance of high-stake grading, particularly in the opening years; and the minimization of "weeding out" courses, insofar as possible. In introductory courses, grading should be light and formative, with plenty of opportunity for feedback and support and, optimally, consequent improvements in performance, and not just on the final examination.

Here, not incidentally, is how colleges can distinguish themselves from their peer institutions. The specific courses and programs they offer, the way that they are presented, the sequences that are featured, the culminating performances—all of these can and should be highlighted. To our mind, that's the proper ground on which institutions should compete with their peers—and not primarily on the size of the gymnasium or the number of meal choices.

Here's a summary.

Takeaway	Recommendation
The primary goal of nonvocational higher education should be to increase Higher Education Capital for a lifetime.	Develop and model a single, powerful mission statement about the importance of teaching and learning, broadly construed.
The ancillary goal of nonvocational higher education should be alignment within and across constituencies about the meaning of, and the means for, achieving the primary goal.	Clearly communicate the importance of this single mission, with attention to both direct and indirect messaging.
"Projectitis," the manifestation of mission sprawl and misalignment, is perilous to students, the institution, and the sector of higher education; in this respect, less *is* more.	Avoid "projectitis" by sculpting programs, projects, and centers that relate to the mission of the institution; drop or radically prune those that are not directly connected to the goals of the institution.

A TOOLKIT FOR ALL COLLEGES

Let's assume that this general approach makes sense and that an institution commits to making it happen.

Here we present two approaches that, we believe, on the basis of our research and reflections, are key to the improvement of nonvocational higher education.

Onboarding There should be a single powerful message present in all information about the school, including the application form and the letter of admission. Each and every student—indeed each and every constituent—should be informed and reminded of the central message.

Key to onboarding, this message should be highlighted and embodied in the opening orientation program, and revisited as often as needed. All students should come to understand and articulate: This is what *college* is about, this is what *our college* is *distinctly* about, here are positive examples, here are problematic examples, here's how we propose to realize our mission with all on campus. Moreover, these same onboarding messages should be highlighted in the first classes—taken by all students, with little grade pressure but ample chance to interact, to ask questions, and to exhibit what has been learned. *Indeed, onboarding need never, and perhaps should never, stop.* It may need to be reinforced to avoid the well-documented "sophomore slump." We should think instead of integrating onboarding—or, if you like, "remaining on deck"—throughout the college experience, through regular reminders and encouragement and embodiment of the principal themes of that college. In the later years of college, students who are farther along can and should share with new arrivals their formative experiences, and they should illustrate the ways in which, over time, these become habits, indeed second nature.

Importantly, *we should never take onboarding for granted*—it's not the job of students or parents to figure out the mission of higher education; such articulation is clearly the responsibility of the leadership, faculty, and staff of each institution.

Think back to our initial campus visit to Greenly College (chapter 1): on the typical campus tour, we found ample discussion of the luxuries and pleasures available on that campus, but relatively little mention of the educational features—labs, libraries, and museums—and equally scant attention to the courses of study, effective teachers, examples of students who are learning and who are exhibiting their learning publicly and productively, or graduates who can exhibit their Higher Educational Capital in an appealing way.

Intertwining Though certainly not necessary (and perhaps not advisable), we acknowledge that a school might choose one additional mission that is not academic in the strict sense—religious, spiritual, communal, civic, ethical, even work-related (engineering, pre-law, preparation for the workplace). One addition is possible.

But in our view, this one additional mission should not, ought not, cannot be simply an option, an add on. It needs to be thoughtfully intertwined into the curricular, cocurricular, and other "messaging" activities and platforms in the school. Moreover, there should be measures of the success of the intertwining, as well as corrections—or even scuttling—if it is not working.

One more summary:

Takeaway	Recommendation
It is imperative to focus on a single powerful mission statement so that every student (as well as other stakeholders) understands and internalizes this mission. Schools can (and perhaps should) compete with one another about the way in which they achieve their learning mission.	From day one, *onboard* students to the mission—display on campus tours and accouterments; capture in courses and in student performances; resonate in extra-curricular activities; reinforce through contact with experienced students who embody its key component.
If something else is important to convey as a mission (e.g., religion, public service, ethics), carefully select one additional secondary mission.	From day one, *intertwine* the secondary mission with the primary mission, both in campus accouterments, and across the course catalog and requirements; foreground the secondary mission in performances both in and outside of class; and have ways of ascertaining that the missions are working integrally and effectively.

In this transitional chapter, nearly all of our discussion is necessarily abstract and paradigmatic. It cries out for practical examples. Accordingly, in what follows, we seek to redeem these promissory notes in a concrete fashion.

Specifically, in chapter 9, we make hypothetical visits to four ideal type campuses. None is exactly like the ten that we studied in detail; each reflects strong and recurring impressions that emerged from our visits and from our analysis of data. In each case, we provide a sketch of each campus's strengths and challenges. And then, drawing explicitly on the scaffolding introduced here, we make targeted recommendations. We believe that these recommendations are appropriate for addressing the alignments and misalignments that we observed; and we believe that, if followed, the campus would be healthier, more centered, and more likely to create an experience that is meaningful and productive for students as well as all others with a stake in the success of the college experience.

In chapter 10, we switch lenses. Rather than focusing on campuses per se, we describe productive and meaningful college experiences to each of the several principal stakeholders of higher education. Specifically, we address presidents and trustees, faculty and administrators, parents, high school educators, students (both college and high school), and job recruiters. Much of what we say should be of interest to policymakers, legislators, and the general public. In the background (and occasionally the foreground), we have in mind what might be done to strengthen alignment across stakeholders.

Finally, in the epilogue, we reflect on our own motivations for undertaking the study, what we have gained from the study, and the stark choices that society now faces.

9 FEEDBACK TO COLLEGES

Before introducing our four specimen feedback sessions, we share an anecdote that should provide helpful context.

Many years ago, Howard attended a master class given by Dorothy DeLay, the leading American violin teacher of the era. A high school student performed, exhibiting many features that did not sound good to Howard's modestly trained ear.

After the performance, Miss DeLay (as she was universally addressed) said only two things to the student. Howard was perplexed and asked why this restrained feedback. She responded, "I said the two things that he *most* needed to hear."

On any college campus, in light of the findings, we could report many problems and make many recommendations. But as with Miss DeLay's student, numerous suggestions and recommendations on a variety of topics are not likely to be heard, acknowledged, or acted upon; indeed, in all likelihood, they would be promptly forgotten.

Accordingly, in each of these "rounds" conducted at four "ideal type" colleges, along with a summary of findings (as presented in chapter 8) and some words of praise (which we have abbreviated), *we focus sharply on a single problematic area and make a few specific suggestions.* Most of these suggestions are based on our investigation of programs at colleges and universities throughout the United States that align various goals of different constituencies. As with Miss DeLay's student, we hope that such highly targeted feedback will prove more useful and will be more likely to be acted on effectively.

A FRAGMENTED CAMPUS: ROUNDS FOR COLLEGE A

Our Report

Without question, it's energizing to become acquainted with College A. There are so many exciting things going on, in so many places, that it looks like you can legitimately claim to be "all things to all students." When we first arrived on campus and attended the admission information session, we heard about the plethora of centers, programs, and services available for students, alums, and also parents.

And yet, paradoxically, *that apparent strength turns out to be highly problematic.* We found that when we speak to various persons— both within and across constituencies—there are few common experiences, few activities and campus resources that are widely shared or even widely known.

And so, we offer, tentatively, a diagnosis. We believe that College A is suffering from what we have termed "mission impossible," or, more colloquially, "projectitis." It seems that whenever some kind of an issue, need, desire, or alumni gift comes up, the school is grateful and accepting—setting up a new department, initiative, or center. (As one cynical faculty member quipped: "Every time I hear of a newly funded center, I think, '*De*center.'")

Our Prescription

Of course, it's easy to come up with mission statements—one can beg, borrow, steal, or even create. The challenge is to come up with one that's *appropriate* for your school; that's readily understandable; that the various constituents are willing to buy into; and, most important, that can resonate throughout the community in many ways and at many times. Then, once agreed upon, the school needs to *embody* the mission—so that even a casual visitor knows what College A is about and can see, hear, or feel it in action. In other words, rather than detailing the range of programs and opportunities for students in an information session, admissions staff could (and should) outline how specific programs are integral to the distinctive experience of College A. Ideally, any significant program should clearly reflect—indeed, embody—the school's announced purpose and mission.

As underscored (in our accompanying report or in *The Real World of College*), we assume that in an institution that is not specifically vocational, the principal mission must be academic. But under that umbrella term, there is plenty of room to highlight what is special, even unique, about your curriculum, your teaching, your assessments, and the kind of graduate that you hope to fashion out of the experience at College A.

Having a mission that is academic, that you embody, and that you live up to is not easy. It is perhaps least problematic at religious institutions, where most members of the campus endorse a particular spiritual mission—for example, Mormon schools, Jesuit schools, Quaker schools, or Jewish schools. In past decades, historically Black colleges had a mission, as did military schools. But as times change and the population becomes increasingly heterogeneous, one cannot count on students and other constituencies knowing the meaning (or perhaps even the name) of the creed. Furthermore, the religious origins of many US colleges and universities are largely irrelevant (if even known) to current members of the community, and invisible in most of its contemporary practices.

And yet, we have found that a historical religious origin can still be advantageous. One of our campuses, DePaul University in Chicago, is a Vincentian school—and the Vincentian mission is known and respected widely. And that awareness extends to students who upon arrival on campus had never heard of the Vincentian creed, which features an emphasis on service and contributing to the "collective good." For more than twenty years, the school offers a Vincentian Service Day for students, staff, faculty, and alums. Similarly, another school at which we spent a great deal of time, University of La Verne in Southern California, was founded by a member of the Brethren—a religious order focused on peace and social responsibility. Now, over a century later, with a highly diverse demography, many students at La Verne talk about these emphases as they relate to their academic program and service work outside of the classroom.[1]

Having a credible and achievable mission might even be the "royal road" to a campus where "I" gives way to "we"—where stakeholders become aligned with one another. Assuming that you've become convinced that a central organizing mission is important and feasible, what steps should you take?

Throughout our work, we have come to value two distinct stances that are also complementary: onboarding and intertwining.

In speaking of onboarding, we emphasize the importance of letting all constituencies know, from day one, what the mission is, why it is important, how it can be achieved, and—more challenging but equally important—the consequences if the mission is *not* pursued, and accordingly, *not* achieved. And so, in descriptions of the school, its central mission should be absolutely, unequivocally central. When students are admitted to the school, they should be reminded of the mission—not in a ham-handed way, to be sure, but in a way that is appealing, alluring, and achievable.

If successful, onboarding should make the mission vivid for all students (indeed, all newcomers) during the first months of college. But such an achievement is by no means certain. And so, we recommend that onboarding continue, as needed, throughout as much of the college experience as feasible (think of it as "omniboarding" or "through-boarding"), and perhaps even thereafter (in which cases, there'll be no need for "off-boarding!").

No one has any doubt about the mission of the Naval Academy. But left to its own devices, the mission can come to seem an occasion for lip service, if not increasingly vestigial. And so, we emphatically embrace a practice that we term *intertwining*. Since, as we have argued, the only major legitimate purpose of an avowedly nonvocational college is an academic one, any additional mission needs to be carefully and thoroughly intertwined with the academic mission.

Let's say that an important mission of the school is civic engagement (as is the case at Tufts University). It's fine to proclaim this mission and to support it with attractive slogans and banners, vibrant artwork, performances, clubs, and the like. But unless this mission also becomes an integral part of the academic curriculum, you are likely to find yourself in a lose-lose situation.

Suppose, building on such a mission, the school chooses to highlight public service. Accordingly, a large swathe of the curriculum should provide opportunities to study individuals and entities involved in public service and—importantly—should make use of any and all disciplines and perspectives that are pertinent to understanding and effectively pursuing of public service.

Clearly, the social sciences offer a ready and appropriate set of tools for understanding and pursuing public service. Our world offers a plethora of problems where the natural sciences can be helpful—whether these challenges focus on climate change, material and cyber-weaponry, pandemics and other diseases, food supply, or other urgent matters. The arts and humanities can also be readily connected to public service, through probing examination of art or literature that addresses or provides context for today's social issues: for example, the plays of Henrik Ibsen or Lorraine Hansberry, the novels of John Steinbeck or Toni Morrison, the art work of Frida Kahlo or Diego Rivera, the dance choreography of Martha Graham or Mark Morris.

In many ways, the First-Year La Verne Experience (FLEX) communities at the aforementioned University of La Verne exemplify both practices: *onboarding* students to a clear mission and *intertwining* that mission with the academic program. FLEX provides opportunities for students to work together as they carry out the school's long-term mission of "service to others." In small cohorts, first-year students (most of whom commute to campus) take a pair of courses that, from different disciplinary perspectives, focus on service; in addition, they take a writing course. Each learning community engages in a service project (on campus or off campus) during orientation week; and some of the learning communities incorporate service work into course assignments throughout the academic year—drawing on knowledge and skills that students acquire in class. The goal of each interdisciplinary learning community is that every student should develop an identity as a student on campus *and* as a contributing member of the local community.

A TRANSACTIONAL CAMPUS: ROUNDS FOR COLLEGE B

Our Report

We've enjoyed visiting College B; it's clearly a pleasant and friendly environment for students, faculty, and administrators. In fact, we found less evidence here of feelings of alienation, or lack of belonging, than at other schools we've visited. Indeed, most of those involved with College B—particularly the students and parents—seem to be quite pleased with the experience. This feeling of belonging is valuable—indeed, invaluable—and you should be pleased with such "customer satisfaction." Bravo!

But you should not—indeed, we would insist you *must not*—rest on these laurels. It's a positive sign that students feel connected to peers and to campus. But we are concerned with the commonly shared perspectives among your students—one that does not mesh with our own core values—about *why* it is important to college; *what* they want to get out of college; and *what* they deem to be the purpose of college. Indeed, to put it dramatically, *whether* there is any valid reason to have college or colleges at all.

What's yielded this disturbing result? In over one hundred interviews with students at College B, we learned that very few of these undergraduates thought of college as a place where they could grow, change, and reflect on the kind of person they want to be and might become. In fact, though pleasant and kind, the students at College B reminded us of the collection of students (described in chapter 3 of our book) who chatted about their college experiences for an hour without ever touching on anything even vaguely academic.

Worrisomely and disappointingly, at College B, we found a sizable majority of students took a "transactional" approach; and the percentage of these transactional students increased rather sharply over the course of college (first year to graduating year). In contrast, those students who had more exploratory or transformational mental models—not a high number at the start—dwindled between first year and the year of graduation.

You might say, "Well, students at College B, and their parents are satisfied customers—and that's what's important—why rock the boat?" Tossing our terminology back at us, you might even say "Hey, we are aligned!"

But we would counter with "Satisfied? That's a low bar, a depressing lowest common denominator for an institution dedicated to learning." For one thing, consider your highly motivated faculty—who—as we learned from speaking to them—came here for the opportunity to work seriously with (and, with luck, to stretch) the undergraduate students. We learned of several professors who left as soon as another career opportunity presented itself and did not look back with affection on their years at College B. Moreover, if it turns out that graduates of your peer schools do better in later life—in terms of professional status, contributions to society, indeed contributions to their school's coffers—than do your own graduates, then, over the long haul you will have to scramble, if not dismantle. And so, we would add: we are struck by the school's current *lack of alignment* with the goals of its own faculty and with the deeper reasons for having an institution of higher education.

Our Prescription

From the moment of admission, students (and their parents) should learn about the many opportunities for change and growth that are accessible during their years at College B (we refer to this as "onboarding"). Of course, this learning should be lively, energetic, and concrete. Students should have the chance to meet and interact with recent graduates who have transcended a transactional stance. Students should also be exposed to experiences that have considerable potential for broadening their perspectives. And you should not hide the costs of remaining in a transactional mode—not only for the four years of college but perhaps throughout life . . . a life that doubtless will spawn—and perhaps hurl—numerous challenges for which students have not been prepared.

Importantly, we have data here. In comparison to other schools of equal selectivity, the majority of incoming students at College B displayed low Higher Educational Capital and, regrettably, the level of HEDCAP exhibited by graduating students was not much higher. Across the range of campuses that we studied, students who are willing to "step forth" in class and "dig deeply" into their academic assignments are far more likely than their peers to display more HEDCAP; to graduate successfully and on time; and to appreciate the aspects, aspirations, and accolades of college other than simply getting a job—whatever that job may turn out to be.

Of course, such growth requires more than a few days of orientation, more than a few seminars during the first months of school. Here is where "intertwining" comes in. Like most other colleges, College B offers many courses that span the disciplinary spectrum. But it's our observation that cheating is rampant on campus; and sadly, neither students nor faculty appear willing to address and solve the problem. (For student views of academic dishonesty, see box 10.2.)

Not only should there be copious assignments and projects where cheating is not possible. Far more important, students should be asked to carry out work that is mind-expanding; projects and problem sets that stimulate them to take on new roles and try out unfamiliar ways of thinking. Moreover, it goes without saying that *all* on campus should understand how handing in work that is not your own undermines the core idea of education (drawing on and displaying what *you* have learned). Those who do not honor this basic precept have no place anywhere on any campus.

A contrast case. At Olin College of Engineering (included in our study as a "comparison" school because of its avowedly vocational focus), where the academic work mainly involves collaboration on projects, students often told us that it was not possible to cheat. Students were being asked to devise and create work that is novel in form and/or content—work that they could not plagiarize, copy, or steal from elsewhere. Furthermore, the collaborative work makes each student feel responsible to contributing to the group's effort—as opposed to a patently competitive atmosphere where students may use dishonest means in a deplorable effort to get ahead of their peers. Instead of encouraging or ignoring cheating, the culture at Olin ostracizes the *thought* of cheating; alignment entails the recognition of each student's contributions to a project.

Other campuses provide helpful examples. In natural science laboratories, students can collaborate on projects in which their teachers have an abiding interest and where the findings obtained can matter for broader society. (As a bonus, the committed student might secure a publication and/or a trip to a conference.) In the social sciences, students can address challenging issues in their community—ones where they have the chance to collect relevant data and make palpable and perhaps even lasting progress with respect to tackling such issues. And in the humanities, students can study works (plays, poems, pictures) that deal with growth and change in various ways; further, they can have the opportunity, in an artistic symbol system (more technically, in a "semiotic" system) of their own choosing, to explore their own life trajectory—where have they come from, what is currently important to them, to what do they aspire and why?

If you have followed us, you may be saying, "Aha, that's the problem. Our students *do not want* to stretch." That may be true, but it's very different from saying, "Our students *cannot* stretch." They can! They should! It's your job, indeed your calling, as trustees, faculty, administrators, counselors to show how *you* have stretched—including recounting efforts in school (or at the workplace) that did not initially work, but from which you nonetheless made gains or learned lessons—and to help these students do the same.

It's timely to mention the Focus Program at Duke University. Optional for first semester students, Focus encourages newcomers to enroll in classes that address a topic that excites their interest. Students apply to "clusters," which consist of two interdisciplinary courses (capped at eighteen students) that make up half of their course load for the semester. (A sample course: The Law and the Human Brain.) Students live in dormitories with their cluster peers and attend weekly dinners with faculty; these gatherings regularly include a featured guest speaker, a student debate, or another relevant activity. Accordingly, these Focus students spend at least half of their classroom time in small groups of students with whom they live, while also receiving individualized attention from faculty. If carefully and explicitly intertwined with the academic mission, these opportunities can draw students out of their "transactional" mindsets, stretching their intellectual, social, and personal comfort zones.

What else might you consider? Invite students out to lunch in a comfortable setting, attend their extracurricular activities (especially the more cognitively demanding ones)—indeed, co-lead their activities: share with their fun, share with their work (optimally, in the spirit of "flow," effort and pleasure will intertwine).[2] Collaborating as a community, you can catalyze the change of your school's culture from transactional to transformational. Indeed, as more students explore, many of them may be transformed in ways that please you, their parents, and the students themselves.

As noted, your "transactional" students see college as a necessary, and hopefully not demanding, transition to work—presumably a job that they can envision at the moment. You can turn this "work focus" into an advantage. Help students get internships or jobs at workplaces that call on and exhibit those skills of critical and creative thinking that are commonly lauded, as well as those "soft skills" that are especially prized in the twenty-first century. Help students understand that the best preparation for a life of rewarding work is to increase and display their Higher Education Capital.

Time for an example. We are impressed by the Minnesota Innovative Scholars Program (MISP). College sophomores and juniors receive a stipend from the Minnesota Private College Council. Their assignment: evaluate a drug, treatment, or prosthetic that is currently being considered for adoption by the well known and

highly regarded Mayo Clinic. In pursuing these genuine challenges, students begin to acquire relevant scientific, medical,
economic, and/or entrepreneurial skills. And, as a bonus, they
present their findings and recommendations to the Mayo Clinic
community, made up of doctors as well as others interested in
possible applications of the recommendations.

MISP constitutes but one way to intertwine work and academic
pursuits—to motivate the transactional student toward exploration or even transformation. As added examples, we cite efforts
at Bates College that help students find broader purpose for their
lives; Berea College, which requires every student to work *on campus*; and Northeastern University, which helps students secure
internships *off campus*, to intertwine work into the academic program. Contact such schools and programs, share with them—you
can learn from one another. Perhaps the most impressive example
of intertwining occurs at Olin College of Engineering (as previously mentioned). Based on the belief that engineering "starts
with people and ends with people," Olin takes a broad curriculum
very seriously. In addition to courses offered (and required) in
the arts, humanities, and social sciences, Olin students are also
encouraged to take courses at neighboring liberal arts colleges like
Wellesley College and Brandeis University.

AN ALIENATED CAMPUS: ROUNDS FOR COLLEGE C

Our Report

In many ways, your school is admirable. You have taken on some
of the most formidable challenges in higher education. You

strive to help students who are largely first-generation college students—many from impoverished backgrounds, on governmental scholarships, and/or lacking adequate secondary school experiences. You stretch to introduce them to the beauty and power of the liberal arts and sciences—a conception of knowledge about which most know little and, indeed, many prove unable to define. Moreover, you have succeeded in inculcating high aspirations in some of them—though, as you know, your completion rate continues to be disappointing. We have visited peer schools that lack your impressive aspirations—and, accordingly, their students achieve and exemplify less than do your students. (Indeed, we think to ourselves, you have done much of what we believe that College B should be doing.)

However, your ambition has come at a severe cost. Across the nation, and in our study, about two-thirds of the student body demonstrate a sense of belonging; some of them identify with the academic agenda, some of them feel close to their peers, and others identify strongly with the mission and spirit of the institution—its aspirations, its goals, and its athletic teams.

Regrettably, however, at College C, this feeling of belonging is far less evident. In fact, only about 40% of the students whom we interviewed indicate a feeling of belonging. And, even more regrettably, nearly a quarter of students went out of the way to convey to us the extent to which they feel *alienated* from peers, from their studies, and from the institution in general. It's no surprise that while mental health has been reported as a problem on college campuses nationwide, its severity seems to be more acute at your campus than at others we studied.

Our Prescription

The last thing that we would recommend is that you attenuate your ambitious goals with respect to an education that is not primarily vocational. In this sphere, you are far ahead of your peer institutions—you are a poster campus, so to speak. You have clearly stated your mission: an institution that focuses on broad education across various fields of knowledge and diverse ways of knowing.

But we encourage you to be more deliberate and explicit in onboarding your students to the academic program and the mission that you have adopted; and, whenever and however possible, to connect it to their activities on campus.

Onboarding first. It is clear that many of your students face challenges in balancing academic work with their outside lives. Many are overwhelmed by the requirements of their courses—often in subjects or in topics that are not familiar to them. Without abandoning this admirable goal, you should strive to smooth their entrance to the academic work.

To begin with, initial courses should be taken by *all students* at the school, and they should constitute a major "talking point" across the campus. We have been impressed by what have been called Explicit Courses—originated some years ago at Amherst College by Jeffrey Ferguson, an English professor. Amherst undergraduates often believe that, because they have graduated from high school, they must be ready for college. But in fact, even students with apparently strong high school education backgrounds do not really know how to read a book critically; how to write a paper that is clear and that displays deep analysis (rather than just repeating back assigned content); how to frame and pursue an effective argument; or how to launch and complete a research project in a timely and organized manner.

Ferguson created a set of courses in which the instructor models and makes explicit each of the steps taken by individuals who are proficient at these tasks. For example, in reading a book, how to make sense of the title, interpret the table of contents, bibliography, index, and the illustrations. More specific skills include reading summary paragraphs, ferreting out questions that the text purports to answer, checking whether and, if so, how these questions are engaged, making use of the preface, as well as perusing published reviews of the book in well-curated publications.

By the same token, when one writes a paper: studying examples of effective and ineffective passages and papers, carrying out critiques of these papers and of those written by classmates, outlining the major points, dissecting abstracts, noticing and summarizing arguments and counterarguments, and so on.

Not only do such explicit courses demystify the agenda of college; they give students common reference points they can talk about, use to support and critique one another, and draw on in subsequent study. Indeed, in the happiest instances, students begin to do some of the work that faculty traditionally do, thereby demonstrating that students have internalized key features of a broad, general education—or, in our terms, strengthened their HEDCAP.

It's worth noting that while these explicit courses were originally developed to help first-generation students, students with apparently more privileged social and economic backgrounds also choose to take them.

As for intertwining: There are numerous ways in which schools can help students feel more connected to the academic program, their peers, and the overall institution. Starting with courses, it makes sense to commence with material familiar to students—their own lives, their own neighborhoods, hobbies, friends and foes; and to encourage debates on topics of interest to them or to current "hot button" topics. Featured might be social issues—ones focused on gender, religion, sexuality, socioeconomic status, race and ethnicity, and/or politics—that students on all campuses confront. Students are more comfortable probing and discussing topics that feel relevant to their lives, and this goal can be readily accomplished through judicious examples drawn from literature, newspapers, films, videos, and podcasts. Students on a range of campuses have told us that they would like more of these opportunities (see box 3.1); indeed these opportunities would help prepare students for "real world" dilemmas. Also, if possible, we recommend inviting graduate or graduating students, or recent alums, to the classroom to model the now polished skills that you are trying to inculcate in today's students.

Turning to the faculty side of the equation, it is counterproductive to lament the lack of preparation of many students. It's not the fault of the students, but rather of earlier preparation, or—more properly—lack of preparation, inadequate expectations, fuzzy standards, and unhelpful messages emanating from the broader society.

It is the college's job to meet students where they are and then to communicate, in as many effective ways as possible, its conviction that students can and will grow. With judicious scaffolding, students *can* do the work. Some students need more regular advising—by faculty and/or staff—to provide support and modeling; and such students may need guidance in how to secure help when it is needed (attending office hours or going to the writing center); how to navigate diverse views in the classroom, for example opposing political or religious views; and how to balance a heavy course load with familial responsibilities. Yes, it is primarily the students' responsibility to manage their own work and lives; but some students might need to be set, and then continually guided, on a sensible path, long before things become overwhelming.

We'll mention some ways this can be accomplished. There's the effective (though costly) program—Accelerated Study in Associated Programs (ASAP) at City University of New York—that provides regular guidance and advising for every student; the semistructured "STEP" initiative (Second-year Transformational Experience Program) at The Ohio State University, in which sophomores and faculty each receive modest stipends to work together on research projects; and the cost-free effort at California State University, Northridge, to connect faculty with students. In the latter case, faculty and staff post stickers on their office doors to let students know they identify with them: "I am an immigrant," "I failed one or more classes in college," "I am multiracial." Importantly, not all approaches need to involve faculty. Students should be encouraged to bond with one another and begin to rely on each other. For example, peer counseling programs (such as the one at Kenyon College) can be extremely useful; students have the chance to talk with one another about common challenges. Also, access to peers is much easier (and less expensive) than access to counselors. Certainly, the "wait time" for a peer to counsel a student is certainly more efficient than "wait times" at a mental health center—provided, of course, that the issue is one that a peer is equipped to handle.

Helping students have constructive dialogue with one another—with respect to navigating social issues, for example—can also enhance peer belonging. Queens College, which represents one of the most diverse zip codes in the country, has developed an approach that catalyzes healthy dialogue. The CERRU Fellowship Program (Center for Ethnic, Racial, and Religious Understanding) creates an intimate but intense space where participants engage in interrogating their own viewpoints while also learning about and probing the perspectives of other fellows. In the spirit of debating, the program entails the establishment of clear ground rules, such as an insistence on respectful and open discussion that avoids accusatory language. Such a program can create strong bonds among the fellows—ones that can be extended to others on campus.

Academics should be central in any college; it's admirable that you have put them at the forefront. The thrill of exploring new topics and ways of thinking, of communicating them to others (including friends and family), and of drawing on them in one's own reflective and productive activities should be at the forefront of every classroom and visible across the campus. But that does not mean that the cycle of studying, learning, and assessing should be drudgery. You—the faculty, trustees, and senior administrators gathered here—would presumably not have chosen to make higher education central in your lives if you did not believe in the mission; we suspect that you would not trade your work for employment in another sector, even one less demanding and possibly more lucrative. You have chosen exactly the right mission for College C; now the challenge is to help your students (and others) feel connected to that mission.

A "FUN" CAMPUS: ROUNDS FOR COLLEGE D

Our Report

No question about it, most of your constituency groups are happy with their experiences at College D. Students have few qualms with the administration, and they describe most of their fellow students as "nice," "fun," and "friendly." They love the weather! In fact, when asked, in the course of our interview, what they might do, given a week without obligations, most students respond that they would do much of what they do during the regular school year—go to the gym, hang out with their friends, or take a road trip to canoe or hike (see box 2.2).

So, what's the problem? Indeed, *is* there one?

Put sharply, students at your school do not seem to view college as an academic pursuit. Indeed, we find that at your school, scores of Higher Education Capital for first-year students are quite low (higher percentage of score of 1 than 2 or 3); but unlike most other schools in our study, the scores of graduating students stay low. At College D, the intellectual needle hardly moves.

To be specific: at your school, while 40% of first-year students have low HEDCAP (score of 1), the same percentage of graduating students also have this score. And, while at most schools, the percentage of high scores of HEDCAP (score 3) doubles between first-year students and graduating students, at your school, we only see a slight increase (20% of first-year students have score 3, compared to 25% of graduating students with this score). Furthermore, young alums from College D don't do much better. We find that only 13% of these individuals are scored as having high HEDCAP.

Note that we score HEDCAP in two ways for each participant: First, without any identifying information, we score the responses to seven individual interview questions; and then we give a "holistic" score based on the entire interview. The responses to the seven questions provide some concrete examples. On the question of which book to recommend to students before they leave college, more students at your school, compared to other schools, *could not name any book at all* or really struggled to come up with a title, often claiming "I don't read that much." Moreover, those who named a book referred to titles that were more suitable to high school (e.g., *Catcher in the Rye* or *To Kill a Mockingbird*) or even elementary school books, like Dr. Seuss (*Oh, the Places You'll Go!*), or popular forms of literature, such as the Harry Potter series. More important than the titles themselves, students did not offer full or convincing explanations for *why* these books are important—the reason that their HEDCAP scores for this question were low. For example, we often heard "I don't know, I just liked it," or "the book helped me to consider important issues," without any further explanation of the important issues (see box 9.1).

Let's turn to the question "Is it important to go to college?" While most students at College D respond "yes"—which pleases

Box 9.1

The Book Question: Surprises and Meanings

Sophie Blumert

What do Dr. Seuss, Harper Lee, and Plato have in common? These authors, though wildly different from each other, are most frequently mentioned by participants in response to our request that they recommend books and explain their choice. The answers yield some of the most varied—and confusing—data from every constituency group in our study. While Dr. Seuss (more specifically *Oh, the Places You'll Go!*) is the top recommendation across all participants, and each constituency group mention him at least once, this response only makes up 2% of the entire sample of titles and authors. And Plato? Only 1%.

We asked all respondents to answer the following question: "If you could give one book to students before they leave college, which book might it be?" We thought this question would provide insight into the respondents' attitudes to scholarly knowledge and aspirations. Privately, we hoped that the books would be worth revisiting—for example, the plays of Shakespeare, the novels of Toni Morrison, or the theories of Karl Marx. In short, we had "Great Expectations."

Our first surprise is the reaction to this question. Our impression is that many participants, from multiple constituency groups, felt like they were being put on the spot by the question. Instead of relishing in the opportunity to think about books, participants appeared vulnerable and uneasy as they racked their brains—and sometimes scanned their bookshelves—for a suggestion. To avoid an embarrassing situation, we sometimes offered an alternative— for example, a film, or a message to students.

The second surprise comes from the high percentage of "non-college" suggestions. For instance, a large number of the suggested books fall into two distinct groups: high school books and self-help books. Approximately 14% of all titles recommended across constituency groups have traditionally been introduced in high school (e.g., *The Catcher in the Rye*, *Brave New World*). While first-year students (understandably) recommend these books most frequently (17%), other participants are not far off—graduating students and young alums suggest high school books 12% of the time; parents, trustees, and faculty 13%; and administrators 15%. While these books may be considered classics, it still is surprising—and maybe disheartening—that a number of participants, students and adults alike, suggest titles that don't necessarily require a college education to read and understand.

But even more popular than high school books are the aforementioned "self-help/personal development" books. This is an exceedingly popular genre for almost every constituency group, a fifth of all title suggestions. We are surprised even further by the number of books about professional success, rather than introspection and self-reflection (e.g., *How to Win Friends and Influence People*, *The 7 Habits of Highly Effective People*). It is possible that the framing of the question led participants to believe that these books could be helpful to students as they go out into the "real world"; however, plenty of books in college-level curricula get at the same meaning (or go even deeper). Put bluntly, and unapologetically, we are disappointed by this finding.

One noteworthy trend is the emphasis on social issues. Out of all of the suggestions across all constituency groups, nearly half (47%) address content explicitly related to race, gender, politics, and more. This result aligns well with our findings about social issues more broadly (see box 3.1). All participants organically raise these topics across the transcript in high frequencies, so it is not unexpected that it appears during this question as well. It also provides us with a possible explanation for the surprising presence of high school books. Texts such as *To Kill a Mockingbird*, *The Great Gatsby*, and *1984* are often a student's first introduction to powerful stories about social issues—still relevant decades after publication.

However, within this context, we find that only 7% of these titles are typically college-level reading (and the number of college books suggested is quite low). An interesting puzzle: students are eager to read books that address social issues, and adults readily recommend them, but the majority of titles come from a high school reading list. Clearly, high school should not be the only exposure that students have to this type of literary content. Knowing that these are salient issues for college students, higher education has the unique opportunity to help them navigate these complex issues through books.

Of course, we did not simply pay attention to the choice of book but also to the rationale. In this context, consider two students.

Peter offers a title that may seem "impressive" on the surface, but he does not demonstrate anything substantive from it:

Well . . . I mean, well, I read . . . earlier this year I took a class on Dante's *Divine Comedy* and . . . that one was interesting I guess. You know, I, it's kind of an interesting way to think about things . . . an interesting way to . . . there's some interesting philosophical ideas in that book and . . . I don't know. Maybe. I don't know if it would, you know, really, you know, really, really teach anyone anything, but, you know . . . I enjoyed reading it and it was also an interesting perspective, I guess.

In contrast, Clara gives a thoughtful answer about a children's book:

Perloo the Bold by Avi . . . So, it's actually my favorite book. What's interesting about the book is you can read it in fourth grade, and that's when

I read it. It's about a rabbit, an anthropomorphized rabbit and these foxes are clashing clans . . . Both cultures treat this certain bird as sort of their deity . . . there's a lot of similarities between how both of these cultures think . . . they're both so focused on fighting each other that they don't realize their innate ability to cooperate. I think that story, kind of, speaks to, I guess, the empathy that we have to have for a lot of other people. The fact that we have to keep an open mind and have a better perspective about not just like what might be important to us, but what other people are thinking, what might be important to other people. Understanding, not just what motivates other people, but also what interests other people.

In an ideal world, we want students to be reading broadly and willingly. With this in mind, we suggest that faculty need to spend more time connecting the meaning of classic texts to issues of the twenty-first century. Why is John Stuart Mill relevant to an impeachment hearing? How did W. E. B. Du Bois pinpoint the defining issue of the twentieth century, and how does it connect with issues today? In addition to these texts, consider also including some contemporary (but still rigorous) books that appropriately complement these classics. No student should leave college without the experience of learning from reading significant texts.

us—they lacked a coherent account about *why* they believe college is important. Students often responded that college is important because it is a societal expectation (it's required nowadays, just like high school), and if one wants to get a decent job, one needs a college degree. Though these responses are understandable, they do not reflect high HEDCAP. Higher scored responses might address how or why societal expectations might be different today than at other times; where in different regions of the country these societal expectations might be different; questioning what we mean by "important"—important for the self, for parents, for employers, and/or for society as a whole.

Clearly, most students seem happy at College D, but they don't exhibit the intellectual growth and depth—critical and creative thinking, questioning, formulating arguments—that college is presumably designed to inculcate.

Rest assured: We are not villains from a novel by Charles Dickens—we don't believe that college should be drudgery, only gradgrindian hard work, hard times, the "worst of times"—and no fun. But we find ourselves in agreement with Plato who contended (we paraphrase) that "the purpose of education is to make you *want* to do, to make you *like* to do, what you *have* to do."

We believe that ultimately your students (and your alums) would be more satisfied—and perhaps lead lives of greater significance—if they experienced "deep" rather than "superficial" engagement with broad-gauged learning. To be sure, college can and should be enjoyable, even fun—friendships made and nurtured, adventures that one might not have at home. But we advocate "deep learning."*

---

*The added value of college inheres in academic and intellectual experiences that come from using your mind well, learning new things, interacting with faculty, arriving at a justifiable conviction that you understand the world better and can build on that understanding to help make a better world.

Our Prescription

Ways to achieve this education goal are easily listed. But its realization requires a commitment to an intellectually rigorous agenda coupled with the personnel who have the competence and the motivation to effect it. To begin with, you need to understand your students and where they are at this point in their lives. And then you need to set an example and to provide lively, vivid illustrations of where you would like them to arrive by the conclusion of their years in college . . . and then help them in every way possible to move toward the wider and deeper use of their mental powers. You—leaders of your campus and your community—would not be where you are today, doing what you are doing, if you had not, at some point, gone beyond the superficial to deeper forms of engagement (which applies to all experiences—basketball, a capella singing, chess mastery, even research in the social sciences). You need to find ways—with student populations that may differ from those in the past or those with whom you grew up—to ignite intellectual curiosity and support its flourishing.

Accordingly, it is necessary to take a step back and to explain to students how a well-rounded education—one that focuses on more than just a strictly vocational preparation—not only helps an individual, but also helps society, for the long term. While most students do not understand the term "liberal arts" (see box 3.2), they can begin to understand its benefits: how knowledge and skills learned in college can be useful for the rest of one's professional and personal lives—from teaching, to raising children, to serving as an engaged citizen. Deep learning endures over time, and gives students a lifelong ability to contribute meaningfully—as well as useful and transferable skills in professional and civic contexts.

No need to start from scratch. We are not committed to a specific curriculum—that is and should remain the purview of your faculty. But bear with us: let's consider how the youthful mind can be enriched by two subjects whose proper academic names may be forbidding—philosophy and semiotics.

It's quite likely that most of your students have not heard of these terms—and virtually certain that they have not come to college specifically to study "big questions" or "ways in which we communicate or fail to communicate" or "ways in which we understand, or fail to understand." And yet, as adolescents or young adults, these students have a capacity—which (according to studies in developmental psychology) most younger persons lack: the capacity to understand the nature and purposes of those disciplines and their key concepts.[3] With lively messaging and inspiring modeling, students should have the motivation to be able to draw on them readily, appropriately, and satisfyingly.

Let's put aside the course catalog. Think about how adolescents or young adults watch a movie or a play or encounter a controversial event in the community, one that blankets the news or is featured on podcasts. It's natural for students to become interested in such a topic; to try to understand; to share their understanding with others—those with whom they agree or disagree, those who understand more or less than they do, those who question or challenge, as well as those who are hesitant to speak.

To be sure, such immersion in "real-life issues" occurs throughout childhood as well. Kids watch movies or television, read magazines or books, talk about a sudden death or an unusual spate of weather; and some can reflect on what they have been saying. But here is where courses like introductions to philosophy and semiotics come in. Only when you are able to think with some distance and some depth about such issues—truth, goodness, love, conflict, prejudice, or anger—are you able to adopt a philosophical stance.[4] And by the same token, only when you can assume some distance from symbols—words, pictures, sign language, mathematical ciphers, various kinds of computational languages, codes, and algorithms—are you able to enter the heartland of semiotics.[5] To adopt a phrase from educational psychology, only during the late teenage years are most students able to "go meta"—to reflect on their learning, what's readily available and what's lacking, and to work directly with abstract disciplines like philosophy and semiotics. They are able to say, "Z claims A, and Y claims B; they agree about C," and the best chance to reach a consensus is to explore D through F." And, to shift from philosophy to semiotics: "It would help if Y could dramatize B, and X could draw a diagram of A, if X and Y could agree on which definition of E they embrace; they then might be able to ascertain common ground as well as genuine bones of contention."[6]

When well done, such an introductory course or two—can open up a universe: one that you can explore as long as your mind remains active. And, to invoke our two favorite terms, it's even better if you have an initial "onboarding course" in Tackling Big Questions (a.k.a. philosophy) and in Making and Communicating Meanings (a.k.a. as semiotics); or, as we observed on one campus, a thought- and controversy-filled introduction to anthropology—followed by "intertwining" of its themes through-out one's subsequent sequence of courses.

To be concrete: Whether you are studying literary epics or microeconomics, brain scans or abstract art, advanced courses on such topics should take advantage of the initial entry onboarding courses; and via such courses, students should have the oppor-tunity to revisit their philosophical and semiotic implications throughout their entire college career—and across the entire course catalog.

You may well be familiar with techniques that have been used successfully to engage students in learning—including learn-ing that can be challenging. For example, history can be taught through the re-creation of debates from the past (dating back to the founding of the United States), the powers that should be afforded to the federal government as compared to those left to the states, à la the program of high school and college discussion developed by David Moss.[7] Or history can be taught through enact-ing the roles that emerge in highly charged situations, like those occupied by different individuals or cohorts in the opening years of the French Revolution, in a widely used program called "React-ing to the Past."[8] In addition, students can be encouraged—or even required—to work on a research project with the guidance of a professor, or an advanced graduate student, or indeed *any* informed resident of a surrounding community who enjoys exploring topics of substance with students enrolled in the local college. Faculty and students can collaborate on inviting stimulat-ing guests to campus and then arranging discussions with those speakers online—perhaps over a meal—as well as offline.

Drawing on rigorous concepts and methods from across the curriculum, learning can take place beyond the campus—for example, in an urban area with museums, libraries, a courthouse. DePaul University's "Discover Chicago" program integrates the city into learning as soon as students arrive on campus. As a result, students begin to acknowledge and attend with increasing depth to their surroundings; and they bond with fellow students as they mutually explore places that might initially be new and unfamiliar to them. Ideally, on campus, students would display their learnings for the community in public ways—through visual displays (such as murals), essays, posted blogs, and talks. And of course, campuses in more rural areas are more likely to feature geographic variation—farms, national parks, bodies of water, rock formations, and a variety of plant and animal life—each of which invite study.

Are such forms of exploration mere frills? Not at all—they often constitute the heartland of deep learning, and, in the best of cases, deep engagement as well as fun. But as adult role models, you need to telegraph your own values. In a less desirable case: Imagine if an instructor allowed athletes to skip the exam at the end of the week, because as he proclaimed "we all want College D to win the championship again." It would be much better if the instructor gave an alternative message to the class: "I'm happy to say that in the exam that you all took at the scheduled time last week, three of the highest grades went to members of our championship team. And, just as important, we had outstanding representation at the Model United Nations."

CONCLUDING THOUGHTS

So much for our imaginary reports to four "ideal type" campuses—along with the important though sometimes delicate messages that we have sought to transmit. Clearly, we could have created more. But our goal was not only to describe or anticipate what might actually arise on a specific campus. We also sought to convey and illustrate the usefulness of the findings that we have documented, along with some of the tools that we have devised, the insights that they can yield, and the exemplary "interventions" or programs that we have observed. Further, the survey we have developed as a result of our study, which can be administered online, may allow campuses to conduct their own investigations and determine which courses of action are indicated.

Visiting specific campuses—and bringing the proverbial good news and bad news—is certainly one way to share our impressions and our recommendations. We can call this "school-specific messaging." But often it may be more appropriate to target insights and recommendations to specific constituencies, even when they happen to be spread across many campuses. Accordingly, we turn next to such targeted messages to several primary constituencies involved in American higher education.

We are frequently asked by colleagues and friends—and even, on occasion, relatives or skeptics—to summarize what we have learned in our study. And of course, with the publication of this book, those who do not have the time or the interest to ponder the entire volume will ask us for "the headlines," which we have sought to provide in our introduction and in various summaries and transitions along the way—most explicitly in chapter 8.

In chapter 9, we provided one form of answer: major points that, we believe, would be of use across an entire college community. We did so through the literary vehicle of "mock" presentations or "rounds" at four ideal-type campuses—labeled by neutral letters as well as by more vivid nicknames.

As much as any sector of the society—such as medical care or legal protection—higher education is a domain in which many groups, segments, and constituencies have clear interests and definite stakes. Perhaps the most distinctive feature of our study is that we have actually examined different constituencies—eight in all. And while some findings and recommendations might prove of interest to all the constituencies, particular constituencies will have quite different interests and, if we dare to say so, may need to hear different messages.

Accordingly, in what follows, having presented the headlines that we believe are most important for *all* constituencies to hear, we provide targeted messages to several of the key stakeholders in higher education. Of course, as with our presentations to ideal-type colleges, these points could be further nuanced for specifically targeted audiences. Throughout, we highlight those messages that we believe will contribute to a sector that is better aligned across constituencies, and more strongly focused on what we consider the central mission of higher education.

HEADLINES FOR ALL CONSTITUENCIES

More similar than different While the United States has thousands of institutions of higher education, differing in selectivity, costs, locations, focus, types of students, and the like, our interviews of over one thousand students show far more similarities than differences. The majority of students exhibit similar concerns, similar aspirations, similar needs—indeed, and surprisingly, they even use the same words, the same linguistic structures. And though of course the students differ in age and in sophistication, most of them are still young, not fully formed, with many of the aspirations—as well as many of the anxieties—that young people have had over the centuries.

Media with a grain of salt It is good to keep up with the sector of higher education—reviewing publications, broadcasts, and podcasts, from reputable providers. But don't assume that what you read or see reflects the totality or even the most important issues of higher education. Journalists and headline writers almost inevitably trend toward the sensational, the timely, and the unexpected. Most individuals on campus are *not* preoccupied with issues of free speech, safe spaces, political correctness, financial costs, or even the upcoming or most recent election, be it national, local, or campus.

The two biggest surprises As we began our study several years ago—with a particular focus on a broad, general, nonvocational higher education—our research group was surprised by two findings: First, the universal reporting of mental health issues across diverse campuses. Second, the frequent laments by students that, in one or more ways, they felt they did not "belong."

In one sense, our surprise was justifiable: neither issue had received much attention in the press (at that time, a decade ago). But this blind spot may also be traceable in part to the background and knowledge base of our research team. It is quite possible that if we had had a more diverse research team, representing several demographies and backgrounds, we might have been more attuned to the pressures that so many students are currently facing. Also, of course, the situation in 2012–2013 (the middle of the Obama presidency) may have been quite different from that in 2018–2019 (the middle of the Trump presidency), let alone the era of COVID-19 (2020 and beyond). What was surprising close to a decade ago, when our study was initially conceived and designed, might well be less surprising today.

The importance of a central mission and the dangers of projectitis While most campuses have a stated central mission, it is hardly ever brought up by most constituents—and it's not even clear whether these missions are even known, explicitly or implicitly, by most of the individuals associated with the campus.

Our comprehensive study has convinced us of this conclusion, perhaps the most important headline from our study: it is *vital* for an institution of higher education that is not explicitly vocational to have a single, powerful stated mission; for that mission to be promulgated and known by all constituents on campus; and, most important, for it to be embodied in the daily life of the campus. To take our own campus as an example, it's laudable that Harvard has for centuries had the pursuit of truth as its stated central mission—"Veritas" is its motto—but it is notable that this mission is rarely articulated or referred to, except perhaps on ceremonial occasions. And when Harvard had a major cheating scandal some years ago, the senior leadership was notable more for its silence than for its direct confrontation of the issue—an issue centrally about honoring the truth.

Speaking of missions, it's lamentable, but worth noting, that some of the major study centers and flagship programs on campuses rarely come up. One can speak to dozens of students on a variety of campuses without hearing a single reference to academic subjects and concepts, scientific laboratories, libraries, museums, the arts, and ethics (let alone the "ethics center"). We hear a lot more about sports and clubs and, indeed, more about the off-campus resources—internships and study abroad—than about some of the most precious resources in direct sight each and every day.

MORE SPECIFIC MESSAGES TO PARTICULAR CONSTITUENCIES

Please note that by no means are these messages intended to be exhaustive. Rather, we strive to convey the *kinds of messages* that might be most useful for members of each constituency to ponder.

For Presidents and Trustees

You have two complementary roles: you are the trustees of the institution, and you are also the trust officers of the mission. It's up to you not only to define, proclaim, and promulgate the mission; you should also do all that's in your power to see that it is embodied and exemplified across the campus and in all media and signage over which you have control or influence.

With this in mind, avoid the tendency to embrace projectitis. It may be easier to get money for a specific center, or project, or interest than for a mission or for "general operating funds," but in the end, that pursuit of "whatever" is self-defeating, if not suicidal, for the institution. When you seek to be "all things to all persons," you likely mean nothing that matters to anyone.

By the same token, while there is no need to eliminate athletics altogether, it cannot and should not be the raison d'être of your institution. And to the extent that you state or imply that this is the case (and there are numerous ways to imply its centrality—compare, for example, the salary of the lead athletic coach and the salary of an award-winning professor of literature or chemistry), you undermine the historical and the contemporary purpose of higher education—indeed, of education in general.

Moreover, the costs of "putting athletics in its place" are not nearly as high as the doomsayers would suggest.[1] Individuals who truly value the institution will rise to the occasion, and those who leave in a huff will search in vain for another cause that is nearly as central to what matters—or what *should* matter—in any democratic society. In fact, in nearly every other developed society on the planet, the excess attention to athletics on secondary and tertiary campuses in the United States is seen as bizarre.

By the same token, you need to honor "truth in advertising." If you want to be a vocational training institution—in effect, if not in name—then you need to announce that fact loud, clear, bluntly. But if you claim to be a broader institution of higher learning—whether you invoke the phrases like "liberal arts," "a broad education," "an interdisciplinary perspective," or (to use the phraseology of the famous Red Book issued at the end of World War II), "general education in a free society" —then you need to accomplish this by deed as well as by word.[2]

Now, some more specific asides:

For presidents   Please don't recommend for trusteeship individuals who are personal friends, or who can be counted on to support whatever you would like to do, however well-considered or ill-considered it is. You need to hear the truth, sometimes the harsh truth, from "critical friends." And don't just select or spend time with those trustees who have deep pockets; learn equally from those who have experience in governing institutions and/or in teaching at such places. And be frank with trustees: in many (though not all) cases, they need to leave their own personal values, their political leanings, and/or their own workplace norms and practices outside the boardroom.

It's fine to send messages to the other constituencies, by whatever medium you find comfortable. But strive to make those messages convergent—consistent with the central mission of the college—and avoid the dangerous lure of projectitis.

For trustees   Don't tolerate meetings that are just "show and tell"—insist on time for frank, full, and substantive discussion of important and difficult issues. (If you and your fellow trustees receive and read the briefing papers beforehand, you can free up many hours!) And don't mix only with faculty or students who are handpicked to present at meetings; seek a broader reach. Most students don't know what a "trustee" is; and most faculty assume that you don't know them, don't care about them, or don't understand them. Get to know at least some of them—invite them to lunch or for coffee, take a walk or run with them. Read the student newspaper as well as broadsheets, go to a class or a public event, spend time in the library, scan the handmade posters, work out in the gym, eat in the café, sample websites and social media postings—all of these experiences will help you to learn much more about the school. Also, familiarize yourself with academic norms and requirements and faculty business, ask probing questions: but don't try to design courses or select faculty—that territory is appropriately delegated to faculty governance.

To end on a positive note, you are leaders and trustees of one of the greatest of human creations—the sector and the institutions of higher education.[3] Universities have existed and often prospered for a millennium (in the Western world, only the Catholic Church has comparable longevity). Rise to the occasion—you will never regret it; and those who come after you will thank you and will be inspired in turn to pass on this precious institution to succeeding generations.

For Students

You are fortunate to live at a time when higher education—which within memory was limited to only the few with status, privilege, and/or resources—is now available to an ever larger number of individuals on the planet. In fact, by some estimates, postsecondary education is now sampled in some form by more than half of those in our own society. In the view of some observers, higher education can and should be as much of a birthright for those of succeeding generations, as K–12 has become across much of the planet. Indeed, as far back as 1947, a commission assembled by then President Harry Truman, made this recommendation.[4] Relatedly, an increasing number of policymakers believe that such an education should be available without cost—as it is in many other societies.

College provides a rare opportunity—one might even say a "once-in-a-lifetime" opportunity—to expand your horizon: to meet and get to know individuals who are very different from most of those with whom you were brought up—and, equally important, for them to meet and get to know you—in person, in class, in the dining hall, playing frisbee, studying for exams, singing in an a capella group, building robots, and having lunch or late-night conversation ... even on Zoom!

You have lived for a while on this planet. Certain traits and aspirations will not change; and perhaps they should not change. But if you want simply to remain the same, then there is little point in going to college.

Now that you have decided to take the leap—and we hope that it was *your* decision—you should be open to change what you think about, how you think about it, what you admire, what you worry about, what kind of a person you are, how you strike others—both those you meet casually (for example, on a bus) and those with whom you have a more sustained relationship (a roommate, a teacher, a coach, a summer employer). As we like to say, *do not* be inertial about your college experience—this is not simply a continuation of high school. *Do not* be simply transactional; instead, *explore* new territories physically, cognitively, socially, emotionally, and remain open to being *transformed* in certain ways.[5]

You—or your parents or someone else (who could be a current supporter of the school, an affluent citizen who pays high state taxes, or a longtime alum)—have spent considerable money for you to go to college. These individuals may well have made genuine sacrifices, and you ought to be grateful and, if possible, express your gratitude directly. But do not think of the benefits of college in the frame of short-term "returns on investment." Think of college instead as a lifetime investment, from which you have the opportunity to achieve dividends of all sorts, including some that you may not have expected. Individuals who receive a broad education—one including the natural and social sciences, the arts, the humanities, the world of computers—accrue capital on which they can draw for decades. And these resources make for a fuller and more meaningful life—for you as well as those for those with whom you come in contact—accidentally or by design.

The faculty and leadership of your school owe you their best efforts to provide a good and rounded education. But even if they strove night and day, they could not merely hand you an excellent education on the proverbial platinum platter. *You need to make commensurate efforts.* And importantly, if your own efforts are not enough, you need to reach out for help—or perhaps take time off until you feel you have the requisite motivation. For many of us, a gap year (or even two or three) can make a significant, positive difference.

The kind of help that you may need on campus can vary—you may need aid with homework, with planning, with stress or anxiety, with feelings of alienation. Do not keep these needs to yourself: speak to others, share with others, solicit their best advice, and then follow it as best you can (and, as well, reciprocate when you can). Of course, it's good to share your aspirations and your anxieties with friends, roommates, family members—but it's *your* life and you need to make the best use of the resources that are available, and not wait until it's too late. Lots of research indicates that *the most important thing that a college student can do is to have a meaningful relationship to a faculty member*, and that won't happen unless you are open to that experience and perhaps even take the initiative. And if, for whatever reason, the first such attempt to reach out does not work, by all means try again.[6]

Of course, you deserve and should have positive experiences, to do things that you have enjoyed in the past. But remember that you don't need to go to college just to hang out. Time in college will disappear more quickly than you can ever imagine. The focus should be on the academic experiences, not just the nonacademic activities. And if you have suggestions about how the academic curriculum might be changed, don't hesitate to speak up and give your reasons.

Nearly all alums with whom we have spoken—close to two hundred—lament that they did not make better and fuller use of the opportunities available during the swiftly passing years in college. Take advantage of your short time in this remarkable place by discovering new ways of thinking about your social context, exploring ideas and concepts, finding your voice and listening attentively to the voices of others, both contemporary and historical.

For Parents, Guardians, and Other Family Members

It's great that your child (who is no longer a child—we'll use the term "youth") has passed the earlier milestones of life—personal, social, educational. That youth has now embarked on the amazing adventure of higher education—be it two years in a community college, four years on a college campus, or the first in a series of steps toward a professional (or a professorial) degree and career.

Of course, you can and should remain in contact with your offspring, providing support, counsel, love, as only a family member can. And to the extent possible, you should be informed about what is happening on *your* youth's campus as well as on other campuses around the land—though please don't assume that the headlines in the media necessarily convey the whole story or even the most important chapters.

This is a time for a major transition—as smooth as possible—to a full and independent life. Rather than trying to understand, address, and seek to solve all the problems, puzzles, and enigmas that might arise, help your offspring to make use of the resources on campus—human, financial, academic, therapeutic. And if the needed resources do not seem to be available, don't try to supply them yourself: instead, encourage your child to make use of personal and social networks—online, offline—that are accessible in the twenty-first century, and, when possible, to help others in the network.

Having spoken to more than one thousand adults connected in various ways to higher education, we are all too familiar with the needs and pressures to secure a job and full employment—to invoke the well-known phrase "return on investment." We (Wendy and Howard) understand these realities—indeed, as parents and grandparents, we are subject to them ourselves. But if the quickest or best route to a job were to go to work directly in the marketplace, we would not need colleges with their trained faculty, well-stocked and attractive libraries, museums, research laboratories, arts centers, student services, and the like.

If you focus solely on "employment" and "jobs," you will undermine your offspring's opportunity to become a broad and well-informed adult, worker, parent, and a citizen. The pressures from the ambient society, and from many peers, are sufficiently powerful and ubiquitous that, if anything, you should bracket the vocational theme song; instead please encourage "stretch," "exploration," the possibility of "transformation." We can assure you, in the end, your beloved youth, soon to be your young adult, will thank you and will be a fuller person as a result.

We'll go further—silence does not suffice!

In fact, it would be desirable to go overboard with respect to the more mind-opening and life-opening aspects of college. Our study documents that most students think that parents are obsessed with jobs. So it's worth going out of your way, as vividly and specifically as possible, to foreground the important *nonvocational* aspects of college: the exciting and mind-opening courses, the traveling adventures (local as much as global), the amazing speakers and campus visitors from many sectors and many perspectives, the variety of art performances and exhibition spaces. If you have the opportunity to visit campus, suggest that you together attend a course in the humanities (or the sciences) or visit the art (or the natural history) museum—the message will be clear, dramatic. Even if, initially, you see frowns on the face of your offspring, the message will be seen, heard, remembered, and perhaps even appreciated, and, in due course, passed down to ensuing generations.

For Educators (and, for that matter, Parents) of K–12 Students

Preparing students for college is an important task—if students are going to make the most of the experience, they need to be ready to do so, with both the requisite skills and the appropriate mindset. And this is where you, educators (and parents) of young students, come in. Ultimately, we should aspire to have students entering college who understand the primary purposes of higher education and who are eager to learn (not just pressured to earn).

Unfortunately, rather than preparing *for* college, getting *into* college has become the focus of many high schools. Indeed, students believe that their predominant *mission* in high school is *admission* to college. And while students can't attend institutions of higher education without gaining acceptance, there needs to be room for other, equally important, if not more important, foci in high school. Indeed, we don't want students to show up for their first year burnt out, disappointed, questioning whether they have wasted their precollegiate time. Students should view college as the expansive opportunity of a lifetime, rather than a reward for a job well done in high school, or a lengthy scenic detour before their first full-time job.

As high school educators (and parents), make it easier for students to pursue their own interests and goals without negative consequences for their sometimes idiosyncratic decisions. For example, encourage students to take humanities classes rather than just STEM classes; to sign up for a challenging academic program, even if it's not a "safe A"; and to engage with the school and wider community by helping to solve problems, and not just in service of burnishing their own resume. Acknowledge the prevalence of mental health issues—anxiety about grades and academic success—and provide appropriate support (use funds to hire an additional mental health counselor rather than another college counselor). These messages will undoubtedly impact how students think about college and beyond.

Moreover, be direct! Speak with your students—in classrooms, hallways, the cafeteria—about the mind-expanding possibilities of college. Highlight the importance of exploratory and transformational catalysts and experiences—and for some, the likelihood of "blended" mental models (see discussion in chapter 5). Discuss your own views as well as your own experiences, high points as well as possible regrets, and your aspirations. Tell students that college is not about building resumes and networks, but principally about encountering and mastering unfamiliar content, trying out new ways of thinking, getting to know individuals who differ from yourself, and exploring issues of diversity more broadly, as well as grappling with social and ethical issues. And, even more than discussion, facilitate new and powerful experiences in high school. Give your youths opportunities to practice—ask them to assume agency for problems (such as thinking through responses to a cheating scandal or how best to support a bereaved student), or to probe social issues (such as silos among peer groups), in the manner of a budding historian or sociologist.

Furthermore, introduce students to the notion of Higher Education Capital (and its fundamental importance for a college education). Give them examples of real or hypothetical conversations with young adults; and finally, let them know that you hope to see their own HEDCAP continue to increase when they visit one day as high school alum.

For Faculty, Senior Administrators, and Staff

You have chosen one of the most important and rewarding roles in our society: the formation, and, in the best cases, the positive transformation, of young people, the future citizens and, in some cases, the future leaders of our country and even of global society. A vital and impressive calling. Some of you focus primarily on teaching in the class; others on providing administrative support of one sort or another (financial, student affairs, administrative, extracurricular). Nearly all of you will have had such a college experience yourselves—hopefully a largely positive one—and many of you will have transitioned from one campus role to another and perhaps back again.

Based on these experiences, you presumably have a view of the mission or missions of higher education. We heard dozens of such mission statements in our interviews. No need to forget or bury those inspiring injunctions: but it is crucial to understand the mission of your particular institution—and if that is unclear, nebulous, too grandiose or too esoteric, to work with colleagues to articulate and then to embody a powerful, plausible, and pithy central mission and message.

Clearly, that's easier said than done. But in the absence of such an agreed upon and embodied mission, your job will be far more difficult, and perhaps will not be salvageable at all. You may not feel that you, yourself, can be the leading missionary—but leadership can be achieved as well as assumed or asserted. We've been inspired by the message of economist Albert Hirschman: we all owe a certain degree of loyalty to our institution; but if the institution is not living up to its potential, then we should speak up, give voice to our dissatisfaction, and, if possible, assume a role that contributes to the articulation and embodiment of the mission.[7] Ultimately, if one feels that achieving a viable mission is a dead end, then the ethical move is to "exit."

Needless to say, exit is not always easy, and it may sometimes not be possible. But unless you articulate for yourself the conditions under which you *would* exit, you are essentially a servant to the whims of others.

Now for some asides.

For faculty Of course, your primary role is to teach, and, to the extent possible, to teach well and effectively. Additionally, on some campuses, you may have a research or student-support mission, as well. But the core of your chosen profession is effective teaching and, as a consequence thereof, effective, demonstrable learning.

While some professions and callings may be distinguished by continuity, teaching in the twenty-first century is not one of them. In comparison to your own education, students today come with new sets of problems and issues—stress and anxiety, feelings of distance and alienation from their college peers and the institution, and the need to negotiate diversity in particular. The students have a decided tendency to be transactional, and to see school as a means toward employment; less of a proclivity toward exploration, let alone toward transformation.[8]* They also read less, write less, and are far more dependent on social and other forms of

---

* Data reported by the Higher Education Research Institute & Cooperative Institutional Research Program at the University of California, Los Angeles, show a decided increase over time in transactional views about why it's important to go to college. For example, in comparing student beliefs in 1976 and 2019 about why college it is "very important": "to get a better job" (71% in 1976 compared to 83.5% in 2019), "to make money" (53.8% in 1976 as compared to 73.2% in 2019), and "to prepare for graduate school" (43.9% in 1976 as compared to 60.4% in 2019).

media—perhaps unreliable platforms—for both information and relationships. (And in the wake of COVID-19—in full force as we write these words—they may be learning largely through online platforms—some synchronous, others asynchronous.)

There is no point in lamenting these trends or in harkening back to the "good old days"—which may not always have been so good. Rather, one needs to take students as they have arrived on campus and address them as best one can. There is a tremendous amount of accumulating knowledge and skill about how to teach effectively and induce genuine learning in the twenty-first century. It's as much an obligation for teachers to be informed about effective pedagogy and informative assessment as it is for physicians to be informed about new diagnoses and new treatments.[9]

Also, it's important to realize that for many students, you appear powerful, even intimidating, and your work—especially outside of the classroom—is obscure, if not impenetrable. Take the time to explain who you are, what you do, and why (and don't hesitate to revisit these points), and be as direct, personable, and performative as possible. Show your human side, including your flaws—and indeed, as appropriate, bring in your children, your pets, your nonacademic hobbies, even your foibles. Once your students see you as human beings, with passions and frailties, you are far more likely to have a real and lasting and positive experience with them and for them.

Whatever your own anxieties, on campus *you* are the adults, and so you have to take the lead—model, coach, embody. But you can't do it alone. It is proper to expect support from your colleagues, as well as some motivation on the part of your students.

Such motivation is much more likely to take place if you make use of three "prescriptions" that we have created (see p. 304).

A final thought: You may have noted that we do not recommend particular courses or curricula. We believe that is properly the prerogative of the faculty at each institution of higher education, and our study confirms that faculty have thought most deeply about this issue. In fact, in our view, schools should compete with each other on the power of their educational vision, and not on the size of the squash courts or luxuries of the dormitories. That said, we favor mind-opening courses early during the students' studies—and one possible set features a course in philosophy (Big Questions) and a course in semiotics (Communicating Meanings). (For amplification, see chapter 9.)

For senior program administrators You may be tempted to think back to the "halcyon days" of college. Those were the times when students allegedly arrived on campus healthy, motivated to learn, and eager to take appropriate roles in student organizations; would graduate on time; and then go on to lead full and responsible lives as workers, professionals, family members, citizens, and perhaps even donors. But if that nirvana ever existed, you might well not have your job—indeed, your job would perhaps not even be needed.

Instead, as our study has amply documented, the biggest problems on campus are issues of mental health and belonging—with uncertainty about how to relate productively to a diverse set of peers being high on the list of tensions as well as aspirations. None of these can or should sideline the overt and long-established mission of higher education—training of the mind

---

in the best tradition of the liberal arts, and the achievement and deployment of Higher Education Capital. But it is your job to provide the supports that allow as many students as possible to take advantage of this opportunity.

And so, for you and your colleagues, we seek to make available three interventions. Drawing on our extended metaphor, we have dubbed these "higher education prescriptions" (or "the prescriptions of higher education").

- The *anti-projectitis* prescription: Campuses are undermined by having too many programs, not well-known to the constituents for whom they have been created and presumably are meant to serve; prematurely launched and sometimes suddenly canceled all too often at cross-purposes with one another. Decide on the most important priorities and associated interventions, publicize them consistently, and, most important, strive to be effective and to demonstrate effectiveness to critical friends.
- The *onboarding* prescription: From day one, in every communication and in every exemplification, students should be helped to understand the chief, the overwhelmingly most important purpose of college and how that can best be realized and achieved. We insist that this mission be primarily academic. This onboarding should include familiarity with the community (town, city, neighborhood), the student population (not siloed in any way), the various adults on campus, and, centrally, the academic expectations and supports for one's entire time in college.
- The *intertwining* prescription: This is probably the most unusual prescription. The academic mission can and indeed must be

absolutely central—just as health is for medicine, or justice is for law. But if there is to be one additional mission, that mission *must* be closely and carefully intertwined with the academic mission.

For Job Recruiters

What you value—and what you fail to value or frankly dismiss—has become a very important signal on every campus. Reflect on your own life (and the lives of those well known to you) and on your own values, and try to avoid shortcuts—for example, selecting only students from certain schools, or only with certain majors, or only with certain internships. Sometimes the very best members of your company or your profession will turn out to have had an unusual background; both your organization and the candidate will benefit from a less transactional choice.

You value communication skills, and properly so. Effect a relationship with faculty and administrators who have direct responsibility for inculcating oral facility and writing skills in students (not that this job should ever be left just to those who have been so designated). Indicate which sorts of features and traits you are seeking and which are not important, or perhaps even counterproductive. And provide feedback to these responsible individuals about which students—or types of students—have been acceptable or even exceptional in the workplaces that you represent; as well, let the school know the students—or types of students—who have been disappointing and why you think that they have not met expectations.

Finally, we know that the job landscape is changing very quickly and that many current jobs will not exist in their current form in a few years. Help students—and, as needed, their parents—to understand this fluid situation. And aid them to think more broadly about the sector in which they would like to work, and the kinds of skills that are likely to have a longer half-life.[10]

GENERAL POINT TO ALL CONSTITUENCIES IN OUR STUDY

As researchers, we have had the privilege of getting to know each of the major constituencies on campus. And if we are clear and strategic, the lessons that we have learned and the advice that we have just offered should be helpful in some way.

But don't just depend on our eyes and ears. To the extent that *you* can get to know the other constituents firsthand, both parties, indeed all parties, will be better off. Put yourself in their shoes, and hope that they will reciprocate this gesture. Better communication among all constituencies will encourage and achieve alignments.

Indeed, over the years, we have presented these findings and interpretations to many constituency groups and have gained much from the ensuing questions and discussions.

Certain skeptical responses have arisen with some regularity. In box 10.1, we summarize the issues and offer brief responses.

ON OUR RADAR SCREEN

What We Have Missed

In this book, we have covered a wide swathe of topics in higher education, some lightly, others in considerable depth. Yet no study can presume to cover all facets of a sector. We have said very little

---

Box 10.1

A Laser-Like Focus on Academics: Responses to Four Skeptics

Skeptic 1: The cost "I have nothing against college per se, or even against academics, but the cost of college has become insane. It's affordable only to the rich and to the rare minority fortunate enough to secure a generous scholarship. If you can get a job without going to college, it's better to just skip college—it's not worth it."

Response College is increasingly out of reach financially for most families. Some of these costs are inevitable; not all of education can be done on a mass scale or online. And there is ample evidence that the costs of college are more than compensated for by higher earnings across the lifespan, even for those who do not major in STEM areas.

But it should also be possible for schools to cut costs. So much of the new money in higher education is for what we would call "frills"—ever more luxurious dormitories, dining halls, student centers, athletic fields, and the like. The explosion of administrative posts and the rapid turnover therein are causes for deep concern. A laser-like focus on academics could be a win economically, as well as a win academically. Moreover, perhaps graduates who succeed financially should tithe a certain percentage of their future income to their alma maters.

Skeptic 2: Political skewedness "I am a traditionalist, a conservative, though not one of those extremists on the far right (or the far left). Our colleges are skewed sharply to the left. Few faculty members are Republicans; most social science courses are closer to socialism than to social science."

Response Without question, faculty tend to be progressive, though the distribution differs across campuses (religious vs. secular) and majors (English vs. engineering). We oppose any kind of political litmus test for faculty appointments. Indeed, other things being equal, it's preferable to have a humanities or science department that spans the political spectrum.

But we are also wary of caricaturing individuals or positions as "liberal/radical" or "conservative/retrograde." Using our book as an example, we discourage a focus on jobs or transactionality, which might be seen as leaning to the left; but we also favor a curriculum in what is traditionally called "the liberal arts," which might be labeled as conservative or even reactionary. We endorse courses in the classics as well as courses on social class. And while we hope that individuals will treat one another with respect, we are against any kind of speech code—again, a position that defies ready labeling.

In short, in good liberal arts fashion, the charge of "skewedness" should be unpacked—and then, if substantiated, efforts should be made to achieve a better balance.

And a reminder: over the centuries, students tend to be liberal in adolescence and become more conservative as they age. Winston Churchill wittily captured this trend: "Anyone who is not a liberal in his youth has no heart. Anyone who remains so as he matures has no brain!"

Skeptic 3: The social and civic purposes of college "Four years, preferably residential, on a college campus are valuable. You meet and network with a diverse group of people, you can participate in organizations, play sports, help out on campus, and in the wider community. College cannot and should not *only* be academic—campus life made college special for me, and I want the same for my children and grandchildren."

Response   We are firm believers in the opportunities afforded by two or four years of higher education—especially available for those who live on campus. Moreover, for most individuals, the college years occur at the optimal time of life, when a certain degree of mental and emotional maturity has been reached but financial and familial obligations are relatively modest.

But we must be blunt: You don't need college just for these opportunities. You can also get such experiences in your neighborhood or through travel, near or far—or through scouting, military, or public service.

Indeed, if these social dividends are your primary goals, then we might as well get rid of the faculty, courses, libraries, research laboratories, museums, and the staff connected to these facilities.

To be clear: these experiences outside of the academic classroom (whether physical or online) are worthy. Indeed, important conversations, discoveries, and learnings take place in dorms, dining halls, and campus centers, in addition to the classroom and the research lab. But if these aspects of college—what we call "student life"—are disassociated from the academic experiences, students will conclude that it's completely up to them to choose the priorities of higher education. If colleges are to foreground specific experiences—ones that encourage exploration and transformation, ones that stimulate students to think in new and powerful ways—then academics must be front and center.

Skeptic 4: It's about getting a job   "Perhaps in earlier times, when jobs were plentiful and the paths to advancement were clear, one could afford to have a college education where you took a range of courses, joined clubs, fell in (and out of) of love, and majored in ancient history. But the world is different now. Preparation for the job market should be the chief, perhaps the major reason for higher education. If the college education does not do that, we should close down college—or at least those colleges that can't prove that they provide a successful return on investment."

Response As parents, grandparents, observers, and educators, we feel your pain. It would certainly be disappointing to go to college for four years, apply for jobs, and end up either unemployed or with a job that clearly did not depend on educational experiences. If a school wants to describe itself in strictly vocational terms, so be it. If General Motors or Goldman Sachs or Google wants to launch a college, let them do so.

But we should not be naïve. Jobs change quickly; young people are not always loyal to jobs or employers, and the reverse is also true. The notion that somehow attendance at a school explicitly dedicated to journalism or to engineering or to pharmacy will magically solve your vocational aspirations is naïve at best and perhaps fundamentally misleading. The decision to go to an explicitly vocational school radically reduces the opportunity to acquire two of the most valuable opportunities inherent in a college education: the opportunity to think differently, to conceptualize and communicate in a more sophisticated way (which we term Higher Education Capital; see chapter 4); and the opportunity to explore and to be transformed (see chapter 5).

We feel that it is unfortunate, tragic, even, to foreclose these precious opportunities for young people who are growing up in the twenty-first century—a time of great possibilities but equally of powerful threats. To understand either of these opportunities—and to give students the right to pursue them—is an obligation that we owe to all young persons who are willing and able to do so.

As should be clear, we feel very strongly about this point. These days it's hard to read any article or watch any media presentation about college that does not explicitly tie higher education to the bottom—or to the first—financial line. And this has disastrous effects on young minds. They are getting the message that college—and indeed, almost any human experience—can and should be judged solely or primarily by its apparent effect on one's pocket book. What a tragic lesson about humanity, about life! To be sure, we are pleased if college graduates do well thereafter (and there's plenty of evidence that they do)—but if the purpose of the experience is simply to raise one's income prospects, there would be much easier and more efficient ways to do so. Clearly that is being done and will be done in the future—we believe that the costs will be severe for the kind of society in which we prefer to live.

To this point, we give the last word to Stephen Hoge, president of the pharmaceutical company Moderna, who reflects on the importance of his liberal arts and science education at Amherst College:

Amherst helped me get comfortable with topics that don't have hard-and-fast answers. That was my liberal-arts experience—taking a class on the history of science, for instance, and engaging the question of whether there is a moral reality to science. Taking biology, and a political-science class on the American presidency, and literature, all at the same time: it teaches you to think across fields. I've always viewed my work as that of a translator, where I'm sitting at the interfaces between science and medicine and engineering and business. That comfort with translating between diverse fields is a product of studying science at a liberal arts college. It also fostered a view that science is a part of the advancement of humanity—and that, in and of itself, is an art.

Growing up, I'd always thought science was cool. But I misunderstood something: I thought science was about things that were known. Amherst fixed that. It helped me understand that science is actually about how you approach the unknown, how you ask questions and use the answers. If you are doing it right, you are always staring into the unknown. For me that brought a willingness to take on risk that I don't think I would have had otherwise . . .*

---

*R. R. Cooper, "The Moderna Era" (Amherst College, 2021), https://www.amherst.edu/amherst-story/magazine/issues/2021-summer/the-moderna-era.

if anything about a range of topics: universities (as opposed to colleges); certain kinds of colleges (military, single sex, historically Black); the financial pressures felt by many institutions, particularly small liberal arts schools; the value of standardized testing before and during college; the role of athletics and Greek life on campuses; whether college admissions should be changed, and if so, how; the pros and cons of an education that is wholly or largely online; the push to increase graduation rates, the case for free college, or at least free community colleges. And because of our decision not to collect certain demographic data, we are not in a position to report research-backed findings about specific racial and ethnic groups as well as students with special needs or other relevant characteristics.

Our study focused specifically on nonvocational higher education. Accordingly, while we clearly acknowledge the importance of jobs and future employment for most constituencies, we have not addressed specifically the ways in which college prepares students for employment.

Yet we speculate that, going forward, many schools will follow the lead of Bates College, Berea College, or Northeastern University, and make explicit efforts to "intertwine" liberal arts with preparation for a vocation if not for a specific job. We have often recalled the testimony of one insightful senior at Olin College of Engineering: "I'm getting the best of both worlds—a liberal arts education and an engineering degree." And perhaps, in the near future, that amalgam will be the aspiration of many institutions of higher learning, both in the United States and abroad.

What We Are Monitoring

We also follow—and expect to learn from—educational experiments at various institutions of higher education; larger ones like Arizona State University, and moderately sized ones like Southern New Hampshire University; schools with highly innovative curricula and living arrangements like Minerva; about-to-be-launched experiments like The London Interdisciplinary School; and still-in-the-envisioning stage like The New Power University.[11] We certainly don't feel that we know or have all the answers on how best to educate young adults in the twenty-first century.

Moreover, we have considerable data on yet other topics that are of interest to us, including methods of instruction, the role of the arts, and we may explore these further at some point. Of particular interest: the lack of concern for ethics, the absence of a such a moral compass, and the prevalence of cheating across campuses and constituencies (box 10.2). We believe that all of the major stakeholders of higher education should be troubled—even outraged—by the nonchalant attitude toward cheating on the college campus. Indeed, shortly after our data were collected, the story of Operation Varsity Blues erupted—perhaps the biggest admission scandal in the history of higher education—involving many constituencies, including parents, students, administrators, and coaches.[12]

What We Are Musing About

Keeping in mind our questions and our doubts, it's also important to acknowledge that our higher education system continues to be

---

Box 10.2

Ethics at Work: The Importance of Academic Honesty in Our Schools

As researchers who have long been concerned with ethical behavior, we were interested in perceptions of academic dishonesty on college campuses. Therefore, in addition to open-ended questions on ethics, we also asked participants to rank the relative importance of academic dishonesty as a problem on campus, as compared to four other issues: safety, mental health, alcohol and drugs, and friendships and romantic relationships.

Across the entire study on ten campuses, one finding is consistent among students and on-campus adults (faculty and administrators): those individuals who consider academic dishonesty as the most important problem are *outliers*. Academic dishonesty is almost always ranked as the *least important* problem on campus.

This "non-finding" is important.

From a variety of studies,* we know that cheating is pervasive; indeed, a majority of our on-campus participants acknowledge that academic dishonesty occurs on campus. At the same time, participants rarely indicate that academic dishonesty is a major issue of concern (both when compared to the other problems and when directly asked to explain views about it). Though incidents of cheating reach the news headlines, our participants seldom elaborate on issues of academic dishonesty on their own. However,

---

* See, e.g., Alexis Redding, "Fighting Back against Achievement Culture: Cheating as an Act of Rebellion in a High-Pressure Secondary School," *Ethics & Behavior* 27 (2017): 156–172, and Donald L. McCabe, "Three Decades Uncovering the Truth about Student Cheating," *Rutgers Today*, May 16, 2014.

when specifically prompted, the majority of students and faculty describe various ways in which academic dishonesty occurs online and offline, in class and out of class.

The apparent lack of concern for academic dishonesty is distressing. College is about learning and mastering content—the major purpose *should be* academic, and everything else, though important, should be secondary. A culture of cheating ultimately lowers the standards and expectations for college, and makes it harder for students to achieve the primary educational goals. Furthermore, if dishonest work becomes the norm for students in educational settings, we can't expect that when students transition to the "real world," their behaviors or attitudes will miraculously change. Clearly, there is a major disconnect between the acknowledgment of widespread dishonesty and the relatively low importance of this issue to our participants.

Why is this the case?

Briefly, based on our study, we find four major reasons:

1. Perception that academic dishonesty occurs more (or less) as a result of professors' attentiveness (or inattentiveness) to the issue
2. Perception that academic dishonesty occurs more (or less) as a result of institutional policies
3. Misconceptions among students about what constitutes academic dishonesty
4. Perception that academic dishonesty occurs more among certain students or groups of students

These perceptions (or misperceptions) emanating from our data—about what constitutes academic dishonesty, the internal attitudes and types of students that might be more likely to engage in dishonest work, and the role that professors and/or institutional policies play in contributing mixed messages—should be concerning to educators as well as citizens. Dishonest work not only mocks the purpose of college, but also perpetuates a society without ethical norms or integrity.

Here are some recommendations for dealing with this vital issue:

First, as explained in chapter 8, schools need to onboard students to a school culture that is positive, but students must also understand the punitive consequences for ethical misconduct. This onboarding process will help introduce students to important values (such as honesty, integrity, ethics) that should be intertwined into the curriculum rather than be treated as a free-standing (and easily dismissed) "extra."

Second, faculty and administrators need to continue the conversation about ethics—including the recognition, reflection, and navigation of dilemmas—over the course of college. While some rules and standards are straightforward, ethics often involve puzzles.

Third, it is important for faculty and administrators to get to know their students—their goals and aspirations for higher education, their mental models—in order to talk with them about "deep learning" and higher education as a lifelong investment.

Accordingly, based on these findings and recommendations, we have now launched an initiative that strives to make ethics a central and visible issue on the college campus.*

*This research has been supported by the Kern Family Foundation. Readers can follow progress on our websites https://www.thegoodproject .org/ and https://www.therealworldofcollege.com.

the envy of much of the world. Indeed, in annual polls, typically more than half (54%) of the top 50 universities cited are American, and less than a quarter (12%) of the other leaders are in the British system, closest to that realized in the United States.[13]

To be sure, these are ratings of universities, which exist all over the world. They are not focused on nonvocational colleges, still largely an American institution at the present time. And these universities are valued largely because of their research capabilities and contributions to the economic welfare of their respective nations or regions.*

But nonvocational colleges in the United States are also admired. Throughout Europe, including Eastern Europe, often aided by Bard College, efforts are underway to emulate or recreate the American college system, and proponents do not hesitate to invoke the terms "liberal arts" or "liberal arts and sciences." Their leaders or funders have experienced and/or studied what is foregrounded at Princeton, or Pomona, or UCLA. We hope that these new and emerging schools will seek to capture what we believe US colleges can and should be.[14]

A more complex situation arises when enthusiasm for the US higher education system is expressed in societies that are not democratic—that may in fact be authoritarian, autocratic, or even totalitarian. Doubts can and properly should be raised about the

---

* For an examination of leading universities across the decades, see William Kirby, *Empires of Ideas: Creating the Modern University in Germany, America and China* (Cambridge, MA: Harvard University Press, forthcoming).

branch campuses of Duke University, Yale University, New York University that have been launched in societies in the middle East and in Southeast Asia—places that clearly do not allow freedom of expression and open debate on a range of topics. Often the US (or Western European) educators at these branch campuses claim that they themselves are not censored by the government; but there may well be considerable self-censorship. And even if students at these branch campuses can express themselves freely within the classroom, they may well get in trouble—even end up in jail—if they voice controversial or contraband opinions once they have left the "protected" campus . . . not to mention what they say online.

We feel it necessary to speak explicitly about China. Higher education there has expanded greatly in the last forty years. Many Chinese nationals have studied in the United States, even as many American students and teachers have spent time in Chinese educational settings (indeed, Howard did so frequently in the 1980s and remains in regular communication with Chinese colleagues and students). We applaud this exchange and hope that it can continue.

But in our view, much of higher education in China increasingly seeks to emulate the surface structures and slogans of Western education: blended classrooms, a range of topics beyond vocational ones, more active student participation in class. At the same time, there is a party line—the Communist Party line—and students cross that line at their peril. When leader Xi Jinping speaks of education with "Chinese characteristics," he clearly indicates that students are not supposed to question government positions and policy on issues of importance—including those treated in economics, politics, psychology, history, and other subjects.

Such challenging strikes at the heart and soul of America non-vocational education—here we should say explicitly, of American education in the liberal arts and sciences. Because unless students can explore openly and freely, and can be open to various forms of self-transformation, they are being deprived of the greatest rewards of higher education.

Alas, writing in the third decade of the twenty-first century, it is also necessary to add that some of these censoring impulses can be found in the contemporary US educational system—from kindergarten through college. These violations of free speech and open debate are noted in the media, and by organizations like the Foundation for Individual Rights in Education, or FIRE.[15] As with other aspects of US society, we can scarcely judge other societies if we do not honor and model our deepest values in our own educational system.

And so we conclude our comments directed to the various constituencies of higher education in the United States. For most of this book, we have spoken to a hypothetical audience—"the general reader of serious books"—and have addressed what we believe are the most important aspirations for the sector. In our concluding epilogue, we reflect on our personal thoughts and aspirations for higher education in the United States and abroad.

EPILOGUE: THE AUTHORS REFLECT

Wendy has been conducting research in psychology and education for a quarter of a century, Howard for twice as long. For both of us, this has been by far our largest and most ambitious project—lasting essentially a decade from the time that the project was first conceived to the moment when the book was finished, and is now in your hands (or on your screens).

We've talked and written a lot about what we learned during the project and what we want to share with the various constituencies. As we wrap up, we'd like to take the opportunity to reflect on what brought us to this work, and what it has meant to us personally. In doing so, we seek to capture some of what we have talked about together thousands of times in the past decade, in person, on the phone, or via email or texting.

Howard   Wendy, what brought you to this project?

Wendy   You! (Just kidding.) As you well know, over the last twenty-five years, we have been investigating how people conceptualize work and how they make important decisions in their work, most especially the ethical decisions they confront.

In 1995, I started to explore students in elementary school and high school as part of our Good Project. Much as in our higher education study, we had the privilege of interviewing hundreds of young people—listening to their stories and personal reflections about work. I became most interested in *how* values for work are shaped, especially by influential people in students' lives—family, friends, teachers—as well as by pivotal experiences in school, in the school newspaper room, on stage, etc. The opportunity to investigate college students and those who influence them (on and off campus) seemed like an incredible learning opportunity. Plus, truth be told, the added bonus for me, as a parent of four children who would hopefully (at that point in time) be college bound, the opportunity to spend significant time on ten different campuses— and to visit others as well—was icing on the cake. Though, as I have now said many times over the course of this project, it wasn't always helpful to my kids that I began to develop views about what we observed and learned. But I have learned to keep my mouth shut about most things (except for one thing—I'll get to that later).

One more note about what drew me to this project: For most people, college is the last opportunity for a formal education, and so I believe that for students, for the professions, for society, and for humanity, the stakes are high. Most people around me describe college as a way to a job, career, success. But I think college needs to be so much more—it needs to prepare students not just for future work, but more importantly, for life beyond.

And you, Howard?

Howard   After conducting lots of research in education that has focused on K–12 in the United States and, occasionally abroad, I became interested in, and concerned about, the state of higher education—and particularly so in the United States. I have spent all of my adult life in higher education, but it's been almost entirely at Harvard—the College (1961–1965), the Graduate School of Arts and Sciences (1966–1971), the research group Project Zero (1967–present), and, accordingly, at the Graduate School of Education where Project Zero is housed and where I taught for several decades. And so, while I have known *one* institution of higher education very well, my knowledge of other institutions of higher education had been quite scanty, and those that I knew the best are ones that are most like Harvard—other Ivy League campuses, for example. (I did a six-year stint on the board of Amherst College in Western Massachusetts, I also taught for two years at New York University and a semester at Clark University in central Massachusetts.) I had not heard of some of the schools that we have investigated and knew almost nothing about several others.

So, this was an incredible learning experience for me, one that I personally appreciated and that I have been gratified to have the opportunity to share with others.

Wendy   I've heard you say that actually some of your interests in this topic go back quite far . . .

Howard   That's right. I had thought that an interest in higher education was relatively new to me. But in fact, as I was writing a memoir, I went back to some of my contributions to my high school newspaper.[1] And I was amazed to find that around 1960, I had actually published pieces about college admissions, about liberal arts, and about what was then called "the new American high school." Some of the themes of those pieces still remain with me—for example, skepticism about standardized tests and enthusiasm about wide-ranging, interdisciplinary curricula.

What educational issues were you thinking about when you were in secondary school and when you went to college?

Wendy   Interestingly, when I think back to my initial interest in studying education, it was in my tenth-grade World History class in high school, in which we could write a research paper about any topic of our choice. We worked on it for the whole semester, and I remember this being a favorite assignment—it's when I first realized that I had a passion for research. And Howard, you might be interested to know (given your earlier personal and professional experiences in China), that the paper was focused on the high-pressure testing in China. Even then, in the late 1980s, I was concerned about how students navigated academic pressure.

In college, as a European history major, I was mostly consumed by the stories of people—rather than by particular events—and also interested in how these stories could help one understand other people's perspectives.

Like you, my early interests very much reflect the work we do now.

Howard   Tell me a bit about your family's educational background.

Wendy   Neither of my parents went to college, and so in my immediate family, I was a "first-gen" student, but I never thought about this when I went to college. Now that I am a parent, working at a university, and studying higher education, I realize that in many ways, this was a big deal—especially because I went to a bigger school (Northwestern University in suburban Chicago) where, in a sense, I had to find my own way. I don't even remember having an advisor!

The good part of being a "first-gen" is that my parents never put any pressure on me—all of my own goals (and stress about achieving them) came from within. My parents were just happy that I was going to college, they didn't care where. Nowadays, that seems rare—I am sympathetic for those young people who endure so much pressure from others. Both my maternal and paternal grandfathers went to college, but my sister and I were the first women on both sides of our families to graduate from college. And yours?

Howard   My parents, who were Jewish, grew up in relative comfort in Weimar Germany in the 1920s. They married in January 1932. When Hitler came to power the next year, they made every effort to leave. They even moved to Milan but returned to their home city Nuremberg after Hitler and Mussolini began to join forces.

After numerous attempts, my parents were fortunate to be able to emigrate to the United States, arriving—as Fate would have it—on November 9, 1938, Kristallnacht. This historic date was the infamous "Night of the Broken Glass" when less fortunate Jewish relatives and friends were attacked or even murdered.

Because of their personal circumstances, my parents were deprived of higher education themselves; but, like others in the family and in their circle, they valued education highly. Our house always had books and newspapers around and the nightly news broadcasts were never missed. My sister and nearly all of my cousins went to college in the United States and several have remained in education in one way or another. In today's lingo, as the children of refugees, nearly all of my generation were also "first-gens." So, as it happens, neither you, Wendy, nor I, had parents who had the opportunity of a college education. Perhaps that's one reason why we are so passionate about this topic!

Wendy   When you think of the concepts that became central in our study, to what extent do you identify with them, and in what way?

Howard   I was fortunate. Growing up in Scranton, Pennsylvania, in the 1950s, I had support and friends—but I was not stretched intellectually. After attending the local high school I transferred to a nearby independent school, Wyoming Seminary, which was more stimulating; but while I valued my classmates there, I never really felt that I was surrounded by highly motivated and academically gifted peers until I arrived at Harvard College in the fall of 1961.

As a "first-gen" from a so-called depressed area of the United States (where my agemate President Biden also spent his early years), I could have been intimidated, but I don't think that I was. I loved college and would have been happy to continue it throughout my life.

Wendy   In a sense you have!

Howard   Point taken. Returning to your question, when I left northeastern Pennsylvania, I already had strong personal values, which I think I have maintained. But in all other ways I was ready to be transformed—as we used to quip in Scranton, the most valuable possession was a one-way ticket out of town! I had good friends in college and never felt alienated. And, to borrow our terms, I was a blend of the *exploratory* student—literally, taking or auditing dozens of courses across the disciplinary terrain—and the *transformational* student—ready to become a quite different person in terms of what I knew, how I thought, how I related to other individuals.

In a word, college really worked for me. (In one respect, it's generally easier to be the child of immigrants; rather than having to cope with goals that your elders impose on you, you end up educating your parents, siblings, and cousins about the "new country.")

But lest I appear to be a pollyanna, I should add that I had classmates who were much less happy in college, and that I myself did not like graduate school at all. Fortunately, I was "saved" by some wonderful mentors. A friend once said to me, somewhat wistfully, "Howard, you have a gift for attracting mentors."

As much as possible, I would like students in the future to have the kind of college experience that I was privileged to have. That's why the book's subtitle speaks about "what college can be." To be sure, I realize that circumstances are quite different now. As just one example, Harvard College tuition was $750 in the 1950s, and $1500 in the 1960s—it is now just shy of $50,000 a year. Moreover, students today have different challenges, different strengths and weaknesses, different ambitions and anxieties. I certainly would not want to return to many aspects of life in the United States that were prevalent sixty years ago.

Wendy So, what about the period for your own family?

Howard My children went to college a few decades ago, and my grandchildren are still too young to be worrying about SATs, college applications and essays, campus tours, and the like. Of course, I have lots of ideas about where they should go and what they should study. But unless I am pressed, I also bite my tongue very hard.

As the mother of four, Wendy, how do you think of the college experience today, in comparison to the way it was when you went to college in the late 1980s? What advice have you given your children and their friends? And what have you learned from their experiences?

Wendy Good question. I am not sure that when I was in college, I *ever* thought about a job, and that's not because I didn't need one or want one. But times were different—it was acceptable and respectable to be a history major. People didn't ever ask me "And what do you plan to do with that?" I am disappointed and saddened that history majors are on a steep decline. I can't imagine ever discouraging someone from this major—I learned how to read carefully, formulate an argument, write, be critical, and ask questions.

In the predigital era, I was trained to do careful analyses—not to make any inferences without consulting multiple sources—certainly the idea that we would treat 280 characters (allowed in a tweet) as fact would have been preposterous to me (and still is).

In terms of my own children, they have been extremely fortunate to go to fine elementary and secondary schools. But the writing is on the wall, so to speak. The kids get the messages: If you are good in math, go to a business school, double up in the hard sciences, but not the humanities (colleges want to see rigorous science and math courses). If you are athletic, do everything you can to be recruited, which occurs even in middle school for some sports! I firmly believe that in addition to thinking about what higher education can be, we also need to be "minding" our high schools—and the intrinsic and extrinsic messages young students receive. I hope to play a role in helping those who are responsible for our high schools think through these issues.

And, Howard, my kids don't want my advice! (As an aside, you once gave me one of the best pieces of advice—"Your kids will not listen to what you say, but they do watch what you do.") Because of our work over the last ten years, they call me Ms. Liberal Arts (an expression we have dropped from our research, but not from our personal lives and vocabularies)—but I take it and grin. I didn't care what kind of college they went to, but I did insist that they go to a liberal arts program or school, at least for the first year of college. If at that point, they wanted to switch because of a particular interest, they could. I'm still holding my breath, but my two oldest children (identical twins), who are now graduating college students, are happy in the liberal arts—and my third child, now a first-year college student, is also in the liberal arts program (at the same school!). There has been no discussion of switching programs. They will never say "You were right," and I will never say "I told you so," but we all know.

I don't give my friends advice unless they ask. But most of my friends and their children reflect the students and parents we interviewed in our study—about half are transactional about the college experience, and fewer are exploratory or transformational. Very few chose to apply to liberal arts programs or schools. Most are focused on how college will lead to professional opportunities (first internships, then jobs). I think they think I am strange to encourage (and even insist on) liberal arts, even though most of them went to liberal arts programs or schools themselves—and valued the experience.

But this is a sign of our times and our society's values. Students (and their parents) are programmed at an early age to become passionate about something—whether it be math, music, or athletics—and to leverage that passion as a ticket to college— hopefully a prestigious college, because what else would all that work be for?—and then eventually that ticket will lead to a job, preferably *the* job. (It's not that I don't believe in the importance of jobs. I love my job, and without going to college, I wouldn't have been able to do my job!)

However, I do hope that one day, people will focus—and obsess—about Higher Education Capital, not just the job. We need students to develop the ability to think about and solve real-world problems, such as climate change, religious and racial divides, and even a pandemic.

Howard, looking back on the study itself, what could we have done differently? What *should* we have done differently?

Howard As I said earlier, we were very fortunate with the study—and we appreciate the generous support of many donors and the excellent advice that we received from our (uncompensated but much appreciated) consultants.

If I had to repeat the study, I would make few substantive changes. In retrospect, it would have been good to have detailed demographic information about our participants (race, ethnicity, parental income and occupation etc.). But such probing might have yielded a different sample or different kinds of answers to some questions—we'll never know. And had we found demographic differences, we would have had to handle them very carefully. With respect to my own well-known investigation of multiple intelligences, I've never regretted my decision to avoid examining *any* differences in the intelligence profiles of different racial or ethnic groups.[2]

Of course, if our time and resources and energies were unlimited, we could have interviewed more participants on more campuses, and in particular, on campuses from which we did not sample: single gender, historically Black, military academies and so on. (We might even have examined some of the experimental programs mentioned in the previous chapter). But I'd go out on a limb and say that I think we would have gotten pretty much the same results even if we had doubled the sample size and quadrupled the number of campuses.

Were we to venture beyond our shores, that might yield a quite different story. American colleges and universities have a distinct history in a specific geographical location at a particular historical moment; and it would be invaluable to be able to compare them with institutions in Western Europe, Eastern Europe, Africa, Latin America, across Asia—and, especially to that selection of schools in Europe, and, increasingly elsewhere, that (appropriately or inappropriately) term themselves "liberal arts" campuses.

And I'm gratified that in the last few years we have formed relationships with educators beyond the United States who cherish a broad education in the liberal arts and sciences.[3] But as we have noted many times, it is unlikely that anyone will repeat a study as ambitious—and demanding—as ours.

That said, armed with our concepts and our questions, it is possible to create a survey. Such an instrument can tap many of the same issues, eliciting findings that could be helpful to all kinds of institutions of higher education. We have, in fact, created a "rough and ready" survey, a sample of which can be viewed on our website (see https://www.therealworldofcollege.com/about-survey). Such an instrument would allow all kinds of institutions of higher education all over the world to learn more about their students—as well as other constituencies—and to compare themselves statistically to similar institutions of higher education around the world. That would make us very happy. And we hope and trust that it would improve the experiences of students, and the range of constituencies with whom they come into contact.

Final words?

Wendy   It's been a privilege for us to be able to carry out this study in the United States in the middle of the second decade of the twenty-first century. We could not have done so without the cooperation of literally thousands of people, the wisdom of dozens of colleagues, and the generosity of eighteen funders. We know how fortunate we are. And we believe that if others, in the future, are to have analogous experiences, and to seek to make comparable contributions, we need to have a strong and independent sector of higher education, and that includes a strong and independent research enterprise.

Together   In the previous chapter we addressed the various constituencies with the most direct investment in American colleges. As we close this book, we offer some thoughts to the broader society—which extends well beyond our shores.

If one had to designate *one* American institution that the rest of the world admires and wants to emulate, it's our higher education system. For close to a century, our colleges and universities have done a good job of preparing students to live in a complex and ever-changing world, to secure steady employment, and to become good and active citizens. Educators from other parts of the world travel routinely to study our institutions—big or small, private or public, highly selective or closer to "open enrollment." When colleges and universities are ranked, the United States dominates the rankings, as we continue to do with Nobel and other prestigious prizes; and when countries attempt to set up new institutions, or to link with those in other parts of the world, the US institutions are their customary target.*

Sadly, as almost all readers of this book will know, that situation has changed rapidly, and not at all for the good. While there are many more students going to college, a great many students are distressed, graduation rates are declining, parents are frustrated, faculty and senior administrators try hard but are all too often

---

*Unfortunately, with the exception of certain model schools and school systems, public K–12 education in the United States is not a subject of admiration and emulation in much of the world. See Diane Ravitch's *Left Back: A Century of Failed School Reforms* (New York: Simon & Schuster, 2000) or Pasi Sahlberg's *Finnish Lessons: What Can the World Learn from Educational Change in Finland?* (New York: Teachers College Press, 2011).

troubled and, by their own lights, not as effective as they'd like to be. Being the president of an institution of higher learning has become one of the most challenging—and all too often, one of the least enjoyable—professions in our society. And that's because the once exalted status of higher education threatens to wane, as has happened with respect to many other contemporary professions and institutions.

The good news: *The situation does not have to be this way*. The country has the resources—indeed, the ample resources—to retain its position as the model of higher education for the world. And it is well positioned to respond to (and even to help improve) a world that is rapidly changing. The hardware—campuses, libraries, museums, labs, playing fields—is already in place; and the software—motivated faculty, skilled administrators, sensitive and sensible therapists—exists on most campuses. As do students and families with hope and aspirations.

Drawing on our ethnographic and clinical skills, we have noted what the sector has contributed and what it can continue to contribute in the future. From an analytic point of view—and put crisply—the rest of our society has a challenging choice:

- Maintain current supports, modest as they are, and leave the sector as is to solve its problems—we could call this the "ostrich prescription."
- Remove support (as so many state legislatures have done), prod the sector to embrace a new economic model, far closer to that of a commercial enterprise than to a non-profit educational institution—we could call this the "neo-liberal" or "corporate prescription."

- Seek to understand the sector as well as possible, to identify its strengths and its challenges, hold the sector to *appropriate* standards—some long-standing, others much more time-sensitive; and then provide the sector the support that it needs to realize its full potential—we could call this the "right prescription."

The last option is the route that we support—with enthusiasm and hope. We hope that the research that we have carried out, and the book that we have written, constitutes a meaningful contribution to that aspiration.

ACKNOWLEDGMENTS

Over a ten-year period, numerous individuals helped us with our study—offering advice and feedback on our research methodology, connecting us with campuses, reacting to early impressions and initial findings, and reading drafts of our book manuscript. We are grateful for the kindness and generosity of family members, friends, and colleagues.

In 2011, Howard Gardner and Richard Light began a conversation about the importance of higher education, particularly nonvocational education, and its current opportunities and challenges in the United States. These exchanges, in which Wendy soon became an active participant, led to the formulation and launching of our ambitious study. We thank Richard (Dick) Light, who quickly became our "chief adviser" and "sounding board" throughout the duration of the project—from conception to the successive drafts of the book.

Our study could not have been carried out without the help of our invaluable research team. Kirsten McHugh helped to launch the study and coordinated a major initiative, Aligned Programs for the 21st Century. We gratefully acknowledge the expertise of three methodologists who guided the qualitative and quantitative analyses of data: Shelby Clark, John Hansen, and Reid Higginson. We also thank our dedicated research assistants, who worked closely with us to interview participants and analyze the data, as well navigate important logistics, such scheduling interviews, travel arrangements, filing, and maintaining both our participant and library database. We especially appreciate those who stayed with us for a long period of time, Sophie Blumert, Kirsten McHugh, Jeff Robinson, and Noemi Schor; in addition, Alina Fein, Dara Fisher, Mindy Kornhaber, Maya Weilundemo Ott, Alexis Redding, Christina Smiraglia, Johanna Tvedt, and Kathryn Webber, each of whom contributed their time and insights. We also appreciate the work of many student researchers: Katie Abramowitz, Deaweh Benson, Maya Collins, Tommy Doherty, Michael Goetz, Ben Kesselman, Becca Leibowitz, Bryan McAllister-Grande, Samuel Myers, Susanna Mykoniatis, Kate Tanha, and Anna Valuev.

At the MIT Press, we thank our editor Susan Buckley, who provided shrewd, helpful, and timely feedback on both early and later versions of our book manuscript; Judith Feldmann for her careful and exemplary copy editing, and Amy Brand and Gita Manaktala for their support of our efforts. In addition, we appreciate the counsel and support of Ike Williams and Hope Denekamp at their literary agency. We also thank Peter Dougherty at Princeton University Press for his collegiality and his friendship, and importantly for his suggestion of our book title!

Of course, we are enormously grateful to our funders who believed in our study, even at exploratory stages. Special thanks to James and Paula Crown, Thomas Lee, and Julie Kidd and the Endeavor Foundation for their lead gifts; in addition, we express our gratitude to the Bezos Family Foundation, Carnegie Corporation (Vartan Gregorian and Jeanne D'Onofrio), Lumina Foundation, Andrew W. Mellon Foundation (Eugene Tobin and Mariët Westermann), Spencer Foundation (Michael McPherson), Teagle Foundation (Judith Shapiro), and three anonymous funders.

We drew on the wisdom and expertise of many close colleagues and friends: Danielle Allen, Larry Bacow, Derek Bok, William Bowen, Steve Brint, Bridget Burns, Richard Chait, Anne Colby, Jonathan Cole, Andrew Delbanco, Bill Damon, Tom Dingman, Drew Gilpin Faust, Ted Fiske, Joel Fleishman, Patricia Graham, Graham Gund, David Handlin, Andrew Ho, Anne Harrington, Ben Heineman, Nan Keohane, Rakesh Khurana, Daniel Kontowski, Helen Ladd, Matthew Mayhew, Judy McLaughlin, Rick Miller, David Oxtoby, John Rosenberg, Henry Rosovsky, Neil Rudenstine, Richard Shavelson, Katie Steele, Shirley Tilghman, and Olga Zlatkin-Troitshanskaia.

Some of our colleagues and friends read early versions of the book and provided helpful critique and suggestions: Susan Engel,

Richard Light (as mentioned earlier), Tanya Luhrmann, Amelia Peterson, Richard Saller, and Ellen Winner (who qualifies as a team member for her important counsel and feedback throughout the study and book project).

At Harvard Project Zero, we thank our close colleagues who patiently listened to weekly updates on our work and provided guidance and moral support when needed: Lynn Barendsen, Courtney Bither (who helped to prepare references and navigated other editorial details), Shinri Furuzawa (who also helped in a myriad of ways), Faith Harvey, Danny Mucinskas, Jordan Pickard, and Emily Raese.

Last, but not least, we thank the colleges and universities that invited and allowed us on campus for interviews, observations, and helped with many logistics, including the sacred parking permits: Amherst College (John Drabinski, Jeffrey Ferguson, Rhonda Cobham-Sander); Borough of Manhattan Community College (Karrin Wilks); California State University at Northridge (Elizabeth Say); City University of New York (Donna Linderman, John Mogulescu, Felix V. Matos Rodrigues, Vita Rabinowitz); DePaul University (Jay Braatz, Dennis Holtschneider); Duke University (Edna Andrews, Elizabeth Fox, Michael Maiwald, Steven Nowicki); Kenyon College (Sean Decatur, Chris Gillen, Judy Holdener, Carol Schumacher); The Mayo Innovation Scholars Program (Elizabeth Jansen, John Meslow); The Ohio State University (David Manderscheid, Blake Thompson, Susan Williams); Olin College of Engineering (Vincent Manno, Richard Miller); Queens College (Aysa Gray, Sophia McGee, Mark Rosenblum, Jailene Ruiz), Tufts

University (James Glaser); University of New Hampshire (Kenneth Fuld, Ted Kirkpatrick); and University of La Verne (Devorah Lieberman, Kathleen Weaver).

Both Wendy and Howard deeply appreciate their spouses and other family members for many conversations and for providing support on the home front when they spent many weeks traveling to campuses.

No doubt, we have forgotten some individuals who were helpful to us—we apologize and hereby express our profound gratitude. Needless to say, we take responsibility for whatever errors remain and will seek to correct them in subsequent printings.

APPENDIX A: LIST OF SCHOOLS AND SCHOOL FEATURES

School	Size of Undergraduate Student Body	Type of School	Selectivity (based on SAT scores)	Location in the US	Residential/ Nonresidential	Special Focus
Borough of Manhattan Community College	Large	Public	Low	Urban (Northeast)	Nonresidential	Community college (Associate's Degree), one of the seven community colleges in the City University of New York system
California State University, Northridge	Large	Public	Low	Suburban (West)	Nonresidential	One of the 23 state schools in the University of California system
DePaul University	Medium	Private	Medium	Urban (Midwest)	Mix of residential and nonresidential	Affiliated with the Vincentian order
Duke University	Small	Private	High	Suburban (South)	Residential	Liberal arts college within large research university
Kenyon College	Small	Private	High	Rural (Midwest)	Residential	Small liberal arts college

LIST OF SCHOOLS

School	Size	Public/Private	Selectivity	Location	Residential	Description
The Ohio State University	Large	Public	Medium	Urban (Midwest)	Residential	Flagship campus in Ohio, member of the Big Ten
Olin College of Engineering (comparison school)	Small	Private	High	Suburban (Northeast)	Residential	Founded in 1997, undergraduate engineering school with an emphasis on liberal arts and sciences, closely affiliated with Babson College and Wellesley College
Queens College	Medium	Public	Medium	Urban (Northeast)	Nonresidential	Liberal arts college, one of the eleven four-year colleges in the City University of New York system
Tufts University	Small	Private	High	Urban (Northeast)	Residential	Liberal arts college within small university
University of New Hampshire	Medium	Public	Low	Suburban (Northeast)	Residential	Flagship state university in New England

APPENDIX B: SAMPLE QUESTIONNAIRE

This is the questionnaire used with all students across the ten campuses in our study. For the other constituencies (e.g., faculty, administrators, parents, trustees, young alums, and job recruiters), the same basic questions were asked but were sometimes slightly reworded as appropriate. For example, whereas we asked students, "What kinds of instruction (in class) are most effective for you?" we would ask adult constituencies, "What kinds of instruction (in class) are most effective for students?" Or, when we asked students "What have been your biggest struggles in college?" we would ask adult constituencies, "What are students' biggest struggles in college?" Finally, some questions only appropriate for students at residential colleges were skipped for those students at nonresidential colleges (e.g., "What would you miss if you commuted to campus?"), and some questions only appropriate for students were skipped for adult constituencies, e.g., questions regarding hometown and high school. We also added a few questions for particular constituencies, e.g., for trustees, "What kinds of topics are most discussed at board meetings? What topics should be discussed?"

WARM-UP

1. Where are you from; where is your hometown? What kind of high school did you graduate from and what activities were you involved with there (how did you spend your time in high school—what were you interested in)?
2. Why did you choose [this school] over other schools? [*If possible*] Do you remember other places you applied?

   [*If not answered above*] Is there anything distinctive about its educational program that interested you?
3. If you were to describe the students in this school in just one adjective, what would it be?
4. How was the transition to college—was there anything that you found surprising or for which you were not prepared?

PURPOSE OF COLLEGE/UNIVERSITY

5. What are your goals for your college experience?

   [*If needed*] What needs to happen/be in place in order for you to realize these goals?

6. Is it important to go to college? Why or why not (and for whom is it important and for whom is it not important)?

CLASS CURRICULA—CONTENT OF CLASS

7. If you were in charge of the academic program—the czar—what are three changes that you might make?

    [Probe if needed] Particular courses that are "time well spent" or "wastes of time."

8. What should you get out of your course of study when you leave here? Do you think there's anything that *everyone* should get out of their college education? For example, specific areas of knowledge, or skills everyone should gain?

    If not already mentioned:

    How did you pick your major(s)? Who was/will be helpful for you in this process?

CLASS CURRICULA—DELIVERY METHODS

9. What kinds of instruction (in class) are most effective for you? Why?

    Have you engaged in any learning experiences out of the classroom—? If yes, please describe.

    If appropriate:

    How do you feel about live lectures? What makes a great lecture?

10. What parts of your education do you think could be done via distance learning, and which not? What would your response be to those who argue that students can get a sufficient education via online courses?

CAMPUS LIFE

11. What are the benefits of living on a college campus?

   [*If not mentioned*] What would you miss if you commuted to campus?

   [*If necessary*] What are some of the resources, programs, and/or major activities at this school that help students make the most of their college experience?

12. What is your favorite campus activity?

   [*Probe if needed*] (a) Why/what makes it a favorite? (b) How did you find this group/activity?

   Probe: Is it something new from what you did in high school?

13. From your perspective, what are the biggest concerns on this college campus?

14. Please rank order the following issues from 1–5 (1= biggest problem and 5=smallest problem), and explain why you put them in the order you did [*Participants will rank on separate sheet*]:

   ___ Academic dishonesty (plagiarism, cheating)

   ___ Mental health issues (e.g., stress, anxiety, depression, eating disorders, etc.)

   ___ Relationships with peers (friendship and/or romantic relationships)

___ Alcohol/substance abuse

___ Safety issues (e.g., violence, sexual misconduct)

Other? Please describe (do not rank order this item).

15. Who is most helpful for you in dealing with these issues (ask specifically for the item ranked at the top in the above question)?

16. Are students on-campus involved in working on or solving these problems on-campus?

    Probe: If YES, describe; if NO, what would help you feel empowered?

17. In what ways does college prepare students to handle moral and ethical dilemmas?

18. What kinds of ethical dilemmas, if any, do students face on the college campus? *[Probe if needed]* Can you give a concrete example from a situation that you have experienced, or from an experience that you heard about?

19. Is there any person or group that serves as a kind of moral compass or conscience on campus, such that students look to them for guidance when confronted with difficult ethical issues? To whom do you go to for guidance in these situations?

20. If you were given a free week on campus, without obligations, but with all of the resources, how would you spend your time?

TRANSFORMATION/WHAT CAN EDUCATION BRING ABOUT?

21. Some people say that college should be a transformative experience. Do you agree with this statement? *[Probe if necessary]* If YES, in what ways should students be transformed? FOR

SENIORS: In what ways have you been transformed over your time at college?

22. Is it important to take risks at college? *[Probe if necessary]* If YES, what kinds?

23. What have been your biggest struggles in college?

24. If you could advise an incoming freshman, what would be the three pieces of advice that would help him/her make the most of his/her college experience?

25. If you could give one book to students before they leave college, which book might it be? Why?

    If student can't name a book, ask for TV show or movie

    [Probe if necessary] Where did you hear about this book? Did you read it for school?

26. In what ways does the college experience influence your own personal development? *Or,* how does college help you grow as a person?

    [Probe if necessary] Who has been influential in this development/growth?

FINAL QUESTIONS

27. What role do you think the college experience most prepares you for in the future—specifically your role in your society or your community?

    If needed, probe: Specifically, what do you hope you will learn here that you will be able to take with you in the future?

28. Please rank order the following statements about why it's important to go to college, and explain why you put each in

the order you did (use separate sheet for ranking). Please rank order the choices from 1–4 (1 = most important and 4 = least important):

___ To get a job

___ To gain different perspectives on people, knowledge, and the world

___ To learn to live independently

___ To study a particular content area in depth

[*Only ask if "To get a job" is ranked as "1" or "2"*] Like you, some people list getting a job high on the list, but what if the job students are training for disappears in the future?

29. How do you think some of the other constituents with whom we will be speaking might rank order these items?

    [*Probe for parents, administrators, faculty, alums, job recruiters, trustees (might need some explanation)*]

30. When you see or talk to friends who don't go to this school, in what ways do you notice a difference between how their experiences have changed them and how your experiences at [this school] have made a difference for you? Are there any distinctions?

31. In thinking about your work and this school, what kinds of things, if any, keep you up at night?

32. Your school defines itself as a "Liberal Arts," institution. What does that mean to you?

33. We haven't yet discussed "the arts" in the college experience. What do you see as the role of the arts at this school and in the overall college experience?

Probe specific involvement if necessary (ask for specifics, e.g. How recently, how often, etc.)

Graduating students: Is this more or less involvement than you had expected or hoped would be the case?

First-year students: Do you expect this to stay the same over the course of your college career, or do you expect more or less interaction with the arts?

34. Can you describe a transformative educational experience you have had to date?

    [Do not specify in college or out of college, unless they ask explicitly]

35. What motivated you or interested you to participate in the interview—?

36. Is there anything else you'd like to add that we haven't touched upon?

APPENDIX C: ALIGNED PROGRAMS FOR THE 21ST CENTURY

As part of our overall study of higher education, we also investigated distinctive programs which bridge some of the major misalignments we have identified. In conducting this systematic research, which we called Aligned Programs for the 21st Century (ALPS for short), we sought to provide recommendations to campuses facing similar misalignments.* We draw on and describe many of these initiatives and approaches in Part IV of this book. (While the ALPs cases were collected in 2013–2018, and we cannot guarantee that these programs still exist in the form described, the lessons learned should be evergreen.)

---

* We are grateful to Kirsten McHugh for coordinating this effort and helping to carry out much of the work described in this summary.

Importantly, some of these programs were at schools participating in our larger study, while other programs were housed at other campuses. In each case, we met with individuals who were involved in developing and implementing the program, as well as students and others who participated (and often benefitted) from the program.

Below, we briefly describe each program, the misalignment the program addresses, as well as the school with which it is associated.

Accelerated Study in Associate Programs (ASAP), City University of New York: Supports community college students towards accelerated and improved graduation rates (ideally within three years). A multipronged approach, ASAP addresses the financial, academic, emotional, and career roadblocks many students face. In order to participate and receive robust support, students need to meet a specific set of criteria.

Center for Ethnic, Religious, and Racial Understanding (CERRU), Queens College: Brings together groups of students and addresses tensions among students who may have historical reasons for conflict—e.g., concerning politics, religion, race, or ethnicity. The goal of the program is to encourage dialogue through structured conversations—challenging students to listen, respect, and discuss other perspectives.

Explicit Course Series, Amherst College: Provides incoming college students (particularly within a highly selective school) the necessary reading, writing, analytic, and research skills that are important, yet are not often directly taught in college courses.

Many students, even those who feel they are prepared for college, do not necessarily recognize their limited proficiency in these areas. Originally developed for use by one faculty member, other faculty members learned in faculty workshops how to use these explicit methods.

The Focus Program, Duke University: Encourages and models a transformational approach to college (rather than a transactional approach). Designed for first-year students, the program places small "clusters" of students in courses that bring together two seemingly disparate fields of study (e.g., Law and the Brain). Students live in the same dormitories as their cluster peers and attend weekly dinners with faculty.

The La Verne Experience, University of La Verne: Intertwines academics with a secondary mission of "good citizenship" through experiences both on and off campus. The Experience features a series of four major initiatives—one for each of the four years that comprises the undergraduate experience. The first-year experience, called "FLEX," provides structured "learning communities," through which students take courses in different disciplines and apply learnings to "real-world" needs in the school community and in La Verne neighborhoods.

The Mayo Innovation Scholars Program (MISP), Minnesota campuses: Incorporates and integrates an interest in jobs, future careers, and entrepreneurship with academic coursework. Teams of select students from several Minnesota campuses work collaboratively on a system, procedure, or technology of interest—one that could ultimately be implemented, licensed, or patented by the Mayo Clinic. While students have access to a graduate student team leader, faculty advisers, and select Mayo personnel, the chosen undergraduates are expected to work largely independently as they develop methods, findings, and a recommended course of action. As a culminating event, the students present their conclusions to an audience that includes other students, faculty, and personnel from Mayo Clinic—as well as members of our research team on one occasion!

Mental Health, Overview of programs and initiatives at various schools: Supports students' mental health by increasing awareness, decreasing stigma, and providing pathways to professional support. These initiatives cover a range of approaches and topics, namely: facilitating grassroots efforts in which students take responsibility for the overall wellbeing of the community (e.g., Kenyon College peer counseling, California State University at Northridge "mental health ambassadors"), hosting gatherings and providing spaces for students of all backgrounds to feel more connected and less isolated (e.g., Tufts University Hillel organization, Second Year Transformational Education Program at The Ohio State University, and Center for Ethnic, Religious, and Racial Understanding at Queens College), and encouraging interdepartmental collaboration to provide individualized strategies for wellbeing (e.g., Massachusetts College of Art, in partnership with the JED Foundation).

Writing in Math and Science Courses, Kenyon College: Integrates oral and written communication training with technical instruction of math and science (in an effort to debunk the "urban myth" that students study either science *or* the humanities). In teaching and coursework, faculty focus on the importance of being able to communicate coherently in their respective fields. As a result, students of the sciences and mathematics can graduate from liberal arts colleges with computational *and* compositional expertise.

NOTES

Chapter 2

1. Wendy Fischman et al., *Making Good: How Young People Cope with Moral Dilemmas at Work* (Cambridge, MA: Harvard University Press, 2004).

2. David Brooks, *The Second Mountain: The Quest for a Moral Life* (New York: Random House, 2019).

3. Christopher Jencks and David Riesman, *The Academic Revolution* (New Brunswick, NJ: Routledge, 1968); David F. Labaree, *A Perfect Mess: The Unlikely Ascendancy of American Higher Education* (Chicago: University of Chicago Press, 2019); "The Best Universities in the World," *U.S. News & World Report*, 2020, https://www.usnews.com/education/best -global-universities/rankings.

4. Andrew Kreighbaum, "Majority of Republicans Have Negative View of Higher Ed, Pew Finds," *Inside Higher Ed*, August 20, 2019, https://www

.insidehighered.com/news/2019/08/20/majority-republicans-have -negative-view-higher-ed-pew-finds; Paul Fain, "In Dramatic Shift, Most Republicans Now Say Colleges Have Negative Impact," *Inside Higher Ed*, July 11, 2017, https://www.insidehighered.com/news/2017/07/11/dramatic -shift-most-republicans-now-say-colleges-have-negative-impact; Pew Research Center, "Sharp Partisan Divisions in Views of National Institutions," July 2017, https://www.pewresearch.org/politics/wp-content/uploads /sites/4/2017/07/07-10-17-Institutions-release.pdf.

5. Roger L. Geiger, *The History of American Higher Education: Learning and Culture from the Founding to World War II* (Princeton, NJ: Princeton University Press, 2016); Julie A. Reuben, *The Making of the Modern University: Intellectual Transformation and the Marginalization of Morality* (Chicago: University of Chicago Press, 1996); Frederick Rudolph and John R. Thelin, *The American College and University: A History* (Athens: University of Georgia Press, 1990).

6. Clark Kerr, *The Uses of the University*, 5th ed. (Cambridge, MA: Harvard University Press, 2001); Clark Kerr, *The Gold and the Blue*, volume 1: *A Personal Memoir of the University of California, 1949–1967* (Berkeley, CA: University of California Press, 2001).

7. Robert D. Putnam and Shaylyn Romney Garrett, *The Upswing: How America Came Together a Century Ago and How We Can Do It Again* (New York: Simon & Schuster, 2020).

8. Ronald G. Ehrenberg, *Tuition Rising: Why College Costs So Much*, rev. ed. (Cambridge, MA: Harvard University Press, 2002); Sandy Baum and Michael McPherson, "Improving Teaching: Strengthening the College Learning Experience," *Daedalus* 148, no. 4 (2019): 5–13, https://doi.org /10.1162/daed_e_01757.

9. "25 Years of Declining State Support for Public Colleges," *Chronicle of Higher Education*, July 26, 2020, https://www.chronicle.com/article /25-years-of-declining-state-support-for-public-colleges/.

10. "Digest of Education Statistics, 2018," National Center for Education Statistics (NCES) (US Department of Education, 2018), https://nces.ed .gov/programs/digest/d18/tables/dt18_330.10.asp.

11. Richard Arum and Josipa Roksa, *Academically Adrift: Limited Learning on College Campuses* (Chicago: University of Chicago Press, 2011); Ernest T. Pascarella and Patrick T. Terenzini, *How College Affects Students: A Third Decade of Research*, vol. 2 (San Francisco, CA: Jossey-Bass, 2005).

12. Cathy N. Davidson, *The New Education: How to Revolutionize the University to Prepare Students for a World in Flux* (New York: Basic Books, 2017); Jeffrey J. Selingo, *College (Un)bound: The Future of Higher Education and What It Means for Students* (Boston: Houghton Mifflin Harcourt, 2013).

13. Stanley Fish, *Think Again: Contrarian Reflections on Life, Culture, Politics, Religion, Law, and Education* (Princeton, NJ: Princeton University Press, 2015); Howard Gardner, *Truth, Beauty, and Goodness Reframed: Educating for the Virtues in the Age of Truthiness and Twitter* (New York: Basic Books, 2012).

14. Baum and McPherson, "Improving Teaching"; Eric Mazur, *Peer Instruction: A User's Manual* (New York, NY: Pearson, 1997); Carl Wieman, *Improving How Universities Teach Science: Lessons from the Science Education Initiative* (Cambridge, MA: Harvard University Press, 2017).

15. Jean Twenge, *iGen: Why Today's Super-Connected Kids Are Growing Up Less Rebellious, More Tolerant, Less Happy—and Completely Unprepared for Adulthood—and What That Means for the Rest of Us* (New York: Atria Books, 2017).

Chapter 3

1. Matthew Mayhew, Alyssa Rockenbach, Nicholas A. Bowman, Tricia A. Seifert, Gregory C. Wolniak, Ernest T. Pascarella, and Patrick T. Terenzini,

How College Affects Students: 21st Century Evidence That Higher Education Works, vol. 3 (San Francisco, CA: Jossey-Bass, 2016); Ernest T. Pascarella and Patrick T. Terenzini, *How College Affects Students: A Third Decade of Research*, vol. 2 (San Francisco, CA: Jossey-Bass, 2005).

2. Howard Gardner, Mihaly Csikszentmihalhi, and William Damon, *Good Work: When Excellence and Ethics Meet* (New York: Basic Books, 2002); Yuval Levin, *A Time to Build: From Family and Community to Congress and the Campus, How Recommitting to Our Institutions Can Revive the American Dream* (New York: Basic Books, 2020).

Chapter 4

1. Derek Bok, *Higher Expectations: Can Colleges Teach Students What They Need to Know in the 21st Century?* (Princeton, NJ: Princeton University Press, 2020).

2. Richard Arum and Josipa Roksa, *Academically Adrift: Limited Learning on College Campuses* (Chicago: University of Chicago Press, 2011); Richard J. Shavelson, *Measuring College Learning Responsibly* (Stanford, CA: Stanford University Press, 2010).

3. Jeffrey Jensen Arnett, *Adolescence and Emerging Adulthood: A Cultural Approach* (Upper Saddle River, NJ: Prentice-Hall, 2000); Charles Nathaniel Alexander and Ellen J. Langer, *Higher Stages of Human Development: Perspectives on Adult Growth* (New York: Oxford University Press, 1990).

4. Arum and Roksa, *Academically Adrift*; David N. Perkins, "Postprimary Education Has Little Impact on Informal Reasoning," *Journal of Educational Psychology* 77, no. 5 (1985): 562–571, https://doi.org/10.1037/0022-0663.77.5.562; William G. Perry, *Forms of Ethical and Intellectual Development in the College Years: A Scheme* (San Francisco, CA: Jossey-Bass, 1999).

5. Mihaly Csikszentmihalyi, *Finding Flow: The Psychology of Engagement with Everyday Life* (New York: Basic Books, 1998).

6. Perry, *Forms of Ethical and Intellectual Development.*

7. Richard A. Detweiler, *The Evidence Liberal Arts Need: Lives of Consequence, Inquiry, and Accomplishments* (Cambridge, MA: MIT Press, 2021).

8. Pierre Bourdieu, *Distinction: A Social Critique of the Judgement of Taste* translated by Richard Nice (New York: Routledge, Taylor & Francis Group, 1986); Pierre Bourdieu, *The Field of Cultural Production*, edited by Randal Johnson (New York: Columbia University Press, 1993); Raj Chetty, John N. Friedman, et al., "The Determinants of Income Segregation and Intergenerational Mobility: Using Test Scores to Measure Undermatching," NBER Working Papers 26748 (National Bureau of Economic Research, 2020); Claudia Dale Goldin and Lawrence F. Katz, *The Race between Education and Technology* (Cambridge, MA: Harvard University Press, 2010); Anthony Abraham Jack, *The Privileged Poor: How Elite Colleges Are Failing Disadvantaged Students* (Cambridge, MA: Harvard University Press, 2019); Frank Levy and Richard J. Murnane, *The New Division of Labor: How Computers Are Creating the Next Job Market* (Princeton, NJ: Princeton University Press, 2006); Bridget Terry Long, "The College Completion Landscape: Trends, Challenges, and Why It Matters," 2018, American Enterprise Institute Research Papers, May 30, 2018.

9. Daniel Kontowski, "European Liberal Education 1990–2015: A Critical Exploration of Commonality in the Visions of Eight First Leaders," doctoral thesis, University of Winchester, 2020, https://winchester.elsevier pure.com/en/studentTheses/european-liberal-education-1990-2015.

10. James O. Freedman, *Idealism and Liberal Education* (Ann Arbor: University of Michigan Press, 1996); Neil L. Rudenstine, *Pointing Our Thoughts: Reflections on Harvard and Higher Education, 1991–2001* (Cambridge, MA: Harvard University Press, 2001).

Chapter 5

1. Jonathan Zimmerman, "What Is College Worth?" *New York Review of Books*, July 2, 2020, https://www.nybooks.com/articles/2020/07/02/what-is-college-worth/.

2. Margot Locker, Lynn Barendsen, and Wendy Fischman, "The Funnel Effect: How Elite College Culture Narrows Students' Perceptions of Post-Collegiate Career Opportunities," unpublished ms., https://howardgardner01.files.wordpress.com/2014/05/funnel-effect-_-may-2014-_-final.pdf; Stefan Collini, *What Are Universities For?* (London: Penguin, 2012).

3. Freedman, *Idealism and Liberal Education*.

Chapter 6

1. "Healthy Minds Network," Healthy Minds Network, 2019, https://healthymindsnetwork.org/wp-content/uploads/2019/09/HMS-Questionnaire_19-20-1.pdf; American College Health Association. *American College Health Association-National College Health Assessment II: Reference Group Executive Summary Spring 2018* (Silver Spring, MD: American College Health Association, 2018).

2. Greg Lukianoff and Jonathan Haidt, *The Coddling of the American Mind: How Good Intentions and Bad Ideas Are Setting Up a Generation for Failure* (New York: Penguin, 2018); Jean Twenge, *iGen: Why Today's Super-Connected Kids Are Growing Up Less Rebellious, More Tolerant, Less Happy—and Completely Unprepared for Adulthood—and What That Means for the Rest of Us* (New York: Atria Books, 2017).

3. Hannah G. Lund et al., "Sleep Patterns and Predictors of Disturbed Sleep in a Large Population of College Students," *Journal of Adolescent Health* 46, no. 2 (2010): 124–132, https://doi.org/10.1016/j.jadohealth.2009.06.016.

4. Richard Arum and Josipa Roksa, *Academically Adrift: Limited Learning on College Campuses* (Chicago: University of Chicago Press, 2011); Richard P. Keeling and Richard H. Hersh, *We're Losing Our Minds: Rethinking American Higher Education*, 12th ed. (New York: Palgrave Macmillan, 2012).

5. Anne Case and Angus Deaton, *Deaths of Despair and the Future of Capitalism* (Princeton, NJ: Princeton University Press, 2020).

6. Anne Harrington, *Mind Fixers: Psychiatry's Troubled Search for the Biology of Mental Illness* (New York: W. W. Norton, 2019).

Chapter 7

1. The President and Fellows of Harvard College, *Final Report: Pilot Pulse Survey on Inclusion & Belonging* (Cambridge, MA: Harvard University, 2020), https://pulse.harvard.edu/files/pulse/files/pilot_pulse_survey_ib _final_report.pdf.

2. Jennifer M. Case, "Alienation and Engagement: Development of an Alternative Theoretical Framework for Understanding Student Learning," *Higher Education* 55, no. 3 (2007): 321–332, https://doi.org/10.1007 /s10734-007-9057-5; G. M. Walton, S. T. Brady (2017). "The Many Questions of Belonging," in *Handbook of Competence and Motivation: Theory and Application*, 2nd. ed., ed. A. J. Elliot, C. W. Dweck, and D. W. Yeager, 272–293 (New York: Guilford Press, 2018); Maithreyi Gopalan and Shannon T. Brady, "College Students' Sense of Belonging: A National Perspective," *Educational Researcher* 49, no. 2 (December 24, 2019), https://doi .org/10.3102/0013189X19897622.

3. Bonnie M. K. Hagerty et al., "Sense of Belonging: A Vital Mental Health Concept," *Archives of Psychiatric Nursing* 6, no. 3 (1992): 172–177, https:// doi.org/10.1016/0883-9417(92)90028-h; Ricardo Maestas, Gloria S. Vaquera, and Linda Muñoz Zehr, "Factors Impacting Sense of Belonging at a Hispanic-Serving Institution." *Journal of Hispanic Higher Education* 6,

no. 3 (July 2007): 237–256, https://doi.org/10.1177/1538192707302801; Terrell L. Strayhorn, *College Students' Sense of Belonging: A Key to Educational Success for All Students*, 2nd ed. (New York: Routledge, 2018).

4. Tierra M. Freeman, Lynley H. Anderman, and Jane M. Jensen, "Sense of Belonging in College Freshmen at the Classroom and Campus Levels," *Journal of Experimental Education* 75, no. 3 (2007): 203–220, https://doi.org/10.3200/jexe.75.3.203-220; Marybeth Hoffman et al., "Investigating 'Sense of Belonging' in First-Year College Students," *Journal of College Student Retention: Research, Theory & Practice* 4, no. 3 (2002): 227–256, https://doi.org/10.2190/dryc-cxq9-jq8v-ht4v; Dabney Ingram, "College Students' Sense of Belonging: Dimensions and Correlate," doctoral thesis, Stanford University, 2012; Angie L. Miller, Latosha M. Williams, and Samantha M. Silberstein, "Found My Place: the Importance of Faculty Relationships for Seniors' Sense of Belonging," *Higher Education Research & Development* 38, no. 3 (2018): 594–608, https://doi.org/10.1080/07294360.2018.1551333.

5. Leslie R. M. Hausmann, Janet Ward Schofield, and Rochelle L. Woods, "Sense of Belonging as a Predictor of Intentions to Persist Among African American and White First-Year College Students," *Research in Higher Education* 48, no. 7 (2007): 803–839, https://doi.org/10.1007/s11162-007-9052-9.

6. Hausmann, Schofield, Woods, "Sense of Belonging."

7. Anthony Abraham Jack, *The Privileged Poor: How Elite Colleges Are Failing Disadvantaged Students* (Cambridge, MA: Harvard University Press, 2019).

Chapter 9

1. Marlin Heckman, *University of La Verne (CA) (The College History Series)* (Mount Pleasant, SC: Arcadia Publishing, 2001).

2. Mihaly Csikszentmihalyi, *Finding Flow: The Psychology of Engagement with Everyday Life* (New York: Basic Books, 1998); Jal Mehta and Sarah Fine, *In Search of Deeper Learning: The Quest to Remake the American High School* (Cambridge, MA: Harvard University Press, 2019).

3. Charles Nathaniel Alexander and Ellen J. Langer, *Higher Stages of Human Development: Perspectives on Adult Growth* (New York: Oxford University Press, 1990); Bärbel Inhelder and Jean Piaget, *The Growth of Logical Thinking from Childhood to Adolescence; an Essay on the Construction of Formal Operational Structures* (New York: Basic Books, 1958); William G. Perry, *Forms of Ethical and Intellectual Development in the College Years: A Scheme* (San Francisco, CA: Jossey-Bass , 1999).

4. Matthew Lipman, "Philosophy For Children," *Metaphilosophy* 7, no. 1 (1976): 17–39, https://doi.org/10.1111/j.1467-9973.1976.tb00616.x.

5. Kurt W. Fischer and Thomas R. Bidell, "Dynamic Development of Action and Thought," in *Handbook of Child Psychology*, ed. Richard M. Lerner and William Damon (Hoboken, NJ: John Wiley & Sons, 2006), 313–399; Deanna Kuhn, *The Skills of Argument* (New York: Cambridge University Press, 1991); Perry, *Forms of Ethical and Intellectual Development*; Bärbel Inhelder and Jean Piaget, *The Growth of Logical Thinking from Childhood to Adolescence; an Essay on the Construction of Formal Operational Structures* (New York: Basic Books, 1958).

6. Thomas Sebeok, *Signs: An Introduction to Semiotics* (Toronto: University of Toronto Press, 1994).

7. "About," Case Method Project (Harvard Business School), accessed September 8, 2020, https://www.hbs.edu/case-method-project/about /Pages/default.aspx; Conor Friedersdorf, "Finding Faith in Democracy at Moments of National Conflict," *Atlantic*, June 26, 2017, https://www .theatlantic.com/politics/archive/2017/06/have-faith-in-democracy-at -moments-of-national-conflict/531564/.

8. Mark C. Carnes, Patrick G. Williams, and John A. Garraty, *Mapping America's Past: A Historical Atlas* (New York: Holt, 1996).

Chapter 10

1. James Lawrence Shulman and William G Bowen, *The Game of Life College Sports and Educational Values* (Princeton, NJ: Princeton University Press, 2001).

2. Harvard University, Committee on the Objectives of a General Education in a Free Society, *General Education in a Free Society: Report of the Harvard Committee* (Cambridge, MA: University Press, 1945).

3. Howard Gardner, "The Three Sacreds—and Their Disruptions," in *Which Side of History: How Technology Is Reshaping Democracy and Our Lives*, ed. J. Steyer (San Francisco: Chronicle Prism, 2020), 204–207.

4. George Frederick Zook, *Higher Education for American Democracy: A Report of the President's Commission on Higher Education* (Washington, DC: United States Government Printing Office, 1947).

5. "Taking Advantage of College (Before It's Too Late)," https://www.therealworldofcollege.com/blog/taking-advantage-of-college-before-its-too-late.

6. Richard J. Light, *Making the Most of College: Students Speak Their Minds* (Cambridge, MA: Harvard University Press, 2004); Brandon Busteed, "The Biggest Blown Opportunity in Higher Ed History," Gallup.com (October 20, 2020), https://news.gallup.com/businessjournal/178082/biggest-blown-opportunity-higher-history.aspx.

7. Albert O. Hirschman, *Exit, Voice, and Loyalty: Responses to Decline in Firms, Organizations, and States* (Cambridge, MA: Harvard University Press, 1970).

8. Brian O'Leary, "Backgrounds and Beliefs of College Freshmen," *Chronicle of Higher Education*, August 24, 2020, https://www.chronicle .com/article/backgrounds-and-beliefs-of-college-freshmen/?cid2=gen _login_refresh&cid=gen_sign_in.

9. Sandy Baum and Michael McPherson, "Improving Teaching: Strengthening the College Learning Experience," *Daedalus* 148, no. 4 (2019): 5–13, https://doi.org/10.1162/daed_e_01757.

10. Richard E. Susskind and Daniel Susskind, *The Future of the Professions: How Technology Will Transform the Work of Human Experts* (New York: Oxford University Press, 2015); Howard Gardner, "Is There a Future for the Professions? An Interim Verdict," The Good Project, December 2, 2015, https://www.thegoodproject.org/good-blog/2015/12/2/is-there-a -future-for-the-professions-an-interim-verdict?rq=%22interim%20verdict %22.

11. Michael M. Crow and William D. Dabars, *Designing the New American University* (Baltimore: Johns Hopkins University Press, 2015); Jonathan Grant, *The New Power University: The Social Purpose of Higher Education in the 21st Century* (Harlow: Pearson, 2021); Ben Nelson, Diana El Azar, and Ayo Seligman. "Creating a University From Scratch (SSIR)," *Stanford Social Innovation Review: Informing and Inspiring Leaders of Social Change*, May 11, 2020, https://ssir.org/articles/entry/creating_a_university_from _scratch; Gabriel Kahn, "How Tiny, Struggling Southern New Hampshire University Has Become the Amazon of Higher Education," *Slate*, January 3, 2014, http://www.slate.com/articles/life/education/2014/01/southern _new_hampshire_university_how_paul_leblanc_s_tiny_school_has _become.html; Kate Whiting, "The First New University in the UK for 40 Years Is Taking a Very Different Approach to Education," *World Economic Forum*, May 13, 2019, https://www.weforum.org/agenda/2019/05/this -new-uk-university-is-turning-learning-on-its-head-to-tackle-the-worlds -most-complex-problems/; Adi Gaskell, "Reinventing Education For The

Future Of Work." *Forbes*, April 2, 2019, https://www.forbes.com/sites/adigaskell/2019/04/02/reinventing-education-for-the-future-of-work.

12. Dan Levin, Concepción De León, and Adeel Hassan, "'So Disheartening': At Colleges Embroiled in Scandal, a Sense of Outrage and Sadness," *New York Times*, March 15, 2019, https://www.nytimes.com/2019/03/15/us/college-admissions-scandal-students.html.

13. "2021 Best Global Universities Rankings," *U.S. News & World Report*, https://www.usnews.com/education/best-global-universities/rankings (accessed June 30, 2021).

14. Daniel Kontowski, "European Liberal Education 1990–2015: A Critical Exploration of Commonality in the Visions of Eight First Leaders," doctoral thesis, University of Winchester, 2020, https://winchester.elsevierpure.com/en/studentTheses/european-liberal-education-1990-2015.

15. See the Foundation for Individual Rights in Education's website: https://www.thefire.org/ (accessed June 30, 2021).

Epilogue

1. Howard Gardner, *A Synthesizing Mind: A Memoir from the Creator of Multiple Intelligences Theory* (Cambridge, MA: MIT Press, 2020).

2. Howard Gardner, *Frames of Mind: The Theory of Multiple Intelligences* (New York: Basic Books, 1983); Gardner, *A Synthesizing Mind.*

3. Daniel Kontowski, "European Liberal Education 1990–2015: A Critical Exploration of Commonality in the Visions of Eight First Leaders," doctoral thesis, University of Winchester, 2020, https://winchester.elsevierpure.com/en/studentTheses/european-liberal-education-1990-2015.

BOX SOURCES

Box 2.2, p. 29, "A 'Free Week' on Campus: The Greatest Gift of All," © Katie Abramowitz 2020

Box 3.1, p. 41, "If You Were the Czar . . .," © Christina Smiraglia 2020

Box 3.2, p. 63, "What Does Liberal Arts and Sciences Mean to You?" © Christina Smiraglia 2020

Box 4.2, p. 107, "College Courses: Time Well Spent, or a Waste of Time?" © Sophie Blumert 2020

Box 5.1, p. 134, "Looking Beyond the Sticker Price: Concerns about Money," © Sophie Blumert 2020

Box 5.2, p. 161, "Trustees: Can They Transcend Transactionality?" © Sophie Blumert 2020

Box 6.1, p. 180, "What Keeps You Up at Night: The 3 a.m. Worries," © Katie Abramowitz 2020

Box 7.1, p. 222, "In a Word: The Adjective Question," © Sophie
Blumert 2020

Box 9.1, p. 273, "The Book Question: Surprises and Meanings," ©
Sophie Blumert 2020

INDEX

Page numbers followed by a "b" or "f" indicate boxes or figures, respectively.